Lagos

World Cities series

Edited by
Professor R.J. Johnston and Professor P. Knox

Forthcoming titles in this series:

Lagos

The City is the People

Margaret Peil

G.K. HALL & CO.
70 LINCOLN STREET, BOSTON, MASS.

© Margaret Peil, 1991

Published in the United States by
G.K. Hall & Co.,
70 Lincoln Street, Boston, Massachusetts

Published simultaneously in Great Britain by
Belhaven Press
(a division of Pinter Publishers)
London and New York

ISBN 0-8161-7299-4

Library of Congress Cataloging-in-Publication Data

Peil, Margaret.
    Lagos: the city is the people / Margaret Peil
        p.   cm. – (World cities series)
    Includes bibliographical references and index.
    ISBN 0-8161-7299-4
    1. Lagos Metropolitan Area (Nigeria) – Social conditions.   2. Lagos
Metropolitan Area (Nigeria) – Social life and customs.   I. Title.
II. Series.
HN830.A8P45   1991   80-25525
306'.09669'1--dc20   CIP

Typeset by Florencetype Ltd., Kewstoke, Avon
Printed and bound in Great Britain by Biddles Ltd.

Contents

List of plates

List of maps

List of tables

Acknowledgements

No book on a city as large as Lagos could be written without the help of a great many people. I was very fortunate in getting this necessary help from friends, academics, civil servants, consular and church officials and the ordinary people whom I met on visits between 1971 and 1989. Particular mention must be made of the Sole Administrators of local governments and Lagos State Director Generals (Permanent Secretaries), Commissioners and Departmental Heads, who took the time to discuss their sectors, directed me to published statistics and gave me permission to consult those under them. The Lagos State Commissioner for Information and Culture supplied several excellent photographs. Numerous civil servants were equally helpful. Much of the data I collected would not have been available 15 years ago, and the quality demonstrates how far local administration has improved since Lagos became a State. An important source on ordinary life has been the survey I conducted in Ajegunle in 1972, sponsored by the UK Social Science Research Council, and subsequent contacts with Cardoso Catholic Community Project there. Shell Petroleum gave me a copy of their Street Guide, which helped to settle many locational problems.

Those who must be mentioned by name include Prof. Tolani Asuni and his wife, Dr Judy Asuni, who shared both their house and their long experience of life in Lagos over many years. Dr A.A. Adefolalu gave permission to adapt his transportation maps; Prof. A. Adeyemi gave me a copy of a forthcoming paper on crime; Dr Tade Aina allowed me early access to his book on popular settlements; Richard Ammann gave permission to use his photographs; Dr G.A. Banjo sent copies of papers on transport planning; Prof. Sandra Barnes started research on Lagos at the same time as I did and has provided much good advice; Kevin Burkill drew the maps; Ms M.A. Johnson gave permission to quote from her poems, 'Nightmare' and 'Electric City'; Dr Nina Mba and Mrs Vera Oshowole, Nigerwives themselves, discussed the problems of Nigerian marriage; Dr Mba also loaned copies of History Department student projects; Dr N. Oloko provided data from her study of working children; Dr D. Olowu sent a copy of his paper on the Lagos City Council, part of a forthcoming book; Mrs Clara Osunulu of the African–American Institute provided data from her study of street traders; Prof. O.A. Oyediran explained how planning works in Lagos; Dr Eunice Oyekanni gave me access to the Sociology Department student projects, a mine of useful information; Prof. D.A. Oyeleye loaned me his last copy of the Geography Department's book on Lagos; William Reilly, S.J. sent a photograph; Mr Thomas, of the Lagos State Population Commission, explained current estimates of Lagos' population and council boundaries; Prof. Lillian Trager gave me information on the expatriate community; and Dr Adebayo Williams provided helpful comments on various chapters.

Margaret Peil
Centre of West African Studies
Birmingham University, UK
1 August 1990

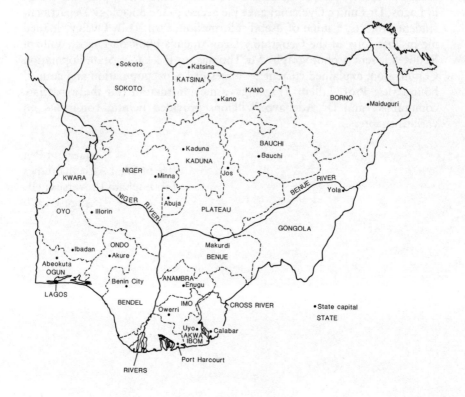

Introduction

'The most awful city . . . I want to go there!'

As the anonymous quotation above points out, those who know Lagos well are often ambivalent about it. Its problems seem intractable and the conditions under which ordinary residents live are at best arduous, yet it has an invigorating liveliness, an entrepreneurial spirit in which anything might be possible, which makes even the unsuccessful loath to leave. This book explores some aspects of the problems, living conditions, and opportunities which make Lagos what it is. As far as possible, this will be done from the point of view of the participants, people who have settled in Lagos at various periods and with differing backgrounds, but usually with the common goal of using Lagos as the route to personal and family success.

At about six million people, Lagos is a metropolis by world standards and one of the largest cities in Africa. Yet, like many other large cities, Lagos can also be seen as a series of provincial towns, providing housing and work for fifty to five hundred thousand people each, in buildings which are seldom more than three storeys high. There is a great deal of interdependence between these 'towns', and between the core (Lagos Island and Iddo) and the suburbs stretching for 21 km on the mainland: from Ajegunle and Maroko to Agege and Alausa. Although a majority of the population have always been Yoruba and some beliefs and behaviour observed in the city may appear to be uniquely Yoruba, Lagos is a city in which much of the world is represented; the working out of ethnic, class, regional, gender and age conflicts can tell us much about how such relationships work in other cities. The dynamism and entrepreneurial vigour of Lagos mean that life is seldom dull.

This book focuses on various groups of people who make Lagos what it is, who shaped its growth from a temporary fishing camp into the capital of tropical Africa's most populous nation. The early settlers were joined by African and European traders, returned slaves, colonial officials and migrants from all over Nigeria and West Africa seeking work or education. The indigenes continue to distinguish themselves from both related groups and outsiders. There are still hereditary chiefs with local authority over people and (to a decreasing extent) land. Political conflicts over power in Lagos led to the formation of Lagos State, with its capital at Alausa on the outskirts of the city. The non–African population of businessmen and diplomats is a significant presence in some areas of the city, but their influence is limited; in spite of tower blocks and international commerce, this is a truly African metropolis.

Lagos has been politically important since the nineteenth century, when commercial and political events shaped its development and the people who led the drive for Nigerian independence. Abuja officially replaced Lagos as the capital of Nigeria in 1983, but the new capital is still being built and only a few ministries had moved there by 1990. Except for special events, such as the Constitutional Assembly, Lagos has continued to be the seat of government; when the Federal Government has moved to Abuja, Lagos will remain Nigeria's economic capital and primate city and the capital of Lagos State. Much of Nigeria's large-scale manufacturing takes place here, and it is acknowledged as the best location for major commercial and service firms. Lagos is also the country's major transportation centre, its largest port and the heart of the airway and railroad system. Small-scale commerce and entrepreneurship also flourish in Lagos.

The national unit of currency, the naira, has been used without international equivalents throughout the book, since its value has varied widely over time and according to circumstances. It replaced a Nigerian pound in 1972 at N2 = £1 sterling. Its value rose during the oil boom but declined in the 1980s. Official rates at the beginning of 1990 were about N12 = £1; N7.60 = $1, though the informal exchange market produces higher returns. One naira = 100 kobo; only 10k coins are available, but there is a 50k note.

Lagos belies the myth that large cities are impersonal; it thrives on personal relationships. Both rich and poor are highly visible here, as in any metropolis, but in Lagos they may live in the same household or rely on each other for favours. Young migrants arriving for education or training get help from relatives already settled there, and politicians at all levels exchange favours for votes. The quantity and quality of health and education are better in Lagos than elsewhere in the country, but there is still a struggle to get what one needs. Most residents maintain close family ties, but also belong to voluntary associations and participate in organized religion – Islam or Christianity. Both social life and business are affected by widespread crime, which reflects societal conflicts and increases personal insecurity.

Urban planning is unpopular in Lagos and has contributed little to the city's formation. The nature of what has been planned and the reasons for failure provide an interesting example of the relationships between people and their rulers. Competition is particularly important in gaining access to land and housing, which is chronically in short supply; in a city growing as rapidly as Lagos, it is notable that the poor have less need to squat illegally than in most African capitals. Transportation has improved in recent years, due to innovative government action, but the mass movement of people across the city every day makes the journey to and from work chaotic and time-consuming. Other urban services are gradually improving, but continue to cause problems for residents.

The city's people appear in many guises in this book, performing a variety of roles. While well-known leaders are discussed by name, fictitious names have been used for reports on 'average' residents. Many people are represented in several chapters: businessmen–politicians, Yoruba suburban landlords, women teachers whose trading sideline helps to pay their children's school fees, city planners who use client networks to find jobs for relatives from home. Thus, while one aspect of the city is being examined, it is well to remember that it is closely related to all the others. Enjoy your visit!

1
Early Lagosians

Madam Efunroye Tinubu (about 1805–1887) was born at Ijukado (Gbagura) and learned trading from her mother and grandmother. In 1830, she moved to Abeokuta with her husband, who died soon afterward. Her second husband became *Oba* of Lagos, but also died. Her third was Yesufu Bada, a supporter of *Oba* Kosoko who went with him to Badagry after his deposition. Her two sons died of malaria at Badagry, and a charm which ensured her increasing wealth as a trader in salt, tobacco and slaves is said to have prevented further child-bearing. When *Oba* Kosoko returned to Lagos in 1852, she and Bada went with him; she became a Muslim in deference to Bada, who built the first mosque in Lagos. Her influence over the *Oba* made her a political power in the city. She owned land at what is now Tinubu Square and other lands in Igbobi and Idi-Oro; a relative ran a farm from her camp at Alase, in the area of present-day Mushin. She built up trade between Lagos and Abeokuta, which brought her into commercial and political rivalry with immigrants from Sierra Leone and Brazil. Her strong influence over *Oba* Kosoko and his son, *Oba* Dosunmu, annoyed the British Counsul, who imprisoned her husband and forced the *Oba* to expel her to Abeokuta in 1856 on suspicion of slave trading and anti-British political activities. (She owed £5000 to European merchants at the time, which ensured that her trading activities continued.) Her entrepreneurial and organizational abilities were a great asset to her hometown; she obtained the guns and rallied the men to repulse the Dahomi in 1864 and provided financial support for the Ikorodu War of 1865. The grateful citizens elected her Iyalode (First Lady). She continued to be a 'power behind the throne' in Abeokuta, and the townspeople compensated for her childlessness by providing a state funeral. Tinubu Square and Tinubu Street remind Lagosians of the importance of women traders in their history (Biobaku 1960; Barnes 1986: 21; Yemitan 1987).

Many strands of early Lagos history continue to be important today. Population growth and areal expansion have brought many changes to Lagos, but peoples who settled there centuries ago and the values which they espoused remain at the core of the twentieth-century city. Farming and fishing, initiated by the Awori, still take place in the lagoons and open

4

spaces. A few of the houses built by the 'Brazilian' returnees can still be seen, and the jobs for artisans and clerks which attracted migrants at the turn of the century continue to provide employment for large numbers of residents. But the most important influence was trading, which drew the Ijebu and Beni to the Lagos area in the fifteenth and sixteenth centuries; their success led to the development of the port that has made Lagos the city it is today. Political rivalry is endemic, and Lagos provided the basis for the country's independence movement.

Founders

The history of Lagos, as of most cities, is one of increasing opening to a wider hinterland. During the fifteenth century, people of the Awori branch of the Yoruba from the west, Egba Yoruba from the northwest, Ijebu Yoruba from the north and Bini (Edo) from the Benin empire to the east moved into the area which is now Lagos. The Yoruba peoples all claimed distant ties to their spiritual home at Ile-Ife, but were in competition with each other for supremacy in the new settlement. As the earliest settlers, the Awori claimed primordial rights to the land and chieftaincy. As Lagos has spread, it is Awori lands which have been taken over.

Settlement was a gradual process. An Awori hunting settlement at Ebute Metta (now an inner mainland district of Lagos) was seen as unsafe, and settlers moved to Iddo Island for greater security from the Yoruba wars to the north. With only one square mile of land, this was too small for a growing population. Tradition records that the sons of the Olofin of Iddo took up land allocated to them by their father on what is now Lagos Island, an area of swampy islands, creeks and lagoons. The growing settlement of farmers and fishermen was joined by others who were developing trading networks in the area (Mabogunje 1968: 238; Baker 1974: 17; Aderibigbe 1975: 3–4).

Indigenes

The first permanent resident is reputed to have been Aromire, whose red pepper farm is now the site of *Iga Iduganran*, the palace of the *Oba* (traditional ruler) of Lagos. Several of his brothers established farms nearby, but the spread of settlement was limited by thick mangrove swamps and further growth was slow. One brother saw the possibilities for trade and established a successful wharf and market at Ebute Ero, in the northwest corner of the island, near what is now New Carter Bridge. These ten (or 16) sons became the 'owners of the land'; their descendents are known as *Idejo* or 'White Cap' chiefs. The Awori practice of capping chiefs is unusual among the Yoruba, but has been important in Lagos local politics. They played an important part in the development of the city through the colonial period and into modern times (Aderibigbe 1975: 3–5; Barnes 1986: 38).

Awori political rule was soon overthrown by Bini (Edo) invaders, who fought several battles with the Olofin and his followers and eventually took control of the area. The *Oba* of Benin rewarded Ashipa, a Yoruba chief, by appointing him ruler of Lagos. His descendents paid tribute to the *Oba* of Benin until the nineteenth century, though in later years it was irregular and largely symbolic. New categories of chiefs were established, not based on the ownership of land. These formed a council which ruled the town until the colonial period (Baker 1974: 7–18; Aderibigbe 1975: 5–9).

In the 1760s, the Portuguese were invited to trade at Lagos. Its superiority as a port led to rapid growth of the slave trade, to the detriment of other coastal centres. The Yoruba and Fulani wars of the period were producing large numbers of captives who could conveniently be brought to Lagos for local use and shipment across the Atlantic. The lagoons and creeks around Lagos made it easy to hide from French and British anti-slave ships, which became increasingly necessary after 1821. Buying and selling slaves brought considerable wealth to the town's rulers. The palace was rebuilt and furnished with imported goods. The *Oba* was not an 'owner of the land', but he was manifestly an 'owner of money', and drew his power from it. Money, superior access to consumer goods and the ability to dispense material and political favours continue to be important factors in power in Lagos today. Income from foreign trade rather than patronage from the *Oba* of Benin was responsible for transforming the *Oba* of Lagos from the head of an oligarchy (a council of chiefs) into the ruler of a Yoruba kingdom, with all the rituals and institutions this entailed (Cole 1975a: 31).

Increasing wealth also provided diplomatic opportunities. Badagry (the nearest major settlement, about 40 km along the coast to the west) became a client-state in the 1790s and Lagos sent emissaries to Bahia and Rio de Janeiro in Brazil and to Portugal early in the nineteenth century. These new sources of power and wealth meant that Lagos rulers, already installed on the site of the Awori palace and intermarried with local people, felt less need to pay tribute to Benin. Their former lord's power was declining, and theirs was rising. The island's original name of Oko (lagoon) was shifted to Eko (camp) by the Edo; after 1854 the town took on its Portuguese name, Lagos (lagoon). The oldest area of Lagos settlement is still referred to as Isale Eko (the town of Eko) (Aderibigbe 1975: 11–15).

Many liberated slaves who returned from Sierra Leone settled in Lagos, preferring trade to repatriation. They were referred to as Saros, in contrast to the Brazilians, freed Yoruba slaves who were repatriated to Lagos after the 1826–35 slave revolts in Brazil. Some of the Brazilians became wealthy slave dealers themselves (Crowder 1962: 77). European missionaries and merchants supported the British drive to abolish slavery and replace it with legitimate trade by interfering in chieftaincy politics – always contentious among the Yoruba. The *Oba* Kosoko supported the slave trade, whereas the uncle whom he had disposed, *Oba* Akitoye, promised to ban the trade if he was returned to the throne. The British bombarded Lagos in 1851, expelled the Portuguese and occupied the island; Kosoko and his followers went into exile. However, Akitoye and his successor Docemo (Dosunmu) were regarded as illegitimate by local people. In 1861 Docemo was forced to sign a treaty making Lagos a British Crown Colony. In 1862, Kosoko made his peace with the British and returned to Lagos. His descendents and those of Akitoye continued their factional rivalry well into this century (Mabogunje 1968: 240–42; Baker 1974: 19–21; Aderibigbe 1975: 15–20; Cole 1975b: 14; Folami 1982: 31–7).

Traders

The substitution of palm oil and other forest products for slaves softened the effects of abolition and maintained the profits of the local elites. The security of British overlordship encouraged European and American traders to move to Lagos for trade. Guns and ammunition, metal, cloth and sugar were among the goods traded for movement inland. Anglican, Wesleyan and Catholic missionaries also arrived, as did Egba Christians expelled from Abeokuta in 1867, immigrants and refugees from the interior. About 10 per cent of the 1851 population were Saros; by 1865 this was up to 20 per cent. The emancipation of slaves in Brazil greatly increased arrivals in Lagos; by 1873, there were about 5000 'Brazilians' in the city. Freed Hausa slaves formed the first police force and army, and escaped slaves from Yoruba areas soon joined. Others were apprenticed to Brazilian artisans. The first census recorded 25 083 residents in 1866 (Mabogunje 1968: 242–4; Baker 1974: 21–2; Barnes 1986: 21).

During this period, residential areas of Lagos were largely in the western quarter of the island. Baracoons (slave camps) were established on the southern side of the island, now known as the Marina, but the many creeks and swamps impeded settlement. The destruction of mangroves (causing erosion along the coast) and the filling in of swamps gradually changed the morphology of the area and increased the land available for residence. Fishing remained an important industry. Three leading women from this period are still commemorated in local place names. Faji market and Ita Faji commemorate a woman of that name who was a large landowner. Tinubu Square, long the centre of commercial Lagos, is named after Madam Efunroye Tinubu, whose biography begins this chapter. Another wealthy woman, Shongbo, had her slaves build a wall and dig a trench at Odi Olowo, a village in what is now Mushin, in which large numbers of people sought refuge during slave raids. Lagos warriors employed by Shongbo were rewarded with land, which their descendents have used for farming and later for housing (Aderibigbe 1975: 11, 20–21; Barnes 1986: 21).

Colonial Officials and Local Elites

Colonial Lagos lasted one hundred years, from 1861 until 1960. The British did not settle here as they did in Eastern and Central Africa, and the city remained in many ways an indigenous African city rather than a colonial creation. This does not mean that Europeans did not influence the structure and interaction, commerce and industry of Lagos, but that knowledge of Yoruba values and customs remains crucial for understanding how the city developed and functions. Governors and administrators came and went, but ideas about success and how it might be obtained, land and housing and how they should be organized, remained remarkably constant. The independence movement which developed in Lagos pitted Nigerians against Nigerians (even Yoruba against Yoruba) as much as Africans against Europeans.

Government

Both officials and administrative structures changed frequently in the early years of British rule. Lagos was under a British administrator (1848–53), then a council (1853–61), a local governor (1861–6), the Sierra Leone governor (1866–74), the Gold Coast governor (1874–86) and finally its own governor and administration (from 1886). During all of these periods, illness and transfers meant rapid change of personnel. The immediate hinterland became a Protectorate of Lagos. This was expanded in 1906 into the Colony and Protectorate of Southern Nigeria, with Lagos as colonial headquarters. The northern and southern halves of the country were unified under Governor Lugard in 1912. Though distinctions were still made between northern and southern administrations, this set the pattern of government until Nigeria obtained its independence in October 1960. The number of people involved in governing Lagos and the country grew steadily, and Nigerians gradually found niches through which they could participate (Crowder 1962: 170, 204, 208).

The city suffered from gross overcrowding of both houses and streets, poor sanitation and endemic diseases, but successive governments were unwilling to spend enough money to rectify an increasingly desperate situation. The greatest improvements were made under Governor William MacGregor, MD, for whom the MacGregor Canal between Lagos Island and Ikoyi was named. He focused on inexpensive reforms to get rid of malaria (including quinine for Africans), courses on hygiene in schools, a Board of Health with African members (1899) and the reclamation of Kokomaiko swamp. Ebute Metta, the first organized area on the mainland, was laid out in 1900 (Akinsemoyin and Vaughan-Richards 1977).

Unfortunately, the governors who followed MacGregor felt that Africans did not need protecting. The emphasis changed to segregation of Europeans; sanitation and safe water supplies for 'natives' were uneconomic. While Lagos was seen as 'the least sanitary' town on the West Coast, the sewer scheme proposed in 1925 has never been built – no government could afford it. In spite of this, the death rate dropped from 40/1000 in 1871 to 17/1000 in 1950. At the turn of the century, the birth rate was 52/1000, but the infant mortality was 450/1000; this fell to 28/1000 in the 1920s (Abiodun 1974: 341; Gale 1979).

Local government in Lagos also underwent considerable change. Until 1900, there was no distinction between local and central administration. The Sanitary Board of Health and a Native Central Council (with appointed members) preceded the Municipal Board of Health, which operated from 1909 to 1917. In 1917, the Township Ordinance made Lagos a first-class township, with a representative Town Council, mainly from the European community. The inauguration of a Legislative Council in 1922 gave the local elites a chance to participate in electoral politics. Since these bodies operated only in Lagos, (though one member of the Legislative Council was elected from Calabar), there was little opportunity for leaders elsewhere to form parties or engage in political activity (Williams 1975: 60–61).

Voting was restricted to males with a declared annual income of over £100, which severely limited the franchise. (Many traders then as now thought it unwise to declare their income.) Herbert Macaulay's NNDP won all three elective seats on the Legislative Council in 1923, 1928 and 1933, and took all the elective places on the Town Council between 1923 and 1935. The early members were all Christian Yoruba immigrants (usually Saro) and either professionals (barristers or engineers) or business managers. The Council got the right to levy rates in 1941 and a measure of self-government, with a mayor and totally elected membership from 1950 (Baker 1974: 286).

Commerce

Lagos was valuable to the British because of its commercial potential; people came from many countries to compete with the indigenes in developing this. The expatriate community remained small in the early years, both because the centre of power was elsewhere and because the Lagos environment was dangerous to health. Malaria and yellow fever made West Africa a 'white man's grave'; the high death rate on the coast meant that officials in charge in the early years seldom lasted more than a year or two. Mr. W.K. Findlay, who spent many years trading in Lagos for McIver's and Lever Brothers, reported that when he told his Glasgow landlady in 1889 that he was sailing for Lagos she warned him, 'Take your coffin with you!' Large numbers of local people also succumbed. Nevertheless, the security fostered by the British and the expansion of international trading links ensured the city's continued growth (Baker 1974: 22–3; Davies 1976: 140).

Commerce made the colony self-supporting; exports of £78 000 and imports of £62 000 in 1862 had risen to £830 000 and £885 000 respectively by 1900. Only 3 per cent of the 1881 population were farmers and 30 per cent were in commerce. Export earnings were much less dependable than the market for imports. Wars between Yoruba towns seeking power and slaves greatly disrupted trade with Lagos in the 1880s, so the British undertook the subjugation of the hinterland. Nevertheless, it is symbolic of the high local demand for consumer goods and of Lagos' success in providing them that exports were already higher than imports at the start of the century. However, there continued to be surplus funds for investment in Britain. Mail boats began regular trips between Britain and Lagos in 1853 which Elder Dempster continued, carrying passengers until the 1970s. Schools, courthouses and a racecourse had already been established by 1860 (Whitford 1967: 87; Mabogunje 1968: 246; Cole 1975a: 42).

The first bank was opened in 1891 by the African Banking Corporation, at the instigation of George Neville. It soon sold out to Elder Dempster and became the Bank of British West Africa (under Neville's direction) in 1893. It has had various names and owners, but it still operates, as the Standard Bank of Nigeria. The introduction of electricity made it possible to install telephones in 1892. The commercial prosperity of the city was sufficient for a Lagos Chamber of Commerce to be founded in 1897 (Fry 1976).

With increasing commercial activities and political power, improved means of transportation were needed. Bridges were built to link Lagos Island with Iddo, Ikoyi and Victoria Islands. A road to Abeokuta was opened in 1887, greatly facilitating trade with the Egba. A railway was built to Abeokuta by 1898; its extension to Kano, over 700 miles to the north, provided a unique opportunity for Lagos to become an African entrepot. The port was initially a major problem. As at Accra, a sandbar at the entrance to Lagos harbour required expensive transhipment of goods in canoes or the risk of wrecks. Either method caused considerable loss of life. The railway brought rock from Abeokuta to build moles out into the channel. The harbour was dredged and wharfs extended; by 1917 the future of Lagos as a port was assured (Mabogunje 1968: 247–50; Echeruo 1977: 106).

Education

It became clear very early that education was an important key to success in Lagos, if not in commerce, at least in government. Muslim education was available from 1816; Western education was introduced in 1852 by James White, a Saro of the Church Missionary Society (CMS), following the success of primary schools in Badagry and Abeokuta. Education proved to be popular, partly because its usefulness was so evident in a town where wage employment was available. American Baptists and Catholics opened mission schools in 1853 and 1868 respectively. In 1862, there were four schools with 406 pupils, of whom 38 per cent were girls, a considerable opportunity for the time. By 1881, Lagos had 29 schools and 2257 pupils, of whom 42 per cent were girls (Adesina 1975: 126–7).

In 1859, another Saro, Thomas Babington Macaulay, founded the CMS Grammar School. The Abeokuta Female Institution (the first post-primary school for girls) was moved to Lagos when the European missionaries were expelled in 1867. Both of these remained very small until the late 1870s, but a start had been made. The importance which both the missions and the local people gave to education in Lagos is demonstrated by the fact that four Christian missions had secondary grammar schools in Lagos by 1882, whereas this level of provision was almost unknown elsewhere in the country. Secondary education did not return to Abeokuta until 1908 (Ajisafe 1948: 104; Echeruo 1977: 51–3).

Few girls went beyond primary school, but those from elite families sometimes got secondary education in Lagos, Abeokuta, Freetown or Britain. British finishing schools for girls were advertised in the Lagos newspapers. Higher education was not considered useful, at least until the 1920s, because most elite women were destined to be housewives on the Victorian model. At independence in 1960, Lagos had 112 primary and 29 secondary schools, with 74 468 and 5714 pupils respectively; 47 per cent and 44 per cent were girls (FMI 1967: 157–8; Mann 1985: 18, 26).

Colonial authority grants to schools began in 1872, and Education Ordinances of 1882 and 1887 formalized grants to and inspection of schools. They found that the quality of teachers and results were often poor, and grants were sometimes withheld until conditions improved. The first government primary school was established in 1899 to cater for Muslim children, who had stayed away from mission schools to preserve their religion. Even with Muslim teachers, government schools continued to be unpopular, so that in 1901 about a quarter of Christian children were in school, compared to 5 per cent of 'pagan' children and only 3 per cent of Muslim children – at a time when half the Lagos population was Muslim. This provided a distinct advantage for Christians, who formed the 'modern' elite of Lagos for the next sixty years and led the drive for independence. The first government secondary school, Kings College, was established in 1909. (Plate 1.1 shows a colonial style building on its campus.) Queen's College, for girls, followed. These were designated federal high schools in 1967 and continue to be the most prestigious schools in the city (Fafunwa 1974: 97, 204; Adesina 1975: 127–30; Echeruo 1977: 58).

From the 1890s, there were demands for more practical education to replace Latin and Greek with bookkeeping and living European languages, and for a local university so that students would not need to be away from home for long periods in pursuit of a degree. It was recognized that jobs were available for the technically trained, and were paid less in Lagos than the same jobs in other British West African colonies. Higher education was necessary to compete with Europeans (Echeruo 1977: 59–65).

The government's response to these demands was mainly in terms of its own needs. In an attempt to lower costs, it established several departmental technical courses, starting with the Government Survey School in Lagos in 1908. This was later merged with Yaba Higher College, which was opened in 1932 to train teachers and provide vocational education for middle-level jobs in engineering, medicine and agriculture. However, the increasing

Plate 1.1 A colonial-style building at Kings College
Source: Richard Ammann

demand for higher education was not satisfied with an institution which did not provide degrees or full professional training. Local students wanted a university, not a technical college. They wanted to become doctors, not medical assistants, and those who were qualified and could afford it continued to study abroad.

Yaba students were required to study for careers for which there were civil service vacancies rather than follow their interests, and drop-out rates were very high. Political agitation over the status of its courses led to wider demands for independence. The College was officially assimilated into the University of Ibadan in 1947, though the Yaba College of Technology was established in 1948 (Fafunwa 1974: 134–5, 141–4).

African professionals trained overseas soon outnumbered European professionals in Lagos. Indigenous clergy and teachers appeared first. Former slaves returning from Freetown were needed as priests and catechists because European missionaries all too often died of malaria or yellow fever. Dr Henry Carr was the first Nigerian appointed to the inspectorate, in 1889; he was appointed Chief Inspector of Schools for Southern Nigeria in 1915 and the first African Resident for the Colony in 1918. As a wealthy supporter of colonial establishment, he was bitterly opposed by reformers such as Macaulay (Baker 1974: 56, 75; Fafunwa 1974: 95).

Law and medicine followed. Legal training was less expensive than medicine, and numerous barristers found the conflicts in Lagos profitable. Health services were first focused on the armed forces. The first civilian facilities were the Colonial Hospital (later to become Lagos General Hospital), the Infectious Diseases Hospital and the Yaba Mental Home, all opened in 1873. Initially, senior staff for these institutions were imported from Britain; the first Nigerian doctors trained abroad, Drs Nathaniel King, Obadiah Johnson and Oguntola Odunbaku Sapara, took up posts in the colonial medical service 1876–96. Dr Sapara joined the Shopona (smallpox) cult to learn its methods and founded a dispensary that later became the Massey Street Children's Hospital. Infant mortality dropped from 450/1000 in 1900 to 324/1000 in 1910 (Ola Daniel 1975).

Africans initially held relatively high positions in the civil service, but by 1895 discrimination kept them in lower-level posts. Saros were often doing much of the work, on low salaries, subject to constantly shifting European supervisors who were not necessarily better qualified than themselves. The lack of opportunity for promotion was widely resented, and led to criticism of the colonial regime by people who would otherwise have remained loyal to it. While Saros wanted education in English, with the same lessons as in England, in order to further their professional aspirations, other sectors of the population argued strongly that children should also be taught Yoruba, their native tongue, as well as African history and geography. Elite Saro families emulated Victorian dress, domestic arrangements and social behaviour, including woollen suits and English-style marriages. They felt a great need to be accepted by Europeans, though with a few exceptions the racism of colonial administrators made this impossible (Cole 1975a: 43, 48; Echeruo 1977: 44; Mann 1985: 20–24).

Indigenes, on the other hand, continued to wear traditional dress and live in their customary fashion, remaining indifferent to both Western education and wage employment, though they developed a taste for alcohol. Some were hostile to the Saros; others merely tried to ignore Europeans and those who followed them. The immigrant elite did not see Lagos as 'home', and those who were educated tended to patronize illiterate indigenes, even though the latter could point out that Saros or their parents had originally left as slaves. Relations with Brazilians were easier, because many were manual workers and their lifestyle incorporated both European and Yoruba elements. Their handiwork is still found in old buildings (see Plate 1.2). The higher incomes available from self-employment than from unskilled labour for the government made it easier to remain economically independent. The government found it difficult to attract labourers because even unsuccessful traders could usually earn more than the minimum wage (Hopkins 1966; Cole 1975a: 43–6).

Politicians

As the seat of the colonial government, Lagos was the prime location for political opposition to it. Both indigenes and educated newcomers took part in this struggle, and aspirant politicians found it necessary to live in the

Plate 1.2 Water House, Brazilian architecture
Source: Richard Ammann

capital. The attempt by the colonial authorities to impose a water rate was an early source of controversy between the government and the indigenes. The authorities took it for granted that amenities must be paid for, but local people resisted paying for services they had not asked for. Dr J.K. Randle's People's Party led a revolt against the water rate and schemes to alienate indigenous land in 1908 and 1911. This agitation united the immigrant elite and local people in a common cause; the elites were now more aware of their African background and willing to defend local customs and rights (Cole 1975b: 70, 85; Mann 1985: 31).

A long history of numerous, diverse and lively newspapers, from 1880 (*Lagos Times*), provided a voice for the struggle for independence and contributed to the relative liberty of the press in Nigeria today. Newspapers such as the *Observer, Record, Echo, Nigerian Spectator* and *Nigerian Pioneer* were started to provide an opportunity for Lagos-based editors to express their views. Some were loyal followers of the colonial authorities, while others virulently attacked colonial officials and decisions. Herbert Macaulay (see below) ran the *Lagos Daily News*, the first daily, from 1920 to 1936. Dusé Mohammed Ali, a colourful Sudanese–Egyptian journalist and associate of Marcus Garvey, ran the *African Times and Orient Review* from 1912 to 1918 and *Comet* from 1933 to 1943 (Duyile 1987: 666–72).

An extensive groundwork for Nigerian independence was laid in Lagos in the period between the two world wars. It was here that people from different parts of the country met and faced the disadvantages of colonial rule most clearly. The colonial administration needed clerks, junior administrators, teachers and professionals, which could not be supplied from Britain. The people who took these jobs began to see themselves as part of something larger than their own hometowns, or than Lagos.

The first major leader of the independence movement was Herbert Macaulay (1864–1946). By birth, he belonged to the Saro elite. Bishop Samuel Ajayi Crowther, a freed slave who became the first tropical African bishop, was his grandfather, and his father was founder of the CMS Grammar School. He trained in England at government expense as a civil engineer and piano tuner, but after returning to Lagos in 1893 he moved from surveying and architecture into journalism and politics. Although he remained a socialite, he was by inclination an organizer and a populist. Indigenes, especially market women, accepted him as a leader and provided financial support for his activities. In 1923, he founded the Nigerian National Democratic Party (NNDP), and through this and his newspaper played an important role in Lagos politics for forty years. While a loyal supporter of the Crown and 'British civilization', he found plenty to protest about in the way these affected people in Lagos.

Macaulay's first notable political act was organizing a mass protest against the Lagos water rate. His support for the Eleko, who was exiled for opposing payment of the rate, continued between 1915 and 1920, and eventually led to the Eleko's return to Lagos. He was also successful in convincing the Privy Council that land appropriated by the colonial government should be paid for and helping the Jam'at Congregation win control of the Central Mosque from their more fundamentalist opponents. (Controversy on this continued from the 1924 decision into the 1940s; see Chapter 6.) Macaulay was an autocrat, capable of opportunism to maintain his influence, and made many political enemies. His personalist style was culturally acceptable to the Lagos Yoruba, but it led to factions, and the NNDP did not survive him. Nevertheless, 100 000 people attended his funeral (Baker 1974: 88–94; Cole 1975b: 109–19).

The Nigerian Youth Movement (NYM) was founded in 1936 and led from 1937 to 1948 by Dr Nnamdi Azikiwe. He had studied in the USA and settled in Lagos in order to play a part in national politics. As a well-educated Igbo journalist, he was able to compete on relatively equal terms with the Yoruba elite of Lagos. His *West African Pilot* was an important focus for nationalist demands for twenty years. He also ran a private secondary school, one of many which have provided openings for the large number of students who could not find room in government schools. Azikiwe expanded his political activities by drawing on his Igbo roots; he founded the National Council for Nigeria and the Cameroons (NCNC) in 1944, and became the first President of Nigeria in 1960. The NCNC was a confederation of many groups which had sprung up in Lagos: trade unions, literary societies, tribal unions. As such, it was hard to hold together, but provided a forum for criticizing the colonial authorities (Crowder 1962: 238–41).

The NYM became a victim of factionalism in the mid 1940s. It was effectively replaced by the Egbe Omo Oduduwa (Society of Descendants of Oduduwa), founded in 1948 to unite Yoruba youth for progress. Under Chief Obafemi Awolowo, this became Action Group (AG), which played an important role in the Lagos Statehood movement as well as in national politics. The NCNC was generally much stronger in the demand for a unified Nigeria than the AG, because a federal structure would provide more opportunities for Igbo who wanted to move out of their poor and relatively overpopulated homeland. Communal tensions based on differences between Yoruba and Igbo political goals threatened to lead to civil disturbances in 1948. The opportunities available in, and Yoruba control over, Lagos were again a focus of contention in 1953, when Nigeria was divided into three regions. The NCNC and the NPC (Northern People's Congress) wanted a truly federal capital, whereas the AG argued that Lagos was a Yoruba city and should be part of the Yoruba-controlled Western Region (Crowder 1962: 248, 255).

The Yoruba won temporarily, when Lagos was officially incorporated into the Western Region. It lost its mayor, and its Council was placed under the regional Ministry of Local Government; the *Oba* of Lagos became Town Council President. This arrangement was unsatisfactory in many ways, since some urban functions (such as policing) were still carried out by the Federal Government and the regional government neglected planning and development of the capital. Lagos was 'renationalized' in 1954 and officially brought under a Federal Government Ministry of Lagos Affairs in 1959. In 1966, Lagos State was created, with the city as its capital (Williams 1975: 62–3). These developments and the more recent political history of Lagos will be discussed in Chapter 3.

Urban Growth and Structure

Although the precise figures are sometimes questionable, there is no doubt that the growth of Lagos in recent times, in both population and area, has been spectacular. The metropolitan area takes up about 37 per cent of the land area of Lagos State and houses about 90 per cent of its population (LSG 1981). It has been a magnet for migrants since its foundation, and the increasing complexity of the modern-day city reflects the various factors in this attraction. There are many neighbourhoods which closely resemble smaller, provincial Yoruba cities, but the whole represents the more heterogeneous influences inherent in a world-class city.

Residents face a hot, wet climate. The temperature varies little from one month to another, with a mean monthly minimum of 23–26°C and maximum of 28–31°C in most years. Average rainfall for 1985–6 was 1532 mm, with the heaviest rains in May–June and September–October and the lightest in December–January. Relative humidity is usually 75–84 per cent in the morning and only slightly less in the afternoon. The city

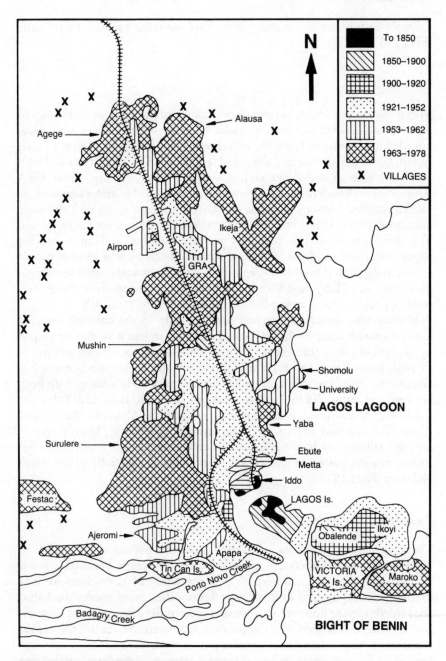

Map 2 Growth of Metropolitan Lagos
Source: Adapted from Mabogunje 1968: 260; *Master Plan* 1980: 10

averages 3–5 hours of sunshine and cloud coverage for 6–7 hours daily (FOS 1987: 6–38).

Growth

Map 2 shows how Lagos has expanded, mainly to the north on both sides of the railway. Growth has been irregular because swamps, coves and canals impeded development. From the initial settlement on Iddo and north Lagos Island, Governor Glover laid out a residential area in Ebute Metta in 1900; Obalende also provided accommodation for Africans. The Ikoyi GRA (Government Residential Estate) was begun in 1918 and expanded as officials needed housing. The rest of Ebute Metta and parts of Yaba were developed in the 1920s and 1930s to relieve congestion on Lagos Island. The development of the port and railway terminal and an estate for expatriates drew residents to Apapa. Across the canal, low-income people settled in Ajeromi (Olodi and Ajegunle). Draining swamps aided settlement on the shores of Ikoyi and Victoria Island; some residents from these areas were moved to what is now Maroko (Mabogunje 1968: ch. 10).

Mushin was already designated a town early in the colonial era, but massive growth came in the 1950s and 1960s. Surulere was also developed at this period, partly through the Central Slum Clearance Scheme and partly through government and private building for middle-income families (see Chapter 8). From the 1950s, there has been considerable infilling with both housing and industries in Ajeromi, Surulere, Mushin, Ikeja and Yaba (see Table 4.2) and large-scale settlement of migrants in Shomolu, Bariga and Agege. The new port at Tin Can Island brought more traffic. Many formerly separate villages (such as Agege and Alausa) have become part of the city. Recent growth has encompassed yet more villages, especially to the north and west (Sada 1970).

Population

There are many problems in getting accurate population statistics in Nigeria, because numbers are a key to power. However, because Lagos is the seat of government and because only a minority of its residents see it as in their political interest to inflate the figures, the census results for Lagos are probably more accurate than those reported for other parts of Nigeria. Because Lagos was seen as an important administrative centre, the census run is much longer than for most other places in Africa. The first census was held in 1866, and more or less decennial censuses have been carried out since 1871, with the exception of the 1940s and the 1980s. Unfortunately, the 1974 census was cancelled as fraudulent and none has been attempted since. In the absence of a recent census, the size and composition of the population are necessarily only an informed guess, though some sample data are available.

Lagos remained a small town by international standards until after the First World War, though even at the turn of the century it was large by the standards of many African countries. In the 1920s, it was only one of many medium-sized Yoruba towns and it was smaller than Ibadan until the 1960s (Mabogunje 1962: 1). Table 1.1 shows relatively slow growth in both size and population in the early years (only about 1 per cent per year), partly because of environmental and health hazards, but also because trading did not require permanent settlement. Nevertheless, it was very crowded for the type of housing and level of sanitation available, and this crowding certainly increased the death rate.

Political and/or economic instability in the 1880s and ethnic conflicts in the 1960s led to temporary declines in the population, but overall growth has been at an increasing rate. The doubling of population and drop in density in the twenty years at the turn of the century was partly due to the annexation of a large peri-urban area on the mainland before the 1911 census. Much of this was initially thinly settled with villages and farms. The 20 years from 1911 to 1931 did not match earlier growth, since economic recession made Lagos less attractive.

Table 1.1 Population size, land area and density of Lagos, 1866–1988

Year	Population	Land area (Sq. km)	Density/ Sq. km
1866	25 083	3.97	6318
1891	32 508	3.97	8200
1911	73 766	46.08	1601
1921	99 690	51.64	1930
1931	126 108	65.51	1925
1952	267 407	69.68	3838
1963	665 246	69.68	9547
1974	2 437 335	178.36	13 665
1988	6 000 000	264.18	20 000

Sources: Population censuses, as cited by Ayeni (1981: 127). 1974 and 1988 are Lagos State Government estimates. From 1952, the figures refer to the metropolitan area.

Lack of opportunities elsewhere during and after the Second World War drew large numbers of immigrants from a wide area. Attempts were made in 1944 and 1945 to limit immigration by denying registration for work to anyone who had not been resident for six months, though this was difficult to prove given the family system which provided for most newcomers; it was also ineffective because a majority of the population were self-employed. A 1945 ordinance required that any employer with more than ten workers must hire ex-servicemen until they formed 10 per cent of his workforce. By 1948, 11 per cent of the civilian wage-labour force were ex-servicemen, and numerous others were self-employed. At that time, Lagos provided 21 per cent of the wage employment in the country (Mabogunje 1968: 261).

Population growth really took off in the 1950s. The quickening political, industrial and commercial life of Lagos, especially at independence and during the oil boom of the 1970s, have proved irresistible, not only to Nigerians, but to emigrants from neighbouring countries. A large proportion of the Ghanaians expelled from Nigeria in 1983–6 had been living in or near Lagos because they could most easily find work there. Growth rates have been largely due to migration, but with a young population the rate of natural increase is high.

Overall figures mask differences between the core and peripheral areas. Between the 1952 and 1963 censuses, the former Federal Territory grew by only 7 per cent per year, while the suburban districts which had formerly been part of the Western Region grew much faster. Ajegunle and Agege had an annual growth rate of 11 per cent, Mushin 18 per cent, Bariga 32 per cent and Shomolu 43 per cent. (Sada 1969: 123; Sada 1970; Morgan and Kannisto 1973: 12; Sada and Adefolalu 1975: 79–82).

A major problem has been increasing density, since housing and transportation could not keep up with such rapid expansion. Housing in many parts of the city has an average of three or more people per room, and the single room which is all that most households have is barely sufficient to store belongings; many activities of daily life necessarily take place out of doors (see Chapter 7). The density of north Lagos Island has always been much higher than the density of the city as a whole. For example, it had 19 305 people per sq km in 1921 and 48 263 in 1963. This was higher than the density of Manhattan Island in New York City, though in Lagos most residential buildings had only one or two storeys. In addition, a large proportion of the 100 000 daily commuters were working on the Island (FOS 1963; Baker 1974: 35).

Two suburbs demonstrate how rapidly population growth and integration into the metropolis took place. In the precolonial era, Mushin consisted of a number of Awori villages ruled by councils and headmen (Baale). The people were farmers and/or traders. The colonial authorities did not pay much attention to the area until the late 1920s, when migrants began to settle there in considerable numbers, buy land for housing and challenge the traditional authorities. Settler leaders united various groups and formed their own patron/client ties with the urban government. A Native Court and a Native Authority were established in 1944.

The town was separated from Lagos, against the will of the residents, when the Western Region government was established in 1951. Since this government saw no political advantage to servicing suburbs of the capital, Mushin continued to be neglected. The administrative status of the area changed fairly frequently, but in 1955 Mushin, with a population of 32 000, was designated a town, headquarters of an elective Mushin District Council. Such was the drawing power of the area and the land it made available for housing that in 1963 the population was 209 000; by 1972 it

Plate 1.3   Grave of a founder of Ajegunle

had risen to 600 000 (Barnes 1987). By then, there was no noticeable boundary between Lagos proper and Mushin. It is now one of the eight local government areas into which the metropolis is divided.

Ajegunle and the contiguous settlements of Araromi, Olodi and Amukoko grew from two villages, Alayabiagba and Onibaba. The latter was founded in 1870 to transfer smallpox patients out of the city to a shrine in this area. As in Mushin, government interest in the area was negligible until the late 1920s, when it was decided to develop land nearby. An attempt to introduce building regulations in 1940 pushed most residents of the area across what became Boundary Road. Some families followed the custom of burying deceased members in the compound (see Plate 1.3). The development of the port and industrial estate across the New Canal at Apapa in the 1950s provided the impetus for rapid growth, since Ajegunle was the nearest area for housing low-income workers.

The population was only 6200 in 1952, but had risen to 18 000 in 1963 and by 1972 was estimated to be about 90 000 in an area of about 3 sq km, pushing out on long fingers of land with swamps between them. The government has reclaimed some land by dumping the city's refuse into the swamps. Recent developments have greatly improved transportation to and from Ajegunle, linking it to urban expressways. Like Mushin, it appears to outsiders to be an integral part of Lagos, though it was only administratively incorporated into the city in 1989 (Sada 1969: 123; Peil 1981: 25).

The large scale of migration to Lagos has had a notable effect on age and sex ratios, since most newcomers are young and until recently males have been more likely than females to migrate. There were only 90 men per 100 women in 1891, when many men were away fighting. The sex ratio rose from par at the turn of the century to 135 in 1921, then declined to 118 in 1951, but rose to 131 in 1963 with the large numbers of male newcomers following independence. With the increasing migration of women and a growing child population, it declined to 98 in 1972. The proportion of the population under 30 has continued to climb, from 62 per cent in 1921 to 67 per cent in 1950 and 78 per cent in 1972. This is partly due to young immigrants, but also to the high birth rate of residents; only 31 per cent of the 1952 population was under 15 years of age, but this rose to 43 per cent in 1963 and 50 per cent in 1972 (HRRU 1972: 1–4; Morgan and Kannisto 1973: 14).

Sex ratios and natural increase vary from one ethnic group to another depending on their stability in Lagos. For example, Hausa migrants are often temporary – middle-aged men who come to trade and leave their wives at home. The proportion of elderly people is low because most of the population are recent arrivals, but numbers are also kept down because most Nigerians plan to return home in their old age. Only 1.9 per cent of the 1972 population were over 60, compared to 3.4 per cent of the national population, and the proportion is probably not much higher today. A survey in the older part of Shomolu in 1982 estimated that about 1.8 per cent of the population were over 60 (Mabogunje 1968: 266; HRRU 1972: 4; Bamisaiye and DiDomenico 1983: 5).

Land use

Differentiated land use goes back to the colonial period. Separate residential areas were developed by Saros, Brazilians, refugees from upcountry and Europeans. This enabled residents of each 'quarter', and especially the indigenes, to maintain their own cultural practices. The Europeans built storeyed houses and missions on the south coast of the Island, along what is now the Marina. This formerly despised area of trading wharfs, slave holding and refuse became prime land, first for residence because it faced the sea, and later for commercial offices when the Europeans, and later eminent Nigerians, moved east to Ikoyi and Victoria Island – the most expensive residential land in the city today (Aderibigbe 1975: 23–4). Saros lived to the west of the Europeans, while Brazilians were established along the middle spine of the island, behind both Europeans and Saros. The indigenes gradually spread from their crowded northwest corner along the north coast of the island, and newcomers found room on the periphery and the mainland.

Since 1989, metropolitan Lagos has been administered by eight local councils; these divisions have built on many earlier ones, as will be discussed in Chapter 3. Administrative distinctions pose many problems for residents, who often work and send their children to school in other parts of the city.

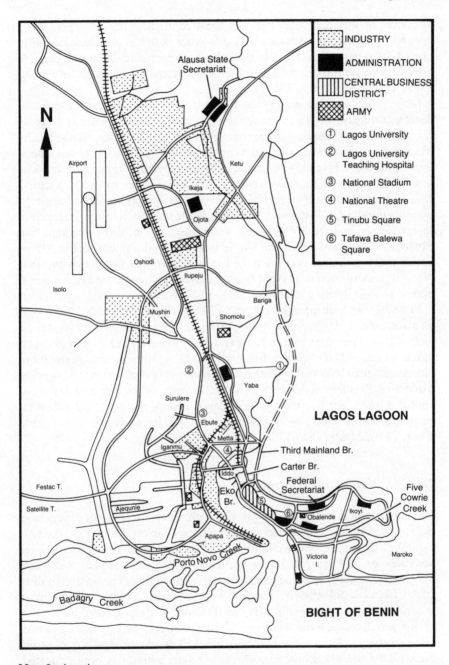

Map 3 Land use

Source: Adapted from Barbour *et al.* 1982: 97; O'Connor 1983: 194

The level of services varies between local councils, with more peripheral ones having the least resources. The difference between an infant mortality rate of 79 in the city and 148 in the suburbs is probably due to the variable provision of sanitation, water and health services (Morgan and Kannisto 1973: 11–12; Peil 1981: 27).

Map 3 shows topography and major locations in the metropolis, demonstrating how islands, canals, creeks, swamps and the railway increase the difficulty of moving from one part of the city to another. The MacGregor Canal was filled to support the Ring Road between Lagos Island and Ikoyi. Five Cowrie Creek, between Ikoyi and Victoria Island, was so-called because it cost five cowries (shells) to cross by ferry. Victoria Island is nearly at sea level and Bar Beach, on its Atlantic coast, is subject to periodic flooding; it lost about a half km to the sea this century. There were severe floods in June 1990, when water rose 1.5 m above normal; one expert has threatened that the whole island may disappear in the 1990s. Given the prestigious occupants of the island, it was not surprising that N115 m was allotted to prevent further damage. An offshore breakwater is planned (*West Africa* 1990: 950, 2058–9, 2286).

In 1976, the built-up area covered 8288 hectares, of which 51 per cent was residential, 19 per cent transportation, 13 per cent institutional or special use, 9 per cent industry, 5 per cent commerce and 3 per cent open space – only 0.01 hectare for each 1000 people in the population. However, much informal trading and recreation takes place on land in other categories. Residential density was 368/h. In terms of the type and density of land use, there are five main zones: Lagos Island, the port and industrial estates, and mainland low, middle and high density residential areas (Sada 1969, 1970; *Master Plan* 1980: 106).

CBD (Central Business District)

The urban core is still Lagos Island, although many government offices have been moved to Ikeja or Alausa on the mainland or even to Abuja, the new capital in the centre of the country. Major commercial and administrative activities are still located on the island, near and often mixed with high-density, low-quality housing and small-scale marketing. The western half of Lagos Island is still the city's central business district. Although the more prosperous stores are now in peripheral shopping centres, retailing is still a major activity along the Marina and Broad Street, and in the warren of streets between Tinubu Square, Nnamdi Azikiwe Street and the Eko and New Carter Bridges. Ebute Ero Market, the city's first, has been relocated, but is still functioning between the bridges. There is also considerable warehousing, wholesaling and small-scale industry in this area, mixed with residential housing on the north side of the island. Residential densities in central Lagos are reputed to average 4 per room, partly because many indigenes do not want to live anywhere else (Marris 1961).

The financial district is more central, with numerous local and international banks and insurance companies grouped near the Central Bank of Nigeria, many in tower blocks along the Marina (see Plate 4.1). To the east of these come administrative, educational and other institutions – headquarters of the Nigerian Ports Authority and the Nigerian Electrical Power Authority (NEPA), the City Hall, the Catholic and Anglican cathedrals, the First Baptist Church and several mission-related secondary schools. The Federal Capital, before its move to Abuja, was most evident in buildings such as the Supreme Court and the Houses of Parliament around the Racecourse and Tafalawa Balewa Square at the eastern end of the island.

Nearby Ikoyi and Victoria Island are closely linked to both government and business. State House, the residence of the Head of State in a civilian government, is on Victoria Island, whereas military government headquarters are in Ikoyi (Obalende). These areas also house the majority of embassies, high commissions and state liaison offices; Federal radio and television services; King's College and the Nigerian Law School; the National Museum and PEC Repertory Theatre; Falomo Shopping Centre, and several churches, banks and private clubs patronized by the elites.

Industry

The industrial areas are not contiguous, but a chain of major estates are located to the west and north of the city, between Apapa and Ikoyi. They include the docks at Apapa and the new port at Tin Can Island; industrial estates at Apapa, Iganmu, Ijora, Ikeja-Oregun and Ilupeju; and smaller areas west of Apapa, in Mushin, Gbagada-Matori, Ogba, Yaba and on Iddo Island (see Table 4.2). Because it houses the richest sector of the population, including large numbers of migrants establishing homes for the first time, Lagos is a prime area for manufacturing consumer goods and items for the construction industry. People in a hurry are prepared to spend substantial sums for processed food and drink, and firms relying on imports of raw materials or kits for assembly also profit from easy access to the Lagos port. The 124 firms reported in Lagos in 1963 had grown to 277 in 1969; by 1989, there were 1134 large industrial firms in metropolitan Lagos (Akinola and Alao 1975: 120–3; LSMC 1989).

The Apapa Industrial Estate, with those at nearby Ijora and Iganmu, covers 900 acres. These house large-scale (often multinational) manufacturers of food and drinks, soap, pharmaceuticals, metal products and motor assembly plants, plus construction firms and a dockyard. A third of the industrial labour force in Lagos in 1959 (some 14 000 workers) were employed in Apapa. Other engineering, plastics, textiles and food industries and transport businesses are located in nearby Iganmu and Ebute Metta.

The Ikeja Industrial Estate, with extensions, has about 400 acres on the north side of the city. Development began 1959, but considerable growth took place during the oil boom of the 1970s. It has a wide range of newer industries on plots of 2 to 10 acres. While some of these firms are locally owned, the largest (with 500 to 2000 workers) are branches of European and American firms; smaller firms (employing 50 to 200 workers) are often run by Syrians and Lebanese, Taiwanese or Indians. Metals, chemicals, pharmaceuticals, food products, beer, textiles, electrical equipment, domestic consumer goods, paint, cement and tyres are produced and vehicles are assembled here (see Table 4.1). By the early 1970s, this area had the largest concentration of factory workers in Nigeria (Mabogunje 1968: 286–9; Akinola and Alao 1975: 114; Peace 1979a: 3–6).

Mushin factories tend to be smaller and more scattered than those on the major industrial estates, though the same mixture of expatriate and locally owned firms produces engineering, construction and electrical goods as well as furniture, mattresses and bicycles. Several large textile firms are located along the Apapa-Oworonsoki Expressway at the western edge of Mushin. The Yaba Industrial Estate was started in 1957 to provide an impetus for small-scale manufacturing; firms share factory buildings, and are expected to move when they grow larger (Akinola and Alao 1975: 115).

Yaba is better known for its shopping centre around Sabo Market and its major industry, education. There was still open land in Yaba at a time when the need for large educational establishments arose. Lagos University was established at Yaba in 1962. In addition to Lagos Polytechnic and Queen's College, there are also Catholic, Methodist and international secondary schools in the area. The Government Trade Centre, the West African Examinations Council headquarters, local offices of the World Health Association, the Secretariat of the West African Health Community, the Registry of the Pharmacy Board of Nigeria and the Federal School of Radiography, various Ministry of Education offices, resource centres and teachers' colleges are also located in Yaba.

Finally, much of Iddo Island is taken up by the Lagos passenger terminal of the railway; another branch runs to the container terminal in Apapa. Large numbers of people cross this island to get to Lagos Island from Ebute Metta on the mainland. A NEPA station, PWD workshops and a wholesale food market are also located here.

Low density

Although housing areas for people of varying income/ability to pay can be differentiated in Lagos (see Maps 6 and 7), there is also considerable mixing in many areas and even within households, so that one's address may say little about one's income or standard of living. There are many wealthy people living in crowded, low-income areas, from Lagos Island and Ajegunle to Agege and other northern suburbs. This is partly a question of where successful men have found land to build and partly the need to stay close to business interests or the desire to remain with kinsmen.

Nevertheless, those who can afford it often seek housing on low-density estates in Apapa, Ikoyi, Victoria Island, Ikeja (the Government Residential area, Maryland, Palm Grove and Anthony Village) and the western periphery (Satellite Town), or in a band on the near mainland (Aguda, Surulere, Ike Ira and Yaba). They have shady, tarred roads and houses have modern conveniences, though the water and electricity supplies may be irregular. Houses are often storeyed, surrounded by gardens and with servants' quarters attached. Many employ watchmen, since armed theft is a continual hazard in Lagos. The government and other major employers rent houses and blocks of flats in these areas, providing subsidized accommodation for professional and high-level administrative employees.

The Apapa estate was built in the colonial era for industrial and commercial executives, who at that time were all expatriates. Victoria Island was developed after independence, at considerable cost in transforming a swampy 1500 acres into a high-quality residential area for top government officials, Members of Parliament and embassies. Government officials are also housed in Ikeja and Ikoyi, though private housing is also available in these areas for wealthy businessmen and professionals. Murtala Muhammed International Airport and the domestic airport take up a large area in Ikeja, and some Lagos State government offices are still there; the main Secretariat was moved out to Alausa (Sada and Adefolalu 1975: 88–9).

Middle density

Mainland residential areas of middle density housing in Ebute Metta, Igbobi, Surulere and Yaba have substantial houses, on planned streets, with frequent public transportation and a reasonably short journey to the city centre. Ebute Metta and Yaba South have lower-quality housing than other parts of this zone, partly due to their earlier urbanization. Older buildings have tended to deteriorate through overcrowding and inadequate repairs; single-family bungalows have sometimes been replaced by storeyed tenements. An extensive area in Ebute Metta is used by Nigerian Railways as workshops, station and residential area, and the National Theatre was built at the north end of the Eko Bridge. Igbobi is a small area, notable mainly for the Orthopedic Hospital, sports ground and army barracks.

Surulere has had several major housing developments, designed for middle and low income residents, though, in practice, most housing went to middle income families. The best known, the Surulere Rehousing Estate, was built by the government in the 1950s to clear the slums of central Lagos. The project is discussed in Chapter 7. The Lagos University College of Medicine and Teaching Hospital (LUTH) and the National and UAC Stadia are in Surulere. Festac Town provides flats for middle income families, and some high income houses. It was built on the Badagry Road for the 1977 Festival of African Arts and Culture.

High density

There is high density housing for low income families, usually in storeyed tenements, in most parts of the city, but they are especially prominent in Mushin and large peripheral settlements at Agege, Ajegunle, Bariga, Isolo, Maroko (until demolition), Oshodi, Shogunle and Shomolu. A major share of recent growth has been in these areas, with little planning or provision of services. They provide low-cost rooms, often in very poor conditions, for a majority of the city's poor, in locations which are relatively convenient to industrial employment or amenable to self-employment. Use of swampy land means that roads and houses may be flooded during the wet season, when open gutters along streets are unable to handle tropical storms. Three days of downpour in 1987 resulted in traffic at a standstill in many areas; overflowing gutters and drainage ditches disgorged debris into houses from Victoria Island to Ajegunle and Yaba. Unusually heavy rains in 1990 left many areas of Ajegunle, Bariga, Gbagada, Maroko and Mushin knee-deep in water. Traffic was paralyzed in many parts of the city (*West Africa* 1987: 1126; 1990: 2121).

Many of these areas had a long existence as independent villages or towns before becoming part of metropolitan Lagos. Many other villages are coming under urban pressure as the city expands to the north and west (Oyeleye 1981; McNulty and Adalemo 1988). The problems of housing and services in these areas and the influence of government planning on them will be discussed in Chapters 7 and 8.

Lagos is well served with a network of open markets, some of them very old (see Chapter 4). Small markets and street trading are common in most residential areas, and there is considerable buying and selling of both raw and cooked food by women from their homes; housewives seldom need to go far to get food. High income areas have modern shopping centres, and there are small and medium-sized shops and supermarkets near the major markets. However, regular visits to open markets remain an essential aspect of shopping in Lagos (Sada *et al.* 1978).

Summary

Lagos' founders and leaders in the struggle for independence are commemorated in its street names: Adeniji Adele Road, Aromire Avenue, Herbert Macaulay Street, Kosoko Street, Nnamdi Azikiwe Street, Obafemi Awolowo Way, Tinubu Square, and numerous streets named after early landowners. The prevalence of Yoruba names testifies to the continuing Yoruba dominance of the city, but the national and international mix is also evident – Alausa means Hausa and Sir Gilbert Carter, the British Governor who secured Lagos' trade with the interior, is still commemorated by his bridge.

The founders of Lagos established patterns that have continued to the present. Lagos has always been ethnically mixed and a commercial and political prize. It remains hot and swampy, overcrowded and underserviced, but a mecca of opportunity which can be richly rewarding to the successful few. The missionaries and colonial authorities introduced new ways of praying and making money, but allowed many traditional customs to survive. The independence movement rose quite naturally among a people who wanted to improve themselves and their families and saw how this could be done. Administrators, politicians and military rulers have come and gone and the pre-eminence of being the national capital has officially been lost to Abuja, yet Lagos is still the main focus of political ambition in Nigeria.

Migrants also flock there for work, education or health care. It continues to be the financial capital and provides a large share of the nation's manufacturing. Yet it remains in many ways a series of neighbourhoods which have their own foci of interest and political factions. National governments, of outsiders, have failed to understand and control this dynamic city; the State and local governments are beginning to come to grips with it. The following chapters will examine various facets of Lagos life: the strangers who share it with indigenes, the types of employment available, family life and the satisfaction of educational and health needs, social relationships, housing and the provision of services which are essential to a functioning metropolis. In each case, the city is made up of the people who share it, shaped by their activities and interests, and dependent on their interaction.

2
Locals and strangers

Oba Adeyinka Oyekan II (1911–) was born on 30 June 1911, son of Prince Kusanu Abiola Oyekan, a Methodist teacher, and great-grandson of Docemo I. He completed his secondary education at Kings College and earned a Diploma from the Yaba School of Pharmacy in 1932. After working for the Methodist Mission in eastern Nigeria, the army during the Second World War and the government in Lagos, he went into private practice. He was crowned head of the House of Docemo in 1950, but a battle over the *Oba*ship of Lagos (which reached the Privy Council in London) was lost to *Oba* Adeniji Adele II. Prince Oyekan had to withdraw as an NCNC Town Council candidate in 1950 because the opposition candidate was *Oba* Adele, backed by the Nigerian Youth Movement and the Action Group. Prince Oyekan ran for Parliament as an NCNC candidate in 1959, but lost. His lively personality and position as a supporter of expanded traditional authority recommended him to the kingmakers in 1965. As 18th *Oba* of Lagos, he was a strong supporter of the statehood movement and is Chairman of the Lagos State Council of *Obas* and Chiefs. Although participating fully in traditional rites, he also taught Sunday School for the Tinubu Methodist Church, and remains a committed member. He has 21 children and numerous grandchildren. He has travelled extensively in Nigeria and in Eastern and Western Europe; in Britain, he was a guest of Queen Elizabeth II (Baker 1974: 120, 212–18, 262–5; Folami 1982: 91–5).

A large majority of the Lagos population, both indigenes and immigrants, has always been Yoruba (Adefuge *et al.* 1986). Between 20 and 32 per cent of the population of Lagos at various early censuses were non-Yoruba immigrants; the 1950 census found that 37 per cent of the population were locally born (mainly Yoruba), 37 per cent were Yoruba immigrants and only 26 per cent non-Yoruba immigrants. Independence increased the flow of Yoruba from surrounding states to Lagos; by 1968 only 16 per cent of the population of the metropolitan area were non-Yoruba (Mabogunje 1968: 263; Morgan and Kannisto 1973: 17). Economic opportunities are the major factor in bringing both Yoruba and non-Yoruba to Lagos. In the early days, freed slaves of varying backgrounds sometimes stayed in Lagos.

Hausa ex-soldiers settled there, especially after the Asante wars. Later, the spread of education and transportation enabled Igbo from southeastern Nigeria to take up opportunities in Lagos. The field has widened in the post-independence period; Lagos provides opportunities that Africans from neighbouring countries cannot find at home. The expatriate 'European', 'Lebanese' and 'Asian' communities are small in numbers, but play an important role in commerce, socially and, on occasion, politically.

Ethnicity is an important factor in Nigerian politics and everyday life. Moving the capital from Lagos to Abuja was designed to place it on more neutral ground. The 1989 Constitution provides that the three most widely spoken languages can be used in the National Assembly; English has remained the national language because by being alien to all it is seen as politically neutral. Nigeria has at least 250 languages, which support local cultures and identities. With the spread of education and migration to the cities, an increasing proportion of the Nigerian population can speak English and find it convenient to do so. Nevertheless, daily life in Lagos is often complicated by the inability of people to communicate with each other (Peil 1976b: ch. 4).

Yoruba

The Yoruba are highly heterogeneous as ethnic groups go, with a wide variety of dialects, identities and forms of social organization. It is often pointed out that they were not seen as a single group until missionaries at Abeokuta produced a written form of their language, and that identification as descendants of Oduduwa was largely shaped by political factors in the struggle for independence. The name itself was given them by the Hausa. Yoruba are renowned for factionalism and for their entrepreneureal and political drive. Lagos is considered part of the Yoruba homeland, and has been largely shaped by Yoruba migrants. Most of these migrants see Lagos as an area to be exploited: Lagos 'is only a farm to us' (Krapf-Askari 1969: 33). The major groups will be discussed here, with the factors that brought them to Lagos and their contribution to the city.

The most important cultural factor for our purposes is the Yoruba cultural preference for living in large urban settlements, even when their occupations can easily be performed in villages (see Plates 2.1 and 2.2). Traditional Yoruba towns are notable exceptions to the accepted definition of 'urban' as large, dense, socially heterogeneous and permanent settlements. Though they were often large (several had 20 000 or more people in the 1850s), dense (with more than 10 000 people to the square mile) and permanent, Yoruba towns were ethnically homogeneous in the pre-colonial period and, except for Lagos and Ibadan, are so today.

The early towns also had a far more homogeneous labour force than they do today; most of the population were farmers in the wet season (going out to their farms as necessary) and craftsmen or traders in the dry season.

Plate 2.1   Fishermen at work

Plate 2.2   A Yoruba woman trader and her child

Many of these towns were political capitals, so rulers and soldiers played important roles; city government and status hierarchies were well-developed. Thus, they had many characteristics of farming villages but also characteristics that are certainly included in definitions of urban and even metropolitan. That the most urban of tropical African peoples should be major contributors to this metropolis can hardly be chance (Mabogunje 1968: Ch. 4; Krapf-Askari 1969).

Age, wealth and political power are the chief bases of status in the highly hierarchical Yoruba society, and they tend to be found together. While certain political roles are only open to members of royal lineages, there has always been scope for choosing the most promising candidate for promotion, often on the basis of wealth. Rich men are also given non-hereditary chieftaincy titles. The Ogboni Society, which uses traditional religion for political ends (on occasion, the government has forbidden civil servants to belong), is open to those who can pay the fees. Cocoa farming provided considerable wealth to many Yoruba families, but commerce has been even more productive. Their early start in Western education provided many opportunities for rising in the civil service and the professions, which have also led to economic and political advancement. Patron–client relationships are important for getting ahead, but there is also scope for individual achievement, providing one can attract followers (LeVine 1966: 37–41).

Yoruba migrants to Lagos have always had a strong contingent of Egba from Abeokuta and Badagry. They contributed about a quarter of the Yoruba immigrants recorded in both the 1931 and 1950 censuses. Of the next two most important subgroups, the Oyo decreased and the Ijebu increased during this period. The Oyo tend to find employment in their own capital, Ibadan, which was the largest tropical African city until the 1960s, whereas the Ijebu have divided their considerable energies between Ibadan and Lagos (Mabogunje 1968: 262–3).

Awori indigenes

Lagos was founded by the Awori people, whose territory stretches to the north and east of the city. The Awori have absorbed peoples of a wide variety of backgrounds who came to the area as slaves, tenant farmers, traders and wives; they are thus very mixed in heritage and identity tends to be socially, politically and morphologically based. As it has grown, Lagos has engulfed numerous Awori villages; this can sometimes be seen through interruptions in a 'grid' street pattern. Some lineages maintain an Awori identity while other lineages identify themselves as Lagosians, though this is flexible and partly depends on the circumstances.

Awori villagers have traditionally supported themselves by supplying food and receiving imported goods in exchange. Patron–client bonds between village elders and city elites have gradually developed over the years. The early participants were chiefs; later they were often political leaders. The Awori had no political institutions above their small villages, and were united mainly through common land and customs, including dialect. Neglect by the colonial authorities, at least until the 1930s, reinforced their autonomy and separation. The village *Baale* or headman, with his (or her) council continued to be responsible for administrative and judicial functions (Barnes 1986: 19–32).

The area was gradually suburbanized through settlement along the railway and the development of army and air installations during World War Two. The proportion of the population engaged in agriculture dropped sharply, so that by independence it was only a small minority. Rising crime encouraged residents to organize neighbourhood groups for their own protection, across inherited village lines. The *Baale* continued to preside over local courts, maintaining the judicial process in Awori hands.

Nevertheless, the numerous, relatively permanent settlers pouring into the area became more and more important through ownership of land and consequent political power in the community. They tended to be better educated than the Awori villagers and more willing to seek outside leadership roles. These newcomers sought to identify themselves as Lagosians rather than as Awori because incorporation into an Awori descent group took a long time. There was no overall Awori territorial identity which might be adopted, and becoming part of the capital was likely to be more rewarding. Thus, while there are still important Awori lineages which can be identified in the area, they are mixed with large numbers of outsiders and have not generally played an important role in the development of the city (Barnes 1986: 36–46).

Ijebu

As was noted in Chapter 1, the Ijebu were among the first arrivals in the village market from which Lagos' commercial power grew. Theirs is an ancient Yoruba kingdom, with a long history of trading as well as success in war, and migration to Lagos was a natural result of their trading interests. The Ijebu were dealing in slaves for the Lagos market by 1807, sent cloth to Lagos by 1823, and were finally conquered by the British in 1892–4 to destroy their middleman position in trade between Lagos and the hinterland. Their capital, Ijebu Ode, is about 100 km north of Lagos, off the main road to Ibadan. It was already large in the early sixteenth century, though the Ijebu as a whole have a more dispersed settlement pattern than most Yoruba subgroups. The *Awùjale* is the paramount *Oba*. Lagos was within easy canoe journey from Ijebuland; the Ijebu towns of Epe and Ikorodu are in Lagos State (Aronson 1978).

The Ijebu have a cognatic kinship system, which allows inheritance through either the father or the mother and consequently the manipulation of kinship links to maximize resources – a good background for entrepreneurial activities. They practised a wide range of occupations and put little emphasis on ascriptive position, giving opportunities for upward mobility through personal achievement. In addition, the farmland in much of the area was not very fertile and not useful for cocoa, which encouraged people to seek better income elsewhere. Many Ijebu went into trade; they dominated markets in many Yoruba towns and even further afield. Their income as middlemen was often considerably higher than that of local farmers, which sometimes gave rise to social and political conflict. During the early colonial period, the Ijebu were in conflict with the Ibadan, who aspired to control a wide area (Akeredolu-Ale 1973; Eades 1980: 25, 43).

On the whole, colonial rule over Ijebu was light; it provided many opportunities for Ijebu craftsmen and traders, and had relatively little effect on values and worldview. Obviously, there were many changes brought about by the introduction of world religions and western education (both very popular among the Ijebu), but there has also been considerable local control and continuity; the Ijebu were relatively undisturbed by the nineteenth-century Yoruba wars and found many ways to use colonial rule to their own advantage. Christianity came early to Ijebu, through traders returning from Abeokuta or Lagos and visits of missionaries from these cities. Education provided by the missions was soon seen as the way ahead.

By 1921, Ijebu Province (a colonial creation which took in only part of the former Ijebu lands) was ahead of every area except Lagos in the proportion of Christians and the number of children in schools; education for girls advanced rapidly. Ijebu Ode Grammar School was founded in 1913, soon after the one in Abeokuta, but many Ijebu were also educated in Lagos and Ibadan, where they often stayed to work. Although the Egba have a reputation for being educated, the Ijebu have higher rates and fill many of the civil service jobs in Abeokuta, their mutual state capital.

Islam was brought to Ijebu Ode by traders and proved popular; about two-thirds of the Ijebu Ode population are Muslim, whereas about two-thirds of the rest of the Ijebu are Christians. Trading has been particularly attractive to Muslims, as it does not require literacy in English; Christians, on the other hand, have found many opportunities in government service and the professions (Aronson 1978: 15–19; Eades 1980).

A survey in 1969 found that about a quarter of the Ijebu population had left home; over a third of these – up to 50 000 people – had gone to Lagos. Christians are especially likely to go to Lagos, as the best place to find non-manual employment, but Muslims also see it as a major source of opportunity. This leaves the home area very short of young adults. Though a substantial number of the Ijebu settle permanently at their destination, many others return home in old age, so that there are large numbers of elderly people in Ijebu towns (Aronson 1978: 20–23; Peil *et al.* 1988).

Ijebu businessmen see commerce as a very natural occupation; they have many relatives engaged in business and outsiders expect them to be successful at it. On the whole, business has considerable status (it often pays far more than clerical work), and young people are socialized into it through helping their parents. A wide network of contacts is a crucial factor for successful business in Nigeria. The Ijebu have had a long time to build up such networks and use them to compete with outsiders. However, the competition in Lagos is increasingly severe, and the Ijebu appear to be rather slow in moving from trading into the larger-scale manufacturing operations which are important for future growth (Akeredolu-Ale 1973).

Egba and Egbado

There are many similarities between the Egba, the Egbado and the Ijebu, who now share Ogun State. The Egbado, whose homeland is to the west of the Egba, are more rural and less educated; they are traditional suppliers of maize, cassava and other foodstuffs to Lagos. In pre-colonial times, the area was ruled from Oyo, the kingdom to the north. In the colonial administrative organization, Egbado Division was about the same size as Egba Division, but had about half as many people. The Egba are found as far south as Badagry on the coast and migration to Lagos goes back to the city's early history. Abeokuta, the Egba capital, was established in 1830 by refugees from the Yoruba wars and grew rapidly. It is distinguished from other Yoruba towns by its political divisions. Where most towns have one *Oba*, Abeokuta has five, with the *Alake* as *primus inter pares*, a result of the continuance of descent group and military interests among the refugees. The present *Alake* was a prominent Lagos businessman before his selection.

Although about half of the Egba population are Muslims, it sheltered many returned slaves and produced the first Yoruba Christians. Refugees from the riots of 1867 were the foundation of the large Egba community in Lagos, which was greatly enhanced by the railway link between the two towns. Both Christian and Islamic education have continued to be very important, the first producing clerks and professionals and the second traders and craftsmen. Egba villages are more closely tied to their city than Ijebu villages; many villagers have links to a family house in Abeokuta and some spend part of the year in the city. This makes it easier for them to adapt to city life should they decide to migrate to Lagos. The pattern may have arisen from the destruction of farm settlements during the nineteenth-century wars, with recolonization of the rural areas when cocoa farming proved profitable. Cocoa is a seasonal crop, which facilitates shifting between rural and urban locations and occupations (Krapf-Askari 1969: 101; Eades 1980).

Other Nigerians

Some 15 per cent of the Lagos population are non-Yoruba Africans, mainly from other parts of Nigeria; only 1–2 per cent are non-Africans. Initially, many non-Yoruba immigrants were Hausa, but by 1931 Igbo contributed a quarter of the non-Yoruba, and this increased to nearly half by 1950. Many Igbo immigrants returned home during the disturbances and civil war of the 1960s (their proportion of the Lagos population declined to less than 3 per cent), but they arrived in increasing numbers in the 1970s. Considering that they have less than 1.5 per cent of the Nigerian population, Edo immigrants are well-represented in Lagos, partly because of their links to its early development. About a seventh of non-Yoruba immigrants 1921–50 were Edo, and expanding education at home since independence has encouraged many peoples from what has become the ethnically heterogeneous Bendel State to seek their fortune in the capital (Mabogunje 1968: 262–3; Morgan and Kannisto 1973: 17; Cole 1975a: 28).

Igbo

The Igbo homeland lies on both banks of the Niger River in southeastern Nigeria, with about two-thirds on the eastern side. The Igbo are similar to the Yoruba in being divided into many subgroups, which only began to see themselves as one people during the political struggles which preceded independence. However, they are quite unlike the Yoruba in many ways, notably in being a rural and (with a few exceptions) a politically egalitarian people, traditionally dispersed in small villages run on democratic principles by lineage elders and leaders of local societies. Igbo 'towns' were essentially groups of villages, cooperating mainly to provide markets and, more recently, services in the form of schools, roads, water supply, etc. for the area's population. There is still intense loyalty to one's place of origin, so that residence 'abroad' tends to be seen as a temporary convenience rather than a long-term commitment to a new location.

Perhaps because most Igbo subgroups had no hereditary leadership, status and prestige are open to individual achievement and facilitated by acquired wealth; this sets the Igbo apart from many more hierarchical ethnic groups, and has proved a good preparation for success in modern Nigeria. One occupation is as good as another so long as it leads to the goal. Achievement can be demonstrated and prestige enhanced by rising in village title societies, which requires increased investment at each level. But it is accepted that an individual cannot succeed on his own, and wealth *per se* is not enough; it must be converted into prestige through benefiting one's family and hometown – paying for relatives' education, building a large house at home, contributing to village development. This cultural and moral expectation is usually fulfilled because it has a strong practical basis; wealth and political power are often ephemeral in modern Nigeria, and those who have used their position to help others will be able to call on them in times of trouble.

The Igbo readily took to Christianity, especially in its Anglican and Catholic forms; pentecostal sects have attracted large numbers in recent years. The mission schools provided an ability to 'read book', which promised the worldly success they sought; the smaller sects provide a friendly community of fellow-seekers. Their homeland has long been densely populated, and many areas are now severely eroded through overuse, so large numbers of young people are forced to leave home for employment. Western education was introduced later than in Yorubaland, but it spread rapidly and has led to large-scale migration, especially to Aba, Enugu and Onitsha (the largest Igbo cities), Port Harcourt (the nearest metropolis), the north (an educationally deprived area, which also had many business opportunities) and Lagos. Whatever the job, the Igbo have a reputation as hard workers (Uchendu 1965; LeVine 1966).

A competitive and manipulative outlook has often made Igbo migrants less acceptable to their hosts than more passive newcomers. They have shown a strong inclination to group together to further their mutual interests, notably in the Igbo State Union, an important political force in the early 1960s. Most of the Igbo living in cities belong to ethnically homogeneous associations, centred on hometown, savings, church and/or recreation. These provide an active social life with people of similar interests and mutual support in times of crisis. They make it possible to keep aloof from other peoples, which enhances the Igbo reputation for exploitation in the marketplace (Barnes and Peil 1977).

Their desire for autonomy and independence of higher authority led other people to question Igbo loyalty to the nation. Mutual suspicion was reinforced in the upheavals of the mid 1960s, which led to Igbo secession and the civil war. Though some remained where they were, hundreds of thousands of Igbo returned home to avoid communal violence. In Lagos, many Igbo who decided to stay moved out of largely Yoruba areas to Ajegunle, the most heterogeneous part of the city. This area also attracted a stream of new migrants once the war was over. They are seldom house-owners in Lagos; there is strong pressure to invest at home, so they rent rooms where they can while living 'abroad'. Many lost jobs in the civil service and had to start over; there is now a wider dispersion of Igbo through the Lagos labour force.

Igbo women tend to be more subservient to their husbands than Yoruba women (possibly because of the influence of mission Christianity), and are less likely to be in the labour force. Igbo women living in Lagos are most likely to be economically active if they have obtained enough education to qualify for teaching, nursing or clerical work.

Hausa

The Hausa kingdoms were conquered by the Fulani in the early nineteenth century, but intermarriage by both the aristocracy and ordinary people makes it difficult to distinguish these groups. About a quarter of the Nigerian population are Hausa, which has made them a political force in the country. The proportion of Hausa/Fulani, and other northerners, in

Lagos has been low in recent years; they are mainly soldiers, politicians or cattle traders, none of whom intend to settle permanently. Large-scale recruitment by colonial powers of a people seen as able soldiers made Hausa the *lingua franca* of several West African armies. Many Hausa are in Lagos on transfer, helping to control the country during times of military rule (Luckham 1971).

Trading and politics fit very well into Hausa culture. They are typical 'backwoods politicians', hierarchically organized by an Islamic aristocracy, conservative in ideology, focusing their hopes for social mobility on the efficacy of patron–client relations. Political power is seen as leading to wealth, and competition is often intense. However, political leadership is an insecure business, subject to sudden retirement or jail. The Hausa have operated in national politics much as they would in local politics, using numerical superiority and mobilizing social/economic networks to dominate. They have been well behind the Yoruba and Igbo in taking up western education and the use of English (one often hears the argument that Nigeria's national language should be Hausa), but have used their own cultural background to good effect in developing efficient long-distance trading networks and flexibly adapting their political structures to the realities of post-independence Nigeria. Several are now listed among Nigeria's wealthiest businessmen. Islam is a basic component of Hausa culture. There have been major riots by fundamentalists in the north in the 1980s, and strong arguments for the Sharia law are made whenever the Constitution is being revised (LeVine 1966: 7, 25–32; Cohen 1969; Whitaker 1970).

In Lagos, they are particularly involved in the cattle trade, accompanying loads of cattle from the north and minding them until they are sold to butchers or exported to neighbouring countries. Temporary visitors who camp out under flyovers are periodically cleared by the government. The longer-term migrants are likely to live in Idi-Oro (Surulere), which is convenient for trading; in the older sections of Ajegunle, where they have set up their own mosques and Koranic schools near the cattle-yard; or in Agege, where much long-distance transportation is organized. Some act as landlords/brokers/bankers for itinerant traders. Others find roles in the Muslim community as mallams or beggars. Begging is an approved occupation for Muslims; a study in the 1940s found that over 90 per cent of Lagos's beggars were Hausa, most of them permanent residents (Cohen 1969: 46).

Many Hausa prefer to follow the Islamic practice of secluding their women, at least during their child-bearing years. While many secluded women in the north earn money through trading from the house (with children as intermediaries) or craft work, this is more difficult in competition with freer Yoruba women in Lagos (both Muslims and Christians). Thus, while older Hausa women may be active as midwives or herbalists or may trade from the gate like Yoruba or Igbo women, the younger ones are often left without a source of income and thus are more dependent on their husbands than these other women. There are also fewer Hausa women than men in Lagos, because short-term migrants often prefer to leave their wives at home. Hausa women without husbands may find prostitution a convenient way to support themselves, though they are more likely to settle in northern cities than in Lagos (Pittin 1983).

Non-Nigerians

The proportion of non-Nigerian Africans and of non-Africans has always been small, though obviously Europeans have had considerable influence on the city. Immigrants from Bénin, Togo and Ghana have been attracted by Lagos' prosperity, especially during the oil boom of the 1970s, when there were many low-paid jobs which Nigerians were unwilling to do. Most non-Africans are diplomats, managers of multinational corporations or middle-level businessmen, though some are wives of Nigerians or are attached to the University or Medical School. Many businessmen are from the Middle East (mainly Lebanon) or India.

In local parlance, residents who are not Nigerian citizens fall into two categories – aliens (who are African) and expatriates (referred to as *oyinbo*), who are mainly European or American, Lebanese or Indian. A majority of the Americans and Europeans in the country – about 20 000 – live in Lagos. Expatriates are usually among the elites of the society in terms of wealth and social position, though they have little manifest power. Aliens, on the other hand, are present in considerably larger numbers and are usually relatively low in economic, political and social position, insofar as they can be distinguished from the local population. They are tolerated because they take jobs which Nigerians do not want or (the better-trained immigrants) for which there are no qualified local candidates.

Aliens

The oil boom of the 1970s brought large numbers of aliens to Lagos, especially from Ghana, where the economy was in collapse; in many places there was not enough food to eat. While Ghanaian teachers and nurses found jobs all over Nigeria, artisans and unskilled school leavers tended to congregate in Lagos because there was work in factories, construction and petty trading. Nigerians were leaving relatively unremunerative manual work for commerce – the goal of most Yoruba, which provided openings for newcomers willing to work for the wages offered. Many of these immigrants came without official papers; these are difficult and expensive to acquire and were not needed by those willing to give a small bribe at the border or able to cross by a bush path. An ECOWAS (Economic Community of West African States) Protocol on Free Movement (signed in 1979) allowed for visits of up to 90 days without a visa; many using this method simply stayed on. The government requirement that aliens have a work permit is ignored by small-scale employers.

In January 1983, all illegal aliens were given two weeks to leave the country or face deportation. This was partly aimed at Muslim fundamentalists who had caused riots in the north, but the other main target was Ghanaians in Lagos. There had been poor relations between Accra and Lagos following the expulsion of perhaps 200 000 Nigerians in 1969–70 and the influx of Ghanaian political refugees into Lagos after the coup of 1981. Both governments had harassed each other's nationals during 1981–2 and deported a few on criminal, economic or political grounds (Peil 1971; Brydon 1985; Aluko 1987).

The Nigerian expulsion exercise was justified in much the same terms and took much the same form as the Ghanaian one. Ghanaians were accused of armed robbery and of being a danger to national security. This ignored the relatively small contribution of aliens to the national or local crime rate; the organizers and perpetrators of crime in Nigeria are overwhelmingly its own citizens. Official crime statistics for Lagos in 1980–3 showed only 328 convictions of foreign nationals, of whom half were Ghanaians. This is not unrepresentative of their proportion in the alien population. Armed robbery has been a serious problem in Nigeria at least since the 1967–70 war, long before there were many Ghanaians to participate. However, some Ghanaians were caught in an abortive attack on the official residence of the Nigerian Vice-President in January 1983 (the number of Nigerians involved was never mentioned), and this strengthened the national security argument (Gravil 1985: 533).

Growing unemployment was a much more valid justification for getting rid of aliens. Lack of alternatives does lead some immigrants to crime, but more important, by the early 1980s unemployment was assumed to be at least 20 per cent in Lagos and Nigerians wanted back the jobs they had left to the aliens. Those without jobs could be deported as 'without visible means'. As has often happened in West Africa, aliens were a convenient scapegoat in hard times, and the expulsion order was popular except to employers who had to pay higher wages to Nigerians (Peil 1971; Aluko 1987).

In practice, having papers and stable employment did not protect aliens. Once the order had been given it was wise to get out if one could. Lagos landlords locked rooms so that belongings could not be reclaimed, workplaces were searched and people suspected of being aliens were attacked on the streets. Some schools, hotels and building contractors had to close temporarily when they lost all or most of their employees; many small firms were happy to welcome returnees a few months later. Given the perennial shortage of housing in Lagos, landlords had little difficulty replacing their former tenants and could raise rents at the same time.

From the Ghanaian viewpoint, the return of about a million citizens, mostly with little more than the clothes on their backs, at a time of severe food shortage was a major catastrophe. They were also unwelcome to families counting on their remittances, and many slipped back into Nigeria as soon as it seemed safe. Some were deported again in 1984 or 1985. By this time, the Ghanaian government was less willing to help them resettle, but opportunities in Nigeria, however risky, were still seen as better than those in Ghana. The ethnic hostility and lack of environmental and personal hygiene in Yoruba cities were additional disincentives for Ghanaians, but had to be borne for the profits to be made (Brydon 1985).

Expatriates

Expatriates are only a small part of the Lagos elites. They are mainly housed in high-income estates. Their social and work lives often keep them separate from ordinary Lagosians; they travel by air-conditioned car, shop in large stores rather than open markets and spend their leisure time away from home in elite clubs or friends' homes. Their children usually attend special schools, often taught by expatriate women. They may attend the same churches and mosques as Nigerians living in their neighbourhoods, but the Lebanese Christians have their own Maronite church and Hindus their own temple.

Lebanese and Indians are notable examples of 'middleman minorities' in West African cities, as strangers exploiting local commercial opportunities, living in a community but not part of it. Starting with small amounts of capital, many have built up substantial businesses. The Lebanese have played an important if minor role in West African commerce since the 1860s, though they arrived in Nigeria considerably later than in Senegal and Sierra Leone. Income tax records for Lagos Colony, 1928–9 show 58 'Syrians', as they were then called, and seven Indians (Bonacich 1973; Baker 1974: 76; Leighton 1979).

Initially small-scale traders, the Lebanese soon moved into transportation, distribution and shopkeeping, filling gaps between local petty-traders and major European companies. Since independence, violence and economic disruption at home have meant that Lebanese born in West Africa have been joined by family members from home, making business expansion essential. At the same time, they have been legislated out of smaller ventures to make way for Nigerian entrepreneurs, and have moved increasingly into manufacturing.

There are about 9000 Indians in Lagos, including families; most are relatively recent arrivals. Some came from East Africa, but others were businessmen in India or England who decided to invest in Nigeria. Indians have also focused on manufacturing as the area in which their capital and experience are most likely to be fruitful.

Indigenization decrees of 1972 and 1977 restricted the areas of the economy in which foreigners can participate and required 40 or 60 per cent local participation in major areas, such as banking and mining, by December 1978. These decrees effectively moved aliens out of market trading and many other small entrepreneureal ventures, and restricted transportation, among other areas, to Nigerians. There has been considerable indigenization of management, especially in banking and insurance, providing many good middle-class jobs for Nigerian graduates.

Unlike the Lebanese or Indians, few Europeans are committed to a long stay in Lagos; their stay is part of a career focused elsewhere. A few European entrepreneurs in Lagos own their own businesses, but they are more likely to be on transfer as employees of multinational corporations, NGOs such as the Ford and Rockefeller Foundations or the World Bank, or attached to the diplomatic community. The same is true of the few Japanese in Lagos. The number of expatriates employed by the University and other educational institutions has declined considerably in recent years, both because Nigeria can now produce its own personnel for higher education and because it cannot afford to hire or house foreigners except for short periods. Some make a serious attempt to understand the society in which they live; others separate themselves from it as much as possible and take frequent holidays at home for shopping, health and 'peace'.

Expatriate wives of Nigerians are an exception to this. Their position can be very difficult, since at least initially they usually know almost nothing about their husbands' language or culture. He has many old friends; she has none. Coping with Lagos life (traffic, crime, electricity and water cut-offs, shortages of imported goods, health problems, etc.) can be very difficult for women from abroad whose previous experience of other cultures has been a holiday in Spain or Greece. Their husband's attitudes toward polygyny or 'outside wives', the amount of support he is prepared to give his extended family and his expectation of an eventual return home in old age often come as a shock. Thus, while some marriages are stable over a long period many do not survive the first two years. Nigerwives, which helps these women with their problems, is discussed in Chapter 6.

Summary

One reason for moving the capital from Lagos to Abuja was to have a city which is not dominated by one ethnic group – which belongs to the whole country. Like any metropolis, Lagos has a very heterogeneous population, but such a large proportion are Yoruba that members of other major and minor ethnic groups feel discriminated against. Ethnicity is only one factor in differentiation, as will be shown in later chapters; the importance of ethnic differences varies from one situation to another and every group has its successful individuals. While the strong Yoruba dominance might set Lagos apart from most world cities and certainly shapes it character, the propensity of the Yoruba to divide into separate sub-groups when close to home makes the issue more complex. The emphasis on personal (or at most family) success means that ethnic groups are seldom cooperative units. Ethnicity is useful in major political contests, such as state or national elections, but everyday social and economic networks focus on smaller groups, as will be shown in Chapter 6.

A study of ethnic attitudes in 1972 found that the Yoruba of Ajegunle were more prejudiced against strangers than other ethnic groups in Ajegunle or Yoruba living elsewhere. An explanation can be given in terms of competition; Ajegunle is the only area in Lagos where the Yoruba are a numerical minority, though they remain the major houseowners. The Yoruba see Lagos as their city (or their farm), and want to reap most of the benefits for themselves. The study was done just after the civil war, so there was probably stronger feeling against the strangers (especially Igbo) pouring into Lagos than would have occurred a few years later, when economic opportunities were better. Nevertheless, at the behavioural level, there was considerable mixing of peoples in housing and, to a lesser extent, in friendship. Most large houses had members of several ethnic groups living together, even members of groups which had been enemies during the war (1967–70). The Yoruba were considerably less likely than members of other groups to have close friends who were not Yoruba, but they had far more people of their own group available (Peil 1976b: ch. 4).

Ethnicity and sub-ethnicity continue to be important in politics (as will be discussed in the next chapter) and limit social contacts because ethnic identity patterns language use. Many migrants to Lagos, and even some people who have grown up there, refuse to learn Yoruba, arguing that since English is the national language it should be the means of communication in the capital.

People who live in Lagos learn to get along with strangers, though conflict which arises over jobs or use of facilities may be expressed in ethnic terms. Once a situation of conflict occurs, the lack of a common language can be a serious barrier to resolution, as when a policeman is called in to stop a fight but cannot communicate with either of the participants. Expanding education helps. Virtually all children growing up in Lagos attend school (see Chapter 5), and most of the younger generation can communicate in basic English as well as in a variety of Nigerian languages. Women are more isolated by language than men, since primary education for girls has lagged behind that for boys and they have fewer opportunities for meeting strangers. Learning Yoruba and taking on local cultural forms can be useful to an alien. Expatriates seldom learn local languages and few learn much about local customs. For most, living in Lagos merely involves temporary inconvenience; more permanent residents such as the Lebanese tend to maintain their own social groups.

Thus there are many ways in which Lagos remains a Yoruba city, but its size and complexity clearly set it apart from smaller and more provincial Yoruba cities. The distinction is less clear in some central and suburban areas where non-Yoruba are rare and links with tradition strong than in industrial or elite areas where Lagos's ethnic heterogeneity is more in evidence.

3
Politicians

Lateef Kayode Jakande (1929–) was born in Lagos and has lived most of his life there. He rose from reporter on the *Daily Service* (a trade union newspaper) at 20 to Associate Editor, then edited the *Nigerian Tribune* in Ibadan. In 1956, he was appointed General Manager of the Amalgamated Press in Lagos, then Managing Director of Allied Newspapers, Chairman of John West Publications and first President of the Newspaper Proprietors' Association of Nigeria. As is common with Nigerian journalists, he has long been involved in politics. He was an active supporter of Action Group during the first republic, and was jailed with Obafemi Awolowo for 'treasonable felony and conspiracy'. While in prison, he wrote *Trial of Obafemi Awolowo* and 'The Case for a Lagos State'. Released in 1966, he headed the Lagos delegation in negotiations over national structural changes under the second military regime. His argument for alliance with the Western Region was not acceptable to Lagos indigenes, who demanded their own state. However, in 1979 he was elected Governor of Lagos State on the UPN ticket, which swept the local elections. Unlike several other governors, he was very popular with the people, since his regime greatly expanded education and improved roads in both the city and the state. He was imprisoned without trial after the 1983 coup, but freed in September 1985. His birthday was commemorated while he was still in jail, with prayers led by the chief Imam that he would soon be released 'to finish the job he had left uncompleted.' He is married with three children, lives in Ilupeju, Lagos and is Chairman of John West Publications (*Who's Who in Nigeria* 1971: 126; Baker 1974:263–7; *West Africa* 1985: 1564, 1880; 1986: 537; Olurode 1989).

Politics is the lifeblood of Lagos, and interest in politics spreads far beyond those who have been elected or appointed to public office. It is the effective national capital (though this function is gradually being lost), a state capital and the seat of eight local governments. All of these are interrelated, and little goes on in Lagos that does not have political implications. Land rights, employment, industry and other sources of wealth rely on political inter-action, involving patron–client relations, bribery, corruption, nepotism and/or 'long-legs' (contacts). Almost everyone knows someone with a link, however tenuous, to those in power.

This chapter focuses on the major political events which have shaped Lagos at the national and state levels and the use made of politics at the local level. Local leadership was important in making Nigeria an independent nation and giving the indigenes their own state. Local councillors and civil servants seek to mould Lagos as a city within the constraints of national and state supervision. Finally, landlords (often of migrant background) manipulate local government links to strengthen their property rights and their place as neighbourhood leaders. Market women are less adept at political manipulation, but occasionally take action to defend their interests.

National Politicians

Agitation for independence started early in Lagos, as described in Chapter 1. Between 1938 and 1950, the nationalist elite largely displaced the 'black Victorians' as the manifest leaders in Lagos. This was the most politically 'advanced' area in Nigeria, and there were political roles and objectives to fight for. The new generation was better educated than their fathers and more interested in joining together and organizing the masses to oppose colonialism.

Since independence, there has been continual conflict over how much power can be centralized in Lagos and how much decentralization to the federated states is consonant with the best interests of Nigeria as a nation. In spite of the requirement of the 1979 Constitution that political parties have a national base, the reality that parties tend to arise in regional political centres such as Kano, Kaduna, Enugu or Ibadan favoured political decentralization. Nevertheless, much of the jockeying for power and deals for coalitions has taken place in Lagos, because this is a relatively neutral ground for all concerned. It is here that representatives of the states meet and negotiate for national power. There has been general agreement (except from the neighbouring southwest) that Lagos is too important to the nation to be under the control of one sector; it should belong equally to all Nigerians. The difficulty of achieving this was a major reason for transferring the capital to Abuja. The two parties inaugurated by federal decree in 1990 are relatively centralized; it remains to be seen how control over them will be achieved.

Two major parties of the colonial period continued to be contenders for leadership during the First Republic. The Action Group (AG) remained a largely Yoruba organization; in Lagos it catered for Yoruba migrants who were settling there in large numbers. The indigenes joined when Lagos was under the Western Region and alliance to AG was necessary for a share in power, but they opposed AG policies which were not to their own benefit (see below). The NCNC drew support from immigrants who had been important in Lagos politics of an earlier period and the mass of non-Yoruba migrants through their hometown associations, though many Lagos indigenes were also attracted (Baker 1974: 56–7).

Plate 3.1 Gates at Tafalwa Balewa Square
Source: Richard Ammann

An important factor in the ability of migrants to Lagos to develop national parties in opposition to the colonial power was literacy. Missions attracted children to schools by promising non-manual jobs in Lagos, and those considering long distance migration to a strange city (notably the Igbo) felt more confident if they had education as a basis for job-seeking. Once established, 'strangers' faced the opposition of indigenes and other Yoruba to their participation in local, and later state, politics, but the more able could find roles in ethnically mixed national politics. Wealth from business or other sources has not been crucial for political success (wealth is often obtained after being elected), but it is handy for those wanting to play a role behind the scenes. This was more true for national than for local elections; there have been few allegations of bribery and vote manipulation in Lagos compared to other parts of the country, perhaps because local office is not worth much compared to the alternatives available in Lagos and because Lagos residents are better informed on political issues and more expensive to buy.

Independence in 1960 brought many new government buildings, especially around the Racecourse at the west end of the Island. These were further enhanced as Tafawa Balewa Square and Remembrance Arcade were developed in the 1970s (see Plate 3.1). The city was initially under the Ministry of Lagos Affairs, which handled all national activities taking place there; considerable city land was alienated to national institutions. The military government of the late 1960s divided supervision between the Ministry of Internal Affairs and the Ministry of Works and Housing. With statehood, some of these functions were devolved to the state government, but others will continue to be under the national government even after it finally moves to Abuja.

Discussions on a new federal capital to replace Lagos started even before independence, but it was not until oil brought an economic boom to Nigeria in the 1970s that it became a practical possibility. In the aftermath of the civil war, it was important that the country have a capital which was relatively central and not under the control of members of any single ethnic group. Immediately after the coup which brought him to power in August 1975, the late General Murtala Muhammed set up the Aguda Panel to find a new Federal Capital. On 3 February 1976 he proclaimed that a new capital would be established at Abuja; a Federal Capital Territory would be developed in a relatively uninhabited area drawn from Niger, Kaduna, Kwara and Plateau States. It was expected to take about twenty years to build (*ThisWeek*, 22 June 1987: 11, 14).

Under the banner of fostering national unity, the Shagari government of the Second Republic spent an estimated N3 billion to speed the building of Abuja, but corruption and inefficiency absorbed far too much of this. Things went more slowly after the advent of military government in 1983. The first Independence Day celebration in Abuja was in 1982, but by mid 1987 only the Ministries of Internal Affairs and Trade had moved north. The transfer of further ministries was delayed by lack of accommodation in Abuja; only 4247 units were built in the first ten years. In February 1988, 5000 civil servants from the Ministry of Agriculture, the National Youth Service Corp, the National Mathematical Centre and the incipient Constitutional Assembly were ordered to move within the next six months. Given the isolation and crowded living conditions for all except government leaders, some civil servants have refused to move. There are fears that the north is making Abuja a Muslim capital, where southerners are consigned to inferior roles. Private firms have been loath to move from Lagos, which is still the most advantageous location for them (*ThisWeek*, 22 June 1987: 19; *National Concord* 26 February 1988).

Indigenes and Strangers: Lagos State

Wherever a national capital is administratively separate from the rest of the country (as in Washington DC and Canberra, Australia), problems arise as to how much political power can be exercised by its permanent residents. This is less of a problem, at least initially, where the capital city is created for the purpose, as in the two cities mentioned and in Nigeria's new capital at Abuja, than where the Federal Territory encompasses a major city with a long history. Moscow, Bonn and Yaoundé provide a better model for Lagos, being both national and state capitals. But control over Lagos is more important than control over Bonn or Yaoundé, because of its primate position in the country's commerce, industry and transportation. To what extent should decisions be made by national politicians and how much say should local people have? There is plenty of money to be made, and decision-makers have considerable control over where it goes.

Baker (1974, Ch. 9) presents a detailed discussion of the Lagosians' struggle for equality with Nigeria's other states, with more control over local affairs than is possible in a Federal Territory. It is notable that the process is being repeated in Abuja, though so far on only a small scale. People who have settled in Abuja tried to get increased local government functions into the 1989 Constitution but failed; for the time being it is to remain a territory under the Federal Government, without the administrative and judicial functions of a state.

Lagos was separated from the rest of the country in 1886, when it became a Crown Colony under direct rule. It lost this independence with the 1951 constitution, coming under the dominance of Western Region in 1952. The drive for autonomy began at this period, when Lagosians experienced the disadvantages of being ruled from Ibadan. The capture of Lagos was a financial bonanza for Western Region; decisions affecting local progress were often taken with an eye to regional rather than local benefits. Developments in transportation and industry tended to favour Ibadan or areas traditionally part of Western Region rather than areas which were clearly in the Lagos municipality. The AG, Western Region's major political party, used its suzerainty to wean voters away from the NCNC, though this did not mean that they followed AG blindly when local interests were at stake. The AG in Lagos soon acquired local leadership, which used it for local ends. Lagos market women remained AG supporters long after the civilian government had been overthrown.

Federal status for Lagos was important for other parts of the country. The north depended on its port for both imports and exports, the east saw Western Region dominance over Lagos votes as a hindrance to its national political position, minority groups in various parts of the country needed an independent centre to which they could appeal and many entrepreneurs resented the monopoly of opportunities available to Yoruba loyalists. Thus, there were strong demands that Lagos return to an autonomous position. In 1954, the colonial government agreed with local negotiators that Lagos must serve the whole nation, not just one region, though the districts of Badagry, Epe and Ikeja, which had been part of the Colony, remained under Western Region control until statehood was achieved.

Local elections in Lagos were the beginning of elective democracy in Nigeria. Middle-level residents began to use political activity in Lagos as a way of challenging the old elite. The first fully elective Town Council, with Dr I. Olorun-Nimbe (a Lagosian Muslim) as Mayor, took office in 1950. It is significant that the main political parties held aloof, allowing parties of workers and market women to back candidates of varied ethnicity and occupation, mainly migrants to Lagos. They were opposed by the indigenes' Area Councils. The new Council signalled that elitist rule was over and that migrants could outvote the locals. The occupations of members ranged from professional (barrister, doctor) to secretary and tailor, but only five of the 24 members were indigenes (Baker 1974: 59–60, 111).

The communal nationalism of Lagos indigenes was similar to that of other minority groups in Nigeria; they resented being controlled by outsiders. It differed in that their distinctiveness was not ethnic or cultural – they were Yoruba, like Westerners – but based on the realization that while indigenes lived mainly in ill-serviced slums and supported themselves by petty trading, well-educated newcomers for whom Lagos was merely a temporary source of opportunity were walking away with the indigenes' land, filling the lucrative jobs which were opening up and manipulating local politics for their own benefit. The city was being exploited and the benefits went elsewhere, to the migrants' hometowns. New roads, water supplies and electricity were installed in strangers' parts of the city. Isale Eko, the core of indigenous residence, was neglected or, from 1955, subject to demolition for 'development'. (This led to riots in 1956; see Chapter 8.)

While the indigenes had been slow to see the benefits of wage employment or Western education, partly because so many were Muslims and traders, the threat to their continued existence as an identifiable unit was a powerful force for mobilization. The struggle took more than 15 years, but in 1967 the low-income, ill-educated community finally succeeded in becoming the core of a new Lagos State.

New organizations, such as the Lagos Aborigines Society and the Egbe Omo Ibile Eko, were formed to present petitions to government leaders. These followed the local pattern of having large numbers of prominent patrons, but also attracted mass support. Muslims from progressive Qur'ânic schools, landowners, market women and chiefs found common cause. Increasing demands for land and jurisdictional disputes between the numerous departments and levels of government servicing Lagos confirmed to the indigenes that autonomy was necessary. The movement 'cut across party lines, religious groups, dynastic factions, and class boundaries' (Baker 1974: 259). They were unsuccessful in 1957, when the government decided that Lagos should remain a federal territory, but the 1959 election showed that Lagosians would reject any party that neglected local interests. The Egbe Eko Parapo or Lagos Citizens' Rights Protection Council (LCRPC) was formed in 1962 by the merger of earlier societies. It was led by Chief T.A. Doherty, who continued active in the movement until statehood was achieved.

The potential breakup of the Nigerian federation in 1966 was seen as a particular threat to local interests, since Lagos would inevitably fall again under Western control. The Lagos delegation to the constitutional review meeting, led by Lateef Jakande, was rejected by the *Oba* and his followers because it ignored their demands for independent statehood. Lagos needed a strong federal government to protect minority rights, not the confederation which both West and East were demanding. Their goal was finally reached on 27 May 1967, when the Head of State, Lt Col. (later General) Yakubu Gowon proclaimed the division of the country into twelve states, including a Lagos state which included Badagry, Epe and Ikeja. Lagos State had only 0.4 per cent of Nigeria's land area and about 3 per cent of the national population (it now has about 6 per cent), but it is the richest, best-educated and most densely populated state (Baker 1974; LSG 1981: 1).

Most governors of Lagos State have been 'strangers' and have served for only a short period. While an electorate can place someone of local origin in control, military governments tend to move men about so they will not have too close ties to local elites. Brigadier Mobolaji Johnson, who governed from 1967 to 1975 and thus laid the foundations for the state, was a Lagosian. He was followed by Commodore Adekunle Lawal (1975–7), Commodore Ndubuisi Kanu (1977–8), and Commodore Ebitu Ukiwe (1978–9), all strangers. Alhaji Lateef Kayode Jakande, whose biography begins this chapter, was elected in October 1979 and served until the military coup of December 1983. He was followed by Air Commodore Gbolahan Mudasiru (1984–6), Navy Captain Okhai Mike Akhigbe (1986–8) and Colonel Raji Rasaki (1988–).

Plate 3.2 Governor's office and Secretariat, Alausa

The capital of Lagos State was initially established at Ikeja, but most of the Secretariat is now in purpose-built accommodation at Alausa (see Map 3; Plate 3.2 shows the Governor's office, centre, and Ministry buildings). As elsewhere in the Federation, the state government controls many local government functions and is a major source of finance for local services. Lagos gets a higher proportion of its income from the Federal Government than other cities because it is paid for the use of land. The loss of rents on government buildings after the move to Abuja will lower the city's income, but many government agencies will continue to need offices in Lagos.

Local Government

Local politics are what national and state authorities allow them to be. Minority parties have little chance with the Lagos electorate, but may manage to reach some of their objectives by other means. As will be discussed below, many activities nominally under the control of local councils are in Lagos either taken over by state or national authorities or strongly influenced by them. For example, the NNDP (Nigerian National Democratic Party, an opponent of AG) was part of the national government alliance in 1964 but manifestly unable to win any seats on the Lagos City Council. Therefore, it tried to infiltrate local institutions through control over appointees to boards for transportation, development, education, etc. (Baker 1974: 129–32).

On the other hand, AG demonstrated the possibilities open to an efficiently organized party which lacked national power. Voluntary ward workers were mobilized to canvass the masses and get out the vote. Initially, links to power in Ibadan made it possible to demonstrate that a vote for AG would bring resources to the locality. But when AG fell from regional power, control of the Lagos City Council made it possible to reward supporters through contracts and other forms of patronage, insofar as these were left in local hands. Since the Lagos AG no longer took orders from national headquarters, it was seen as less of a threat by the federal parties in control and allowed to continue as a local party (Baker 1974: 146–8).

Structure

Lagos State was initially divided into 19 local authorities: 1 city, 2 divisions, 12 districts and 4 local councils. Since many of these were too small to raise revenue or carry out services efficiently, they were reorganized in 1970 into 7 local government areas: Lagos City Council, Mushin Town Council, and Epe, Awori/Ajeromi, Egun/Awori, Ikeja and Ikorodu District Councils. Structural reforms in 1976 raised this to 8, and the revision of May 1989 produced 12 – 1 for each Representative in the next Federal House of Assembly. The Lagos Metropolitan Area has 8 local governments and the

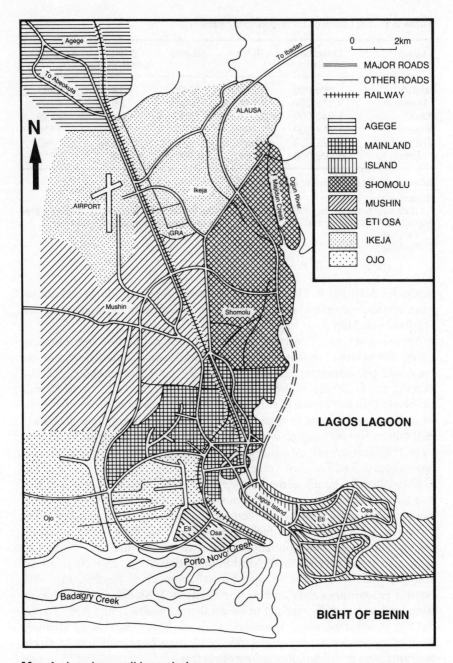

Map 4 Local council boundaries

Source: Adapted from Famisjo Surveys 1983; Lagos State Survey Division 1987

Table 3.1 Statistics of local councils, 1988

Council	Estimated population[a]	Births	Deaths	Primary health clinics	Employees
Island	595 000	28 440	5145	14	2447
Mainland	1 029 000	30 313	2000[b]	36	1770
Ikeja	1 640 000	22 718	1486	na	1189
Mushin	1 414 000	14 955	1151	17	1410
Shomolu	1 022 000	12 416	328	7	797
Total	5 700 000	108 842	10 000	74[c]	7613

Sources: Local government offices.

Notes:
[a] 1989 estimates, using 1988 local government areas. The Ojo part of Badagry area had about 1.4 million people in 1989, with only one government health centre.
[b] Estimate.
[c] Plus Ikeja.

rest of the State has 4. The boundaries between Agege and Ikeja had not yet been established several months after the official announcement. The rest are shown in Map 4.

These Local Councils vary considerably in size, population and resources. Using the relative proportions of the Population Commission and the estimated population of 6.5 million, Lagos Island houses about 260 000 people; much of the Island is now commercial rather than residential property. Eti-Osa (formerly part of Island) and Ikeja have substantial areas of industry and middle or high density housing, producing populations of 300 000 to 500 000. Agege, Mainland and Shomolu Local Councils all have over 1 million people; Mushin and Ojo (formerly part of Badagry) each have about 1.5 million (see Table 3.1).

Island Local Council is the best served in buildings, staff and facilities, due to its long history and central position. Its population is not growing, but staff are needed to handle commercial and industrial activities. The birth and death rates appear high because many outsiders use its hospitals, but it also has an older population than the rest of the city. Birth rates appear to be relatively low in Mushin and Shomolu given their relatively young populations (reflected in the small number of deaths), but birth control programmes took on new popularity in 1988 due to the recession. Mainland is especially well-off in hospitals and health clinics (see Chapter 5), but is short of other resources, such as Xerox machines; Shomolu Council caters for a poor population, including large numbers of recent migrants, and is still building its infrastructure.

Local Councils follow a common organizational model, as shown in Table 3.2 opposite. The Committees of Councillors, under the Local Council Chairman, correspond to the civil service Departments under the Director-Generals (Permanent Secretaries). The Education Department handles primary schools, adult education and libraries. Health and

Table 3.2 Organization of local governments in Lagos State, 1989

Units	Committees
Information ―――――*Chairman*―――	Finance & General Purposes
Political & Chieftaincy	Finance & Economic Planning
Internal Audit	Works and Housing
	Agriculture, Rural & Social Development
	Health & Environmental Services
	Education
Legal ―――――――*Secretary*―――	Departments: Education
Council Secretariat	Health & Environmental Services
	Agriculture, Rural & Social Development
	Works and Housing
	Finance, Supplies, Planning, Research & Statistics
	Personnel Management
Area officer	

Environment includes health education, family health, disease control, medical records and pharmacies. Social welfare, youth services, cooperatives and community development come under Rural and Social Development. All but Island Local Council have some rural areas (Ikeja claims to be 50 per cent rural), and get state funds for rural development. The Works and Housing Departments are responsible for building, mechanical and electrical work; some road repairs; and parks and cemetaries in their areas. The Finance and Planning Department has separate branches for expenditure, revenue, financial accounts, supplies, research and statistics. The Personnel Department is responsible for establishment, manpower development, industrial relations and staff welfare. Finally, large councils have area offices, with officials corresponding to headquarters departments.

Functions

Services which would be the responsibility of local authorities in Britain are often handled by higher authorities in Nigeria for financial, political or technical reasons. For instance, the Lagos State government has taken over property rating, which is the chief source of local income, on the grounds of having more technically qualified personnel. The National Commission for Primary Education distributes funds, including 65 per cent of teachers' salaries, to local governments and says how they must be spent. Education beyond primary school is considered a state responsibility because of the desire to promote more even standards. Planning and land allocation in Lagos are mainly handled at state level; state and federal governments are responsible for public housing (see Chapters 7 and 8). Water supplies and waste disposal are state functions, and the police and prisons are federal organizations. Markets, motor parks and bus terminals remain the responsibility of local governments, but the state can also build markets and the city's bus service was taken over by the state.

Services involving the basic needs of ordinary citizens (education, health, water supplies, roads, markets) attract the most interest from the general public and give rise to considerable bribery and corruption, especially in the allocation of jobs and contracts for buildings and roads, assessment of taxes and maintaining sanitary and other regulations. Local councils have tended to respond to the demands of interested parties (well-connected individuals and groups) rather than those of the mass of the population (see FGN 1966).

Political action by ordinary people is difficult in a heterogeneous and mobile city such as Lagos, where most residents see themselves as transient and continue to identify with their hometowns. However, functions which concern the daily lives of residents often arouse political activity, chiefly protests and demonstrations or delegations sent to 'big men' who might be able to do something. The person approached may be well above the level of the complaint (i.e., market women might see the governor to complain about decisions affecting their market) because they rightly perceive that hierarchical power will be necessary to get what they want. Students, trade unionists and market women are most likely to engage in such activities; businessmen handle their political needs more privately. Older and more educated men are most likely to feel politically efficacious and thus take action to contact officials, whereas, for women, personality and economic success seem to be the most important factors in political activity (Peil 1976b: 148).

A major problem in Nigeria, as in the rest of Africa, is that local authorities seldom have enough resources to handle their responsibilities. Lagos is more fortunate than most; about two-thirds of its budget in the 1970s and 1980s came from local revenue, mainly taxes on land and buildings. This is likely to continue after the move to Abuja, though the city may grow more slowly. An average of 62 per cent of total expenditure of the Lagos City Council between 1957 and 1967 came from general rates, while this income rose from N1.4 m to N5.2 m. In 1972–3, the Lagos City Council had an income of N15.2 m or an estimated N17 per person and even the relatively poor Awori/Ajeromi District Council had N626,000, about N7.6 per person, compared to about N1 per person in most other parts of Nigeria. The per capita sum was actually less because the population was considerably larger than the accepted figure, but the margin of benefit was still considerable. The majority of Lagos State's 1989 budget of N1.079 bn was spent in the city and its suburbs (Okpala 1983: 6; Orewa and Adewumi 1983: 75; Olowu 1990; LSG 1989c; The Guardian, Lagos, 9 January 1989).

Table 3.3 Local government financial resources, 1962–87

	1962–3	1972–3	1987[a]
Revenue			
Lagos City (Island & Mainland)	5 356 800	15 200 000	68 454 201
Other[b]	na	626 000	52 773 535
Income: tenement & ground rents			
Lagos City Council	na	7 800 220[c]	12 509 405
Expenditure: recurrent			
Lagos City (Island & Mainland)	2 091 000[d]		25 046 816
Other[c]			20 277 681
Expenditure: capital			
Lagos City (Island & Mainland)	315 536		38 132 711
Other[c]			49 402 932
Emoluments: salaries & allowances			
Lagos City Council	1 758 620[e]	1 095 630[d]	8 900 242

Sources: FGN 1966: 179, 183; Orewa and Adewumi 1983: 75, 130, 199; Olowu, 1990.
Notes:
[a] Rates, emoluments and overheads 1986.
[b] Awori/Ajeromi in 1972/73; Mushin, Shomolu and Ikeja in 1987.
[c] 1973/74 estimates.
[d] Total expenditure.
[e] All local governments in Lagos State.

Local governments have become big business, with budgets of millions of naira (see Table 3.3). Overall revenue has gone up more rapidly than property taxes. Revenue and expenditure have multiplied about 12 times since 1962–3, whereas wages are up only about 5 times. For example, in 1985 Mushin Local Council had an income of N30 357 164 (48 per cent from federal and state grants) and expenditures/liabilities of N20 842 631. In the late 1980s, budgets rose only slightly and income hardly at all, whereas inflation made wages and services more expensive. In the 1988 Mushin budget of N31 301 338, 33 per cent came from locally generated revenue (rates, licences, fees, earnings from commercial undertakings, interest) and a healthy cash balance. Expenditure was N27 260 086, and recurrent expenditure was three times the 1985 figure, up to 57 per cent of the total.

In his 1989 'grassroots briefing' (for 'Your Highnesses Obas and Chiefs; My Lords Spiritual and Temporal; Market Men and Women; Members and Officers of the CDC; Gentlemen of the Press; Members of the Academic Community; Distinguished Guests; Ladies and Gentlemen'), Mr K.O. Aina, Chairman of the Mushin Local Council, pointed out that the money was spent on improved health services; road construction and resurfacing, culverts and drains; electrification and rural water projects; police posts, a post office and community halls; modernization of markets, meat slaughter slabs and motor parks; street lights and public toilets; and maintenance of primary schools. Mushin Local Government had to reimburse the State

Politicians

Government N10.9 m for primary schools – far more than it received from the State; it also had a large bill for waste disposal.

Councillors

While membership on a local council can be a stepping-stone to higher political office, this does not often happen in Nigeria. Local government is not seen as a political opportunity except during military rule, when no other elective offices are available. Getting elected to a local council requires much less money and contacts than higher office, and local prominence is an important qualification. Baker (1974: 61–70) found that between 1950–59 and 1959–66 there was a shift to councillors who were younger (24 per cent and 67 per cent respectively under 50), Muslim (32 per cent and 50 per cent) and self-employed, especially contractors or traders (18 per cent and 34 per cent). The share of indigenes rose slightly, but there was a notable shift from Christian to Muslim indigenes and the proportion who had spent less than twenty-five years in Lagos rose from 1 to 16 per cent. Traders and merchants kept about 1 in 7 seats, but the proportion of professionals, managers and clerical workers dropped from 65 per cent to 51 per cent. By the end of the period, Lagos Muslims had gained control of the Council.

Almost all of the councillors had some formal education, but in both periods about 1 in 6 had not gone beyond primary school; the proportion with university education dropped from 25 per cent to 18 per cent. This suggests that many lacked the background to deal with the complex policy issues facing the council. Turnover of councillors can be a serious problem because individuals do not stay long enough to learn how the system operates. A third of councillors in the 1950–59 period and 59 per cent in the 1959–66 period served up to three years, and only about 5 per cent served for ten or more years. Thus, the long socialization period which many British councillors enjoy is seldom possible in Nigeria. Both the electorate and the councillors are in a hurry, and local government tends to be seen as an area for rapid exploitation rather than an opportunity for service to one's neighbours.

In the 1970s and 1980s, turnover was exacerbated by changing government regulations on local authorities. At various times, elected councils have been replaced by civil servants or special appointees. The latest case was in 1989, when councils were abolished in favour of Sole Administrators until new local elections could be held in 1990. On the whole, ordinary people feel that they get somewhat better response from elected politicians than from appointees, who are more concerned with their own careers and feel less need to answer to the public. The problem of public service is greatest where suburbs are under a rurally-oriented local authority. The Awori/Ajeromi District Council and later the Badagry Local Council were primarily concerned with rural development, even though a majority of their residents lived in Lagos suburbs and worked in the city itself. Urban services were not extended, leading to widely acknowledged deprivation. Having now been given an urban local council of their own (Ojo), there is a better chance of responsive development.

Elected local councillors are frequently investigated and/or castigated for neglect of their duties or manipulation of functions for their personal benefit. For example, the first freely elected Lagos City Council was soon accused of inefficiency and irregularities. The Bernard Storey Commission of 1952, the 1966 Tribunal and the Ogunnaike Commission of 1970 all found cases to answer, though the 1966 Tribunal found that the threat of dissolution by the Federal government (controlled by another party) deterred independent action by councillors (FGN 1966; Orewa and Adewumi 1983: 63–6). Given the scale of Lagos and the pace of growth in both population and revenue, it is hardly surprising that local councillors find the task daunting. Since they are elected to represent local areas, their concern with market stalls and motor parks is likewise understandable, though their interest in projects likely to give rise to bribes rather than more abstract and unremunerative planning for the future is a hindrance to development.

Councils and committees of the Council are supposed to meet at least once a month. A major problem with the committee system is that councillors do not want to miss anything. A 1963 report complained that many councillors saw it as in their political interest to attend meetings even if they were not members of the committee concerned. The committees had thus become debating chambers rather than handling detailed material to save time for the full council (cited by Williams and Walsh 1967: 42–4). A later report suggests that 'polemics and repetitions which feature at some Council meetings' are not useful, and the problem could be best handled by having fewer meetings (Adamolekun and Rowland 1979: 222). However, this is partly a problem of having a meaningful role and the proper background for the job. In practice, many decisions must be left to experts in the civil service, who are permanent employees engaged in specific tasks, for which they should be qualified.

As local councils have become larger and richer and as more qualified people are available and willing to run for election, the quality of councillors is likely to rise. There are now many experienced business owners and managers in Lagos, and some are attracted by a position on the Local Council. Chairmen earn N20,000 a year, plus N300 a month for expenses in what has become a full-time job.

Civil Servants

Running a local authority with financial and human resources as large as those in Lagos cannot depend on elected councillors; it requires qualified staff. However, there are widespread problems with the recruitment, discipline and promotion of local authority staff and their relations with councillors. Civil servants constantly face 'the caprices and arbitrary demands of local councillors' and staff are often as guilty as councillors of 'personal prejudice, nepotism and favouritism' (FGN 1974: para. 499). The scope for authority and opportunities for promotion are much greater for those employed by the state or the federal government, and local council employees often feel, with some justification, that they are underpaid and underappreciated by the public.

Administrative officials are only part of the problem; surveyors, accountants, engineers, experts in waste disposal and road repair, planners, lawyers and financial specialists are all needed. In Lagos, most of these people can make far more money either working for themselves or employed in the private sector. But this is not just a question of money. The continual political interference experienced by local government employees (from councillors, higher officials and the more powerful sectors of the general public) can deprive them of work satisfaction and encourage them to accept prevailing customs of bribery, nepotism and corruption. Turnover is high.

Civil servants tend to resent political interference with their work and to assume that the job would be better done if they were left to get on with it. This can cause friction with higher governmental authorities as well as with the general public, who often find civil servants aloof and unhelpful. Williams and Walsh (1967: 159) report that higher officials in Lagos often treated local authorities with contempt; they were to be controlled, restrained or neutralized whenever possible; communications were poor and higher authorities often delayed decisions. As a result, they were seen by local officials as 'an interfering nuisance'. The quality and integrity of civil servants appears to have risen considerably in the intervening years, but pay, promotion and scope for independent action continue to be problems. Complaints offices encourage the general public to make their needs known.

Women have a growing role in the Lagos civil service at state and local levels. Well-educated professionals in senior positions include Mrs Eniola Fadayomi, State Attorney-General; Mrs Modupe Folashade Adeogun, Commissioner for Information and Culture; Mrs A.O. Idowu, Permanent Secretary of the Ministry of Youth, Sports and Social Development; and female medical officers and accountants. While there are still many men in clerical positions, women often have the important gatekeeper role, granting or hindering access to office-holders. Many lower-level clerical workers find an opportunity to trade on the job, supplying their colleagues with easily transportable goods in order to increase their income.

Public Political Action: Case Studies

The people with the most interest in Lagos are its permanent residents. A minority of the population even if one includes migrants who intend to remain in Lagos in old age as well as indigenes, these are the people who have the most stake in the development of the city. The people who decide to take political action may not be wealthy, but they are not the poorest residents either. They often run successful businesses and have invested in housing. Some of the women have moved up from hawking or petty trading from the house to ownership of a shop or market stall. They have interests to protect and a commitment to Lagos as a place to live. The other major source of political activity, university students, will not be discussed here because their interests and sources of discontent do not usually concern the city *per se*, though their protests about corruption or the economy may attract public support. How people use the informal political system – manipulate political networks – is the major concern here. Patron–client relations are important regardless of who runs the formal political system. These two case studies concentrate on the informal side of politics.

Landlords

Barnes (1986) provides an extended study of how Mushin landlords manipulate patron–client ties to develop neighbourhood power and leadership roles. Political skills are important in acquiring and developing land in Lagos (see Chapter 7). Their behaviour stems from Yoruba traditions of chieftaincy and the insecurities of dealing with alternating elective and military governments. Power over others is an important component of Yoruba culture which has not changed as Lagos has become a metropolis; the struggle for power and its rewards have merely intensified. The rewards for success are considerable; the penalty for failure may be loss of one's house and land to someone with better political connections. The most successful houseowners become middlemen between the Lagos political elite and neighbourhood residents.

Clientalism is very important in Nigerian politics; it provides the major links between the public and their rulers. It can foster nepotism and corruption, but keeps people far more satisfied with the system than they would otherwise be. It is based on reciprocal but unequal long-term relations between 'big men' or 'big women' and their followers, involving informal contractual ties developed from personal, usually face-to-face, relationships. Patrons invest considerable time maintaining these relationships – attending weddings, funerals and other social events and servicing individuals who come to them for help or just for the social contacts which maintain the link. The clients give more than they get in the long run, but patrons provide a security net which can be essential to continued residence in town (Peace 1979b; Barnes 1986: 8).

In many cases, there are middlemen or brokers between patrons and clients; resources and obligations may be exchanged over several levels. Thus, a man who wants permission to run a business contacts someone he knows who has higher contacts; if the broker has the right links, permission will be granted. At some point, the obligations incurred must be repaid in gifts or actions, deferring to the needs of the patron or broker; part of this repayment may be mobilizing votes or popular support. In the process, resources are allocated more widely than would be the case if the elites did not need the support of numerous followers. Political aspirants can acquire legitimate authority as well as increased resources for themselves (Barnes 1968: 8–11).

In a crowded, heterogeneous neighbourhood, it is profitable to be well-known, trusted, generous with patronage and skilled at settling disputes. The person (usually a male landowner) who can develop widespread sources of information and contacts with the city's powerful will quickly acquire clients of his own. This need not require much initial wealth; the ability to build relationships and deliver the goods is more important. The local terms for these people are 'godfathers' and 'long legs'. They are the people who know where to find a job for a newly arrived nephew, who controls the supply of whatever is currently scarce and who to see if one is in trouble with the police. They are the initiators and mobilizers of projects, opinion formers and role models for the neighbourhood. They provide information, distribute resources, contact officials and maintain the peace. Earning their displeasure can be hazardous (Barnes 1986: 78–85).

Chiefs

The goal of many leaders is a chieftaincy title. While some of these are hereditary (such as the *Oba* of Lagos and Awori lineage titles – *idile* – in Mushin), many (such as ward chiefs and subward chiefs) are rewards for achievement. The symbols and rituals fit into Yoruba culture, but are manipulated for present-day ends. They enhance the holders' legitimacy and prestige, can be used as a stage to political office and provide links through chieftaincy meetings with other important people. Since governmental recognition of each new title-holder is required (signified by an *imuye*, or public initiation ceremony), there is considerable scope for political manipulation; title-holders cannot function efficiently unless community leaders at a higher level have formally approved them. As the area's permanent residents, houseowners select chiefs for their ward, as *idile* chiefs are selected by lineage members. In both cases, the older and more important electors have more influence than younger, less important members (Barnes 1986: 98–116, 189).

Other titles may be granted to reward achievement, but it is important for both the grantor and the receiver of the title that the achievement be widely recognized. Religious groups (both Christian and Muslim), market leaders and secret societies may also confer titles on their leading members, though these have much narrower influence than people holding community titles. Public participation in the system is necessary so that the chief's superiority is legitimated and their followers are not alienated. This is partly structured through chieftaincy councils, at which non-title-holders present issues and sometimes join in the discussions. Younger members of an *idile* expect to be part of the decision-making process on important issues such as the alienation of land. Tenants, who are only temporary residents of the area, are usually less involved, but can approach community influentials through their landlord or some other patron (Barnes 1986: 119–25).

Although the chieftaincy system is structurally separate from the government system, the two are interlocked and the functions of the first change as the personnel and rationale of the government changes. Under civilian rule, the chieftaincy system provides access to political leaders, and chiefs who support the opposition may suffer loss of influence. Overt political influence is less important during periods of military rule, but the need for links with those in power remains. The chieftaincy hierarchy may take on some political functions which are not being carried out by the army, and factions may be restructured to reflect new sources of power and influence. When military governments make civilian appointments, leaders mobilize their followers to seek these positions, and people at the bottom of the system align themselves with whoever is successful (Barnes 1986: 156–7).

Market Women

Southern Nigerian women have a long history of political activity (Mba 1982). While some women's politics involves house ownership and chieftaincy titles, their main demands are for more and better markets. Men trade in certain sectors of Yoruba markets, but most of the selling is done by women. The attainment of success in trading will be discussed in Chapter 4; the major concerns here are the political leadership exercised by successful traders and the articulation of ordinary women traders (most of whom do not have market stalls) with local and higher community leaders.

Baker (1974: 223–43) provides a detailed case study of the 'unassertive influence' of market women. She found them socially cohesive and highly organized under market leaders, but concerned mainly with market affairs rather than with the wider issues of the day. Nevertheless, they can influence government decisions through their control over the food chain (raising prices in anticipation of a wage settlement, for example, or joining a general strike against government mismanagement) and their ability to marshall a large number of votes in local elections.

Lagos market women are organized under the *Iyalode* (Mother of Markets), a chieftaincy title conferred by the *Oba* of Lagos with a status immediately below his own. Alhaja Rabiatu Eyiowuawi, a prominent Muslim exporter, held this title for more than a quarter of a century, joining it with the title *Iyaeko* (Mother of Lagos). Though the title is not hereditary, the present *Iyalode* is a granddaughter. Under the *Iyalode* are the *Alaga*, heads of markets and their subsidiaries. These titles must be achieved by general consensus; they require both wealth and personal popularity, so aspirants need skill in trading, but also recognized capacity for leadership. There is no pay, but fierce competition suggests that the greatly enhanced status is good for business. Below the *Alaga* are the *Iya Ẹgbẹ* and the *O-lo'ri Ẹgbẹ*, the leaders of traders in a range of products and of sellers of one item, such as tomatoes or onions. Each market in Mushin has its own *Iyalode*, with *Iya Ẹgbẹ* under her, but there is no overall 'Mother' for the whole area.

In a situation where there are large numbers of competitors selling similar products, dispute settlement is the most important function of market leaders. But they also meet regularly, both formally and informally, to discuss supplies, prices, discipline, credit, and other issues. Overall, they exercise considerable control over the whole market enterprise, and can quickly contact all market traders if mobilization is necessary. Overt political activity by market women has been sporadic. The Lagos Market Women's Guild supported Herbert Macaulay's agitation against the water rate and *Oba* Adeniji Adele II's Area Councils in the 1950 election, the first in which women could vote. The AG assiduously courted them in the 1950s, using its ability to allocate market stalls and collect fees to reward followers and punish opponents. AG branches were established in markets to recruit women members; their vote was seen as crucial in 1962, when the AG was out of power nationally but won easily in the Lagos Town Council elections.

A major problem for market women in acquiring greater political influence and official representation has been their lack of education. The only market woman who achieved a place on the Town Council through the AG was Mrs Elsie Femi-Pearce, a former teacher. When the military asked for a representative on the administrative committee which replaced the Town Council, the Lagos City Market and Women's Organization proposed Chief E.O. Dare, a male herbalist who was their administrative secretary. Two rival organizations proposed women, but one of these was an AG activist who was illiterate and not a trader. The government finally selected the wife of a High Court judge who was also *Alaga* of Tejuoso Market, Mrs Modupe Caxton-Martins.

Illiteracy and adherence to Islam led Lagos market women to favour traditional leaders and face-to-face politics. Their experience is that impersonal bureaucratic structures are of little use for furthering their interests. Patrons and brokers can be used to approach the bureaucrats, but they do not realistically expect much return for such activity. They lack the time to cultivate politicians, and have little in common wth the educated elite women who are active at higher political levels (Baker 1974: 241–3).

Part of the political ineffectiveness of market women is also due to factionalism, whether this is based on party allegiance, as on Lagos Island, or on the indigene-settler struggle, as in Mushin. Unlike chieftaincy titles, market title-holders can be replaced and status can be lost. Since the rules for leadership are not clear-cut, there is plenty of scope for competition, attacking the character and authority of the present incumbent and rallying support to one's own faction. Personal animosity is also a factor, which may predate or follow a competitive situation. Wider political issues are fought out by backing competitors for market leadership. Thus, although women leaders are elected by the women, men can interfere and use the process to further their own goals (Barnes 1986: 163–80).

Summary

Political leadership in Lagos operates at many levels. There is considerable interaction (some would say interference) between leaders at national, state and local levels and at least some sectors of the general public. National politicians are the most transient, since power can be lost overnight through a coup. Their allegiance is rarely to Lagos and they use it merely as a convenient base of operations, but this does not negate their effect on its development. Their argument, and that of people all over the country, has been that Lagos, as the national capital, belongs to all Nigerians and should serve the interests of the country. It remains to be seen how much of this function will be transferred to Abuja when the government finally moves there. Given Lagos' continuing importance as a primate city, port and major industrial centre, the national interest in Lagos may not decline as much as those favouring the move hope it will.

State politics gives far more importance to the Lagos indigenes than their proportion of the population would warrant. They must answer to national politicians to the extent that they need federal financial resources to maintain the city. State attention is also increasingly being given to residents of rural areas, helping villages to develop to improve the local food supply and stop at least some people from migrating to the overcrowded city. Nevertheless, the city was the major reason for creating the state. Its government is located in the city's northern suburbs; a large share of state personnel comes from and state financing goes to the city.

Thus, local politicians play an important role in state decision making. The role of the *Oba* of Lagos is largely ceremonial, but behind the scenes influence can be brought to bear. Chieftaincy councils, landlords' and market women's associations, trade unions and other pressure groups operate through particularist, face-to-face networks to further the goals of members and clients. These lower-level groups are particularly efficacious in local government, pressuring for building permission, exceptions to sanitary regulations, licences and tax reductions. Councillors are necessarily dispensers of patronage, and civil servants are under considerable pressure from kin, friends and neighbours to humanize the bureaucracy. Frequent investigations and even penalties for those found guilty of bribery, corruption, nepotism and so on are unlikely to change the system radically, insofar as it serves the needs of many people who would be ignored if bureaucratic norms were followed and civil probity were more widespread.

4
Workers and entrepreneurs

Alhaji H.P. ('Horse Power') Adebola (1920–82) was born in Ijebu Ode and claimed to have studied law at the Inns of Court. He was initially employed as a railway station master, but switched to a career of trade union leadership about 1960. He was a colourful, domineering and effective leader of his own Railways and Ports Transport and Clerical Staffs Union (R & PT & CSU), of the United Labour Congress (ULC, 1962–1976) and of the International Confederation of Free Trade Unions. He was active in the early days of political parties, being appointed by the NCNC to a House of Chiefs. But he argued that ideology and politics are a luxury that Nigerian workers cannot afford. They must live with both government and management, though they should be free to use strikes or other methods (in which he was inventive) to further their cause. He rejected both Soviet and American influence on Nigerian unionism and broke with the ULC over CIA influence. Flexible in adjusting to the needs of the time, he has been characterized as a radical, a nationalist and an egalitarian populist. His aim was not to replace those in charge, but to improve conditions for those below. A believer in equality, though not always a practitioner, he could joke with Chief Justice Adebiyi about their experiences as railway workers and give both management and subordinates the rough side of his tongue. His militancy and success brought many members to his union, yet his suspicious, arrogant personality made it difficult for him to retire and for the union to find a successor. He had a wife and six children, a large house in Surulere and land at home. Proud of his refusal to take bribes, he was the only national trade union leader exonerated by the Adebiyi Tribunal in the late 1960s. He was a model which should be more widely followed (Waterman 1983a: 202–3; 1983b).

It may seem from the previous chapter that the business of Lagos is politics. This one will demonstrate that the business of Lagos is business; politics is merely one form of the prevailing entrepreneurship. Business takes a wide variety of forms, from trading shares on the Nigerian Stock Exchange and large-scale manufacturing by both indigenous firms and branches of multi-national corporations to children hawking bread or tape cassettes to passers-by. While a majority of men in Lagos earn most of their income from wage employment in government or industry, their goal is often self-employment. Many combine the two, using the wage or salary for security while they build up a business in their spare time. Their wives and often their children are already self-employed, supplementing the father's meagre wages.

Lagos had 87 per cent of the headquarters of leading industrial and commercial firms at independence, and this primacy has been maintained. The metropolis claimed about 70 per cent of the nation's industrial investment and over 20 per cent of the gross national product in 1975. Gross output was N2433 m and value added per worker N8619 in 1976. It had 27 per cent of large industrial establishments in 1979, including 53 per cent of capital goods firms. In 1985, the Lagos labour force was estimated to be about 2.8 million, excluding many in part-time self-employment (LSG 1981: 6; Nwafor 1982: 80; McNulty and Adalemo 1988: 222–6).

This chapter examines the nature of commerce and industry in Lagos and the people involved in it, including large-scale businessmen, port and factory workers, market women and craftsmen. Major employers (both government and business) attract migrants and thus are indirectly responsible for the high level of unemployment. Many workers moved from wage to self-employment during the oil boom of the 1970s; major redundancy programmes of the 1980s have pushed others into the informal sector.

Industrialists and Financiers

In spite of talk of decentralization and its political attractiveness to voters in other parts of the country, major businesses still find Lagos the best location for both headquarters and production. Much Nigerian manufacturing requires imported raw materials, and access to the Lagos port cuts costs. Access to government officials is often essential, and this is the largest and wealthiest consumer market in West Africa. Hiring experienced personnel is relatively easy because the best educated and trained people often prefer Lagos in spite of its high cost of living and physical disadvantages.

ThisWeek 100's list of 35 'Supreme Achievers' (1989: 110) includes 12 banks or financial firms, of which the top achievers are First Bank, Union Bank and United Bank. The 13 branches of multinational firms include many long-established British and French conglomerates (CFAO, Lever Brothers, Nigerian Tobacco, PZ, SCOA and UAC) as well as Irish, German and American relative newcomers (Guinness, Hoechst, Johnson's Wax and National Cash Register) and 3 major international oil firms (AGIP, Mobil and Total). All of these have their head offices in Lagos. It is interesting that Shell, with its tall building on the Marina, is not on the list.

Lagos is also the natural place for innovations. The Stock Exchange has trading floors in Port Harcourt, Kaduna and Kano, but the major action is in Lagos. Even though the capital required was doubled from N100 000 to 200 000, there were 50 applications for dealerships in 1988. There is plenty of room for small buyers – only N50 is needed, but the government is a major shareholder because initially there was not enough local capital. The main problem is the small number of firms listed – only 113, valued at N12 bn. Many multinational companies handled the 1976 indigenization decree requiring them to reduce their holdings to 40 per cent by forming a local firm (e.g., Barclays Nigeria) and selling shares locally. These offerings were greatly oversubscribed and stockholders have earned a good return on their investment; few are anxious to sell. Lagos State's 31 million shares in 22 companies (most originally purchased 1972–8) have earned a 122 per cent return. Turnover was N716 in 1989 and N800 m capital was raised – 15 per cent by the government. A commodities exchange has been suggested, but Nigeria is not yet ready for this (*West Africa* 1976–7; 1990: 591; *Guardian Financial Weekly* 10 August 1989; LSG 1989a: 61).

Another innovation has been the 'People's Bank', inaugurated by President Ibrahim Babangida in Ajegunle with N150,000 to be loaned 'to the common man without security or collateral'; it is hoped that craftsmen will be able to use loans to set up small industries. This was a popular move; there will eventually be branches throughout the country. The loans must be repaid with 5 per cent interest within a year. It remains to be seen whether this will happen; experience with other government loans suggests that many will take the money as a gift. On the whole, craftsmen are more often held back by lack of raw materials and inadequate marketing experience than by lack of capital, and those in greatest need do not get the loans (*West Africa* 1989: 1737; see also Akeredolu-Ale 1975; Kennedy 1988).

Location

Commercial and industrial activities take place all over the city, in every residential area and along most roads as well as in the few places set aside for them (see Map 3). However, large-scale commerce is increasingly being differentiated spatially from industry. With a few notable exceptions, the former has remained on or near Lagos Island, whereas large-scale, capital-intensive industry has moved to the periphery where land is cheaper and facilities have been provided for it.

Table 4.1 shows the increasing outward movement of industrial estates, extensions of Ikeja and at Ogba, Amuwo-Odofin and Ojo as the inner areas at Apapa and Ijora were filled. Most industrial estates are small, and many industries are not on estates. This is partly dictated by cost and the need for special resources not available elsewhere in the city. Ikeja/Gbagada/Oregun will probably be linked to Ogba eventually, increasing the concentration of industrial employment on the north side of the city and requiring even more cross-town transportation (see Chapter 8). Governor Jakande put a heavy tax on land in the early 1980s; in response, some industries moved to the Agbara Industrial Estate, across the border in Ogun State.

Table 4.1 Industrial estates

Location	Begun	Area (h)
Apapa	1951	100
Mushin	1957	30
Ijora	1958	138
Yaba	1958	1
Ikeja	1959	180
Ilupeju	1966	110
Iganmu	1968	80
Oregun-Ojota[a]	1971	0.5
Agidingbi[a]	1972	40
Isolo	1972	45
Matori[b]	1972	57
Oshodi[a]	1972	57
Gbagada[a]	1974	121
Ogba	1978	414
Amuwo-Odofin	1980s	
Ojo	1980s	

Source: Master Plan 1980: 97.
Notes:
[a] Extensions of Ikeja Industrial Estate.
[b] Extension of Mushin Industrial Estate.

Table 4.2 Manufacturing firms in Lagos, by local government area and product, 1989

Product	Agege	Eti Osa	Ikeja	Island	Mainland	Mushin	Ojo	Shomolu
Printing, paper containers	9	6	46	11	27	41	12	11
Food, beverage	21	19	14	8	21	47	12	12
Metal products	7	7	61	0	6	47	11	6
Textiles, leather	1	7	24	15	24	50	9	3
Rubber, plastics, petroleum products	10	11	38	2	16	34	12	9
Wood, furniture	8	2	12	3	35	18	20	6
Concrete, glass, clay	6	3	18	0	6	31	7	2
Chemicals, paints	5	1	21	2	9	13	3	1
Electronics, electrical	2	1	16	0	4	15	2	1
Soap, cosmetics	4	2	14	0	2	16	1	2
Pharmaceuticals, drugs	1	3	9	0	10	14	2	1
Motor vehicles	0	1	1	0	2	5	2	0
Ship building, repair	0	0	1	0	0	0	2	0
Miscellaneous	6	1	14	0	3	11	2	0
Total	80	64	289	41	165	342	97	54

Source: Lagos State Directory of Manufacturing Companies 1989.

Table 4.2 shows the distribution of large manufacturing firms in Lagos. Of 1132 firms listed in 1989, 30 per cent were in Mushin, 26 per cent in Ikeja and 15 per cent in Mainland Local Government areas. Eti Osa, which contains Apapa, had only 6 per cent of these firms, confirming the move to cheaper land in the northern suburbs. Agege and Ojo each have more manufacturing firms than Apapa. The proportions would be somewhat different if the base were the number of workers or if small firms (under ten workers) were included. Though the *Directory* does not indicate how many workers each firm has, many of Mainland firms are relatively small compared to those in Ikeja or Apapa. The proportion of wage employees in manufacturing in Ikeja and Apapa is greater than their proportion of firms, as shown in Table 4.2, and the proportion of firms in Agege and Ojo would be greater if small firms were included. In 1970, Ikeja had 24 607 workers and Apapa 15 660, compared to only 6739 in Mushin; Ikeja and Apapa had 70 per cent of the employees of firms with ten or more people in Greater Lagos, but only 56 per cent of the establishments in 1972. There are more and larger firms in the Ikeja area today (Federal Office of Statistics 1970; 1972).

Areal specialization is partly because Ikeja has so much space. Metal products are concentrated in Ikeja (42 per cent), as are chemicals, paints and electronics (38–9 per cent) and nearly two-fifths of the miscellaneous firms, often the only large-scale producer in Nigeria of their product. Concrete producers (which are mostly small and need unskilled labour) are likely to be in Mushin (42 per cent); textiles and leather goods are over-represented in Mushin and Island, factories producing soap or cosmetics are mostly in either Ikeja or Mushin (73 per cent) and the few firms producing motor vehicles or spare parts are mainly in Mushin (45 per cent), though the Volkswagen plant is in Ojo. There is some concentration of pharmaceutical firms in Mainland (25 per cent).

Large-scale commerce is more concentrated than industry. About 85 per cent of Nigeria's skyscrapers are located on the south side of Lagos Island; most of these were built to the greater glory of Nigeria's banking industry. Of the top 20 Nigerian financial institutions by assets at December 1988, 11 had their main offices on Broad Street or the Marina, near the Central Bank of Nigeria, and only 2 were not in the Island/Eti Osa areas; many of the smaller banks are setting up offices in Ikoyi and Victoria Island. These central institutions include the First Bank of Nigeria, the country's second most profitable firm (see Plate 4.1).

In the same area, and sometimes sharing their bank buildings, are the offices of the National Stock Exchange, the National Oil and Chemical Company, the National Insurance Corporation and Great Nigeria Insurance Corporation, multinational companies, accountants, consultants and lawyers who can afford to pay at least N350 per square foot for office space. Many of these skyscrapers were built since 1975 to symbolize the success of companies able to pay N1–35 m for a corporate image. (*ThisWeek*, Lagos, 26 January 1987; Asuquo 1987; *ThisWeek 100* 1989).

Plate 4.1 First Bank of Nigeria headquarters, Marina

Local Leaders

Nigerians have sought commercial opportunities in Lagos from its foundation. The Lagos Chamber of Commerce and Industry, founded in 1888, still aims to help both small and large businesses. Local business leaders operate on a much larger scale today, but their activities mix traditional ways with the imperatives of international commerce.

ThisWeek's summary of 100 'Achievers of Repute' (1989: 89–106) tells us something about the background and characteristics of top Nigerian businessmen (only three women are included). Their background was not always adequately described, but it is clear that outstanding financial success is largely based on employment by banks, large industrial firms or the government. Most of the men and all three women had worked their way to the top from modest managerial or clerical positions. A few had remained in the same corporation throughout their working lives, or only moved after reaching the top. Transfers from the government and armed forces to industry or banking included five Permanent Secretaries, seven retired generals (ex-Head of State General Olusegun Obasanjo, two Army Chiefs of Staff and four generals), one man who started in the Police, and a former government archaeologist. There was also a former Vice-Chancellor, at least 11 lawyers, 14 accountants and 7 doctors, but only 2 men who were reported to be engineers.

The majority for whom age was given were in their 50s, but 3 were in their 30s and 2 were over 70. Ten had studied in the UK, from Oxford and Cambridge Universities to London polytechnics. Five had studied in the USA; the 39-year-old graduate of the Harvard Business School was one of the few with the academic management training which has become important for managerial employment today. Others had obtained higher education in Canada, Egypt, France and Germany as well as the older Nigerian universities, though the majority do not appear to have gone beyond secondary school and a few had very little formal education.

Seven had started by organizing their own companies; others had become entrepreneurs after salaried employment. Diversifying resources by participation in more than one enterprise has long been seen as a problem for West African entrepreneurs, but obviously quite a few are able to succeed in this way. Once one is recognized as an 'Achiever', there are numerous calls for membership on boards of Directors. Several men were chairmen of more than one board and 32 belonged to more than one. This is not seen just an intermittent advisory role; many appear to be actively involved in building up companies in which they hold large blocks of shares. There were several multimillionaires, including one who made his first million in trade at 19 and one who was 78 but still active on numerous boards and committees.

Several men were patrons or participants in professional associations, advisors to government or had international links to the World Bank or ECOWAS. But successful businessmen are not allowed to segregate themselves from their communities of origin; status is still tied to active participation in local activities. Communal activity is often rewarded with the traditional title of Chief or *Otunba* (36, including 1 woman); 2 or 3 of the 'Achievers' belong to royal families and 13 were Alhaji, having made the pilgrimage to Mecca. A few were noted for their recreational activities – leadership of the Lagos Lawn Tennis Club or the Island Club, writing plays or novels. At least 6 were active in politics and more will be, publicly or behind the scenes, as the next elections approach. Women were expected to run their homes efficiently; at least they could afford to pay for help.

Expatriate Owners

International investment remains important, though most of the personnel are Nigerians. Large-scale construction firms have tended to be in expatriate hands because considerable capital is needed to maintain a company between contracts and through the wait for payment. Smaller expatriate companies have left, since they were unable to compete with local firms. The large firms also manufacture (paints, plastics), which helps to maintain profits when the construction industry is depressed. Julius Berger (German-owned, with Nigerian management) specializes in roads, whereas Cappa and D'Alberto (Italian management but Swiss-owned) specialize in major buildings. Costain and Taylor Woodrow are both British-owned; the latter has declined considerably in recent years due to an inability to collect N78 m from governments for work done – a problem shared to a lesser extent by other firms (*Business* II:5, 1989).

Dutch interests have investments in about 100 companies – from Philips electronics and Shell to banking, harbour works, packaging, paint and milk products. There are enough businessmen for a Nigeria–Netherlands Chamber of Commerce (*Business* II:5, 1989). British investment is mainly in long-established conglomerates. In addition to those mentioned above, Beechams, Cadburys, Dunlop and Glaxo manufacture in Lagos. Germany's largest investment is the Volkswagen plant, which turned out 42 000 cars in 1979. The Czechoslovakians are considering assembly of Skodas (popular taxis) on the Volkswagen line. The French Peugeot plant is in Kaduna, but SCOA assembles Peugeot trucks in Lagos. The Dumez construction firm is also French-owned. Japanese investment in Lagos is still small, but growing.

Indian-owned firms tend to be run by individuals rather than multi-national companies, but they are equally flexible in moving to another country if conditions become too difficult. The long-established Chellerams has shifted from marketing goods to manufacturing. Import controls have stimulated backward linkages in Indian textile businesses – from cloth to spinning, yarn mills and even cotton plantations. The Lebanese community has diversified industrial interests, mostly run by long-established families. Leventis and Mandilas are among the top industrial firms (Nwafor 1982: 88).

While the management of large Lagos businesses is mainly in Nigerian (especially Yoruba) hands, many large firms also have expatriates at or near the top. In branches of multinational firms, the Chairman of the Board is probably a Nigerian, but the Managing Director or General Manager may be from corporate headquarters, as with AGIP, Bata and SCOA. Some local firms have also hired a managing director from abroad, using a specialist to provide overall supervision until Nigerian managers are fully trained. Indigenization decrees have made it difficult to recruit managers from abroad except for specialized technical posts and for non-citizens settled in Nigeria to find employment outside their own national community. Lebanese firms now have Nigerians among their managers, but also recruit from the local Lebanese community. Some Lebanese have taken Nigerian nationality, including a managing director included in *This Week*'s top 100 businessmen.

The quality of interaction between Nigerian and expatriate managers depends on ability to adjust to cultural differences. Expatriates are usually given more responsibility (power), and have less confidence in their Nigerian colleagues than the latter have in them. Nigerian managers tend to be highly ambitious and expect faster promotion than would be the case in Europe; this can be a source of friction, with Nigerians leaving one firm for another which seems more promising. Nigerian managers in a Lebanese firm were frustrated by the lack of a clear career pattern, the low level of interest in staff development and the slow transfer of technological information. This partly reflects young Nigerian's aspirations for a rapid rise to affluence. They do not want to spend long years in middle-level positions (Ezeala 1983; Faseyiku 1988).

Public Corporations: Lagos Port

Many large industries in Lagos are under government control. These include the Nigerian Electrical Power Authority (the notorious NEPA), the Nigerian Ports Authority (NPA), Nigerian Railways and Nigerian Telephones (NITEL). The State government owns the major bus company (Lagos State Transport Corporation, LSTC), Lagos State Development and Property Corporation (LSDPC), Lagos State Bulk Purchasing Corporation (LSBPC) and its own insurance company (LASACO Assurance Company). The public continually complains about poor service and public corporations are frequently under investigation for corruption, mismanagement and general inefficiency, but privatization is only gradually getting underway. They are an important source of employment. For example, Nigerian Post and Telegraph had 10 555 employees at its Lagos headquarters in 1983, including 2412 middle and senior managers; this was one-third of its whole workforce (Ehimiagbe 1983). Several of these corporations are discussed in Chapter 8; this section focuses on the NPA.

Lagos Port, the fifth busiest in West Africa in terms of arrivals (1088 in 1983–8, a third of the arrivals at Nigeria's nine major ports), handles about 80 per cent of imports and 70 per cent of foreign trade. Nigeria is 21st among developing countries in container traffic (Ivory Coast is 20th). The port is owned by the NPA, whch was created in 1955. In the 1960s, there were two major quays, Apapa Quay (8000 feet, accommodating 14–24 ships) and Customs Quay (1500 feet), as well as a number of specialized wharfs (Fishery, Petroleum, Ijora Coal, Bulk Vegetable Oil, Sea School Jetty) (Waterman 1982: 35–8; *West Africa* 1990: 711). Though communications are good (a railway terminal and the expressway), some consider its operations a national secret; I was arrested by a soldier for taking a photo (Plate 4.2). Fortunately, the harbour police did not consider it an offence.

Plate 4.2   Entrance to Apapa Port, streetside shoemaker

The port at Tin Can Island was opened in 1977 and the third Apapa Wharf extension (50.8 h of land) was commissioned in 1979. Tin Can Island has roll-on-roll-off (RORO) equipment, seven break-of-bulk general cargo berths, one dry bulk cargo berth and accommodation for six container vessels. Apapa's 1005 m of container berths can accommodate four to six ships and its 525 m of multi-purpose berths will handle three cargo/ RORO ships. The 6400 sq m of covered storage and 450,000 sq m of container storage (including the Ijora depot) can be insufficient when agents are slow to collect imports. The container terminal handled 242 vessels in 1989 (down from 343 in 1986), with 43 548 TEUS (tons per equivalent units) (*West Africa* 1990: 711–19).

There has been continual criticism of the NPA for redundant services, malpractices and inefficient use of staff and equipment. It has been suggested that some departments, such as dredging, dockyard operations, engineering services and properties/estates be privatized as limited companies. The NPA employed about 10 000 workers in Lagos Port in the mid 1970s. Much of the manual labour was daily paid or in even lower categories of temporary or casual work. Though there were regulations for transfer from these categories to more permanent employment, this was obviously not happening in many cases. In 1990 there were about 11 750: 3320 at headquarters, 5599 in the Lagos Port Complex, 2183 at Tin Can Island and 650 at the Ijora Container Terminal. This was 60 per cent of the total NPA staff for the country (Waterman 1982: 35; 1983a: 62, 69; McNulty and Adalemo 1988: 224; *West Africa* 1990: 724, 945).

A major example of port problems is the great cement holdup. Stimulated by the oil boom and the prospects of profit, the military government ordered 16 million tons of cement in a 12-month period. During 1976 and 1977, the seas off Lagos were full of ships waiting to off-load; 400 were reported in April 1976. Fees for transporting goods to Lagos rose rapidly. Some carriers found it cheaper to dump their cargoes in the sea than to wait; others suffered piracy. Though the wait is now much shorter due to more space and the decline in orders resulting from financial recession, there are still many hazards associated with delivering goods to Lagos; theft from ships and docks remains common. A task force was set up to decongest both ports in early 1990; 148 000 metric tonnes of cargo were being held, including 8000 cars. Orders had been rushed through to beat tax increases; paperwork was very slow and clearing agents often could not pay import duties. Most freight lifters were out of order. Threats to auction any goods not collected brought the number of cars down to 30 by mid June (*West Africa* 1976–7, 1990).

The use of local contractors for dock labour began in 1918 and was complete by the 1960s. Given the money involved, competition for contracts was fierce. Many managers and politicians had an interest in who got the contracts. The largest contractor in the 1970s was Associated Stevedoring Services. This was founded by the Ghanaian William H. Biney, who began contracting dock labour at home and maintained interests on the Tema docks while building his business in the more prosperous Lagos. His son, Hamilton Kweku Biney, inherited the business. H.K. achieved a prestigious position in the local business community by acting the part. He was described in the *Lagos State Directory of Modern Business* as 'The Otun Ba'loro of Lagos, Lawyer, Zoologist, Stevedoring King, Philanthropist and the Biggest Business Big-Wig of our Time' (cited by Waterman 1982: 63).

The Bineys used a particularistic management style, running the company like feudal chiefs. Their methods included employing men personally; receiving visitors and negotiating at home where they could hold court; giving gifts on the occasion of marriage, births and deaths; and helping with domestic problems. H.K. allowed a certain amount of union activity, partly to play workers off against supervisors and thus maintain personal control. Union leaders were assisted to make the *hajj* to Mecca. These fringe benefits attached workers to him in spite of low wages and hard conditions. Biney was reported to use gangsters to keep subordinates in line; even senior staff could be instantly dismissed, and labourers never knew which of their colleagues was a management spy (Waterman 1982: 60–61; 1983a: 74–5).

The service was rationalized in 1977 with the creation of the Integrated Cargo Handling Scheme to handle both stevedoring and shorehandling. There were to be only five contractors, of which the largest was the National Cargo Handling Company (NAHCO), owned by the government. The managers of this new company were inexperienced civil servants, who needed considerable time to learn the job. NPA policies made it very difficult for contractors to make a profit (less important for a state enterprise), and the labour force continued to be squeezed. However, dockworkers found that the NAHCO and the National Dock Labour Board (which supervises employers) improved their position considerably; they objected when the government suggested privatization in 1986 (Waterman 1983a: 69–74; *West Africa* 1986: 851).

Wage Workers and Trade Unionists

Detailed recent figures on the Lagos labour force are not available. Fapohunda and Lubdell (1978: 5, 24) estimated that in 1964 40 per cent of Nigeria's high-level manpower, not including teachers, 39 per cent of senior staff, 21 per cent of intermediate employees and 41 per cent of clerks worked in Greater Lagos. In 1970, about 44 per cent of manufacturing employees were found there. There were 57 832 employees of firms with ten or more workers in Lagos in 1972. A third of those surveyed worked for private firms, 18 per cent for the federal government, 10 per cent for the state government, 10 per cent for federal or state corporations and 7 per cent for educational institutions. Two per cent had other employers and 21 per cent were self-employed. But many people have more than one job; a 1978 study found that over 40 per cent of every category (gender, occupation, income) had supplementary employment (FOS 1972; Fapohunda *et al.* 1977: 98).

The civil service grew rapidly until the 1980s. In 1986, Lagos had 97 620 federal employees (22 per cent female and 38 per cent of the national total); many of these will move with their ministries to Abuja, but others will choose to remain in the metropolis. There were 20 000 staff on the Lagos State Civil Service payroll in 1989, 8113 local government staff and 27 386 primary or secondary teachers in 1988 (FOS 1987: 104; LSG 1989c, t.5, 11,12).

The 1984–5 Household Survey found that about 33 per cent of adults in urban areas of Lagos State were self-employed, 14 per cent were keeping house and 21 per cent were in school. This reflects redundancies and the greater availability of secondary and higher education since 1972. Of those who were in the labour force, 54 per cent were clerical, sales or service workers, 28 per cent were in professional or managerial occupations, only 14 per cent were reported to have manual occupations (skilled, production or labourer) and 4 per cent were looking for a first job (FOS 1986: 43, 45, 49). Unfortunately, these sources do not provide separate statistics for men and women; most women are self-employed traders (Peil 1979a).

There have been several notable studies of workers in Lagos – in the factories and port and as trade unionists. The wage work that attracted men to Lagos was often unsatisfying, to judge by the Public Works strike of 1897 and the attention given Lagos by trade union organizers. The presence in the city of so many categories of workers, with a wide range of incomes and lifestyles, encouraged comparison of one's lot with more successful residents, and migrants' strong desire for success encouraged occupational mobility and combining jobs in an attempt to reach their goal (Hopkins 1966; Hughes and Cohen 1978).

The majority of men and the more educated women who come to Lagos seek wage employment, at least initially. Their eventual goal may be their own business, which is seen as providing both independence and possibly greater wealth than can be earned in wages unless one is both well educated and lucky. Skill and hard work are not enough for successful entrepreneurship; to grow and compete under present conditions a business requires substantial capital. Unless one has generous relatives or patrons, this demands more than most people can save from their wages. In practice, rising inflation has made saving increasingly difficult just at the time when rising capital costs have made them essential. This has locked many workers into wage employment, cutting them off from their goals. One response to this has been the development of militant trade unionism (Peace 1979a). An examination of unionism in Lagos throws light on many problems faced by those organizing African workers.

The first recorded union in Lagos was a Mechanics Mutual Aid Provident and Improvement Association, active in 1897. Major strikes reported in Lagos up to 1940 include hospital warders (1899), railway clerks (1902 and 1904), printers (1913), dockworkers, engineers and railway workers (1919), Marine Department (1920), railway and public works labourers (1920), bus drivers (1934), transport owners and drivers (1935) and railway foundry workers (1939). There were undoubtedly many smaller strikes which did not attract press or government attention, but it is clear that government employees, having enough education to establish a formal association and relatively easy communications, led the way in militancy. Though the Railway Workers Union was not founded until 1939, earlier unions serving the same workers date from 1919. The NPA workers formalized their union in 1940, though there have been many splits and reorganizations since then. Employees of private firms had much more difficulty organizing; small house unions were common and not very effective (Hughes and Cohen 1978: 37–40; Waterman 1982: 72–4).

Various attempts were made to establish wider unions in Lagos, starting with the Nigerian Labor Organization (1930) and the African Workers Union (1931). These and the many later 'national' organizations have been plagued by factionalism and the self-interest of leaders. Trade unions in Nigeria have tended to be run by entrepreneurial organizers rather than arising from the work force. Even the notable exceptions to this rule have suffered through competition from men who thought themselves better qualified to run the union, either on the basis of ideology or personality. Leadership in the early unions was often supplied by radical journalists, such as I.T.A. Wallace-Johnson, who moved between his native Sierra Leone, Ghana and Nigeria from the 1930s to the 1960s in an attempt to stir up working-class sentiments, and Frank Macaulay, Herbert Macaulay's eldest son (Hughes and Cohen 1978: 44–6).

Employer–employee relations were not a clear racial issue, either during the colonial period or after independence, since African employers often exploited their workers in spite of official labour regulations and African merchants and professionals often sided with the government in industrial disputes. Nevertheless, political leaders of the independence movement saw the usefulness of urban (especially Lagos) workers as allies. Macaulay's NNDP and the NYM championed worker grievances, encouraged reforms which would decrease unemployment and supported local industrialization, though in none of these causes were they very successful. From the 1940s, trade union leaders who wanted political support for their activities tended to look to the NCNC for help (Hughes and Cohen 1978: 48–51).

After independence, the government tried to move trade unions away from politics. However, even consumptionist goals can have political implications in a country where a large proportion of the work force is in government employment (including education, health and state-owned corporations) and where government wages set the pattern for private industry. Governments which are trying to encourage investment from overseas inevitably oppose wage demands which will make local products uncompetitive in world markets or, by raising the cost of living, lead to political dissatisfaction. (Market women are quick to seek their share of an official wage rise; local food prices go up at least as much as wages).

Workers, on the other hand, face inflation and job insecurity and see government and managerial corruption as a direct threat to their livelihood. Strikes for higher wages are directed as much at government as at private employers; the General Strike of 1964 helped to bring down the first civilian government. Whereas the General Strike was organized mainly by government unions and supported by market women and other workers, increasing unionization meant that workers in private industry were much better organized for the battles of the 1970s (Peace 1979a: 170). As the home of a large share of Nigeria's industry and the city with the highest cost of living, Lagos has led the way in each round of wage demands; workers in other cities learned from it.

But unions suffer from internal factionalism and find it very difficult to join for common goals. Twenty-eight organizations of dockworkers, sometimes joined with port and/or railway workers, registered between 1948 and 1977. There were ten unions or associations of employees of the Nigerian Ports Authority in 1973, ranging in size from 4523 to only 67 members. They often catered for single departments (such as Harbours) or categories of workers (foremen,'officers). The NPA Workers Union catered mostly for manual workers in the engineering and stores departments; many smaller groups had split from it. The largest union, the Railway and Ports Transportation and Clerical Staff Union (R & PT & CSU), attracted a wider clientele, from beyond the ports/docks. Some of these organizations were joined for negotiation purposes to the Nigerian Maritime Trade Union Federation, but others were 'independent' and not even registered as trade unions. This factionalism makes it easier for government and employers to control the workforce, but it may also give workers somewhat more control over the leadership (Waterman 1983a: 118–9, 140–1).

The 1970s saw a rising tide of strikes and of government legislation to control them. In many cases, strikes were short; they often lasted only a day or part of a day, protesting a specific action of management rather than demanding better pay or conditions. (Such demands were more common in the 1980s, when inflation was more severe.) NPA workers not only did not picket; they often sat at their workplaces but did no work. A more effective method of complaint devised by the R & PT & CSU was to acquire incriminating documents (through clerical members) and release these to the press or government with demands that action be taken against offending managers. With widespread corruption in the NPA, it was not difficult to find out something to the disadvantage of a manager. Sometimes blackmail was used instead of public release; in either case, the union often achieved more, at less cost, than they would have through striking. Their complaint was against incompetent management, and they wanted the government to improve it (Waterman 1983b: 37–8).

Lagos workers often distrust their national union leaders as exploitative and not sufficiently interested in helping members; many union organizers move into government or management positions. Workers may ignore the union for some time, then become militant when this seems likely to improve their position. Peace (1975) shows how Ikeja workers ignored national union officials (who sided with management and government) and supported local leaders to demand their share of the 1971 Adebo pay awards. Their strikes were largely successful in forcing private managements to pay government wages. However, this did not increase workers' commitment either to the union or to wage employment. They see clearly that unions are in most circumstances ineffective; occasional successes should not be taken for organizational strength. Their main focus of discontent is government, not management, since they wish to escape the factory for self employment and since they are well aware of excesses of government elites (Peace 1979a). Chapter 5 will examine the relationship between wages and the cost of living.

The Self Employed

About a third of jobs in Lagos are in distribution, followed by services. A majority of this work is done by the self employed. A large proportion of women in Lagos are self employed, mainly in various forms of trade. There are also large numbers of self employed male craftsmen and traders, and many men who are officially wage employed also carry on other income-earning activities. A study in Ajegunle in 1971 found 26 per cent of men and 74 per cent of women in the labour force were working for themselves, not including those whose major source of income was from wage employment (Peil 1981: 95). Self employment was highest among both men and women

Plate 4.3 Small shops on Herbert Macaulay Street, note open drain
Source: Richard Ammann

from the north, who had little education or training. Women who had grown up in Lagos were also heavily involved in trade.

Self employment can be conveniently divided into commercial and artisanal activities. It is not always possible to distinguish between the two, as many producers such as tailors and carpenters also sell their goods to the public, but the distinction between those whose primary focus is manufacturing or repairing and those whose primary focus is commerce is a useful one in assessing capital and spatial needs and methods of operation. While young people may learn trading through an apprenticeship, many learn through experience as they grow up. Training for artisanal activities is usually more formalized and longer, taking between one and five years after leaving primary school. Women who prepare food for sale are included among traders, since their main focus is sales. Because of the time needed to prepare Yoruba meals, purchasing both cooked and convenience food from petty traders is widespread among people at all economic levels.

The functional separation which results from town planning in industrialized countries has been only very partially achieved in Lagos because of the disinclination (or in recent years, inability) of the government to control petty traders and self employed producers. Small-scale commerce, manufacturing and services are widely practised in residential areas, especially by individuals working alone. For example, in 1972, there were 1083 'firms' providing products and services along the streets of Ajegunle/

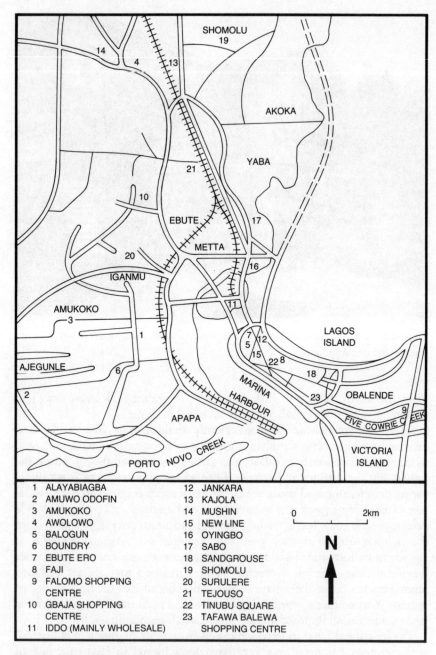

Map 5 Major markets and shopping centres

Source: Adapted from *Lagos Street Finder* 1981

Olodi – from furniture to photography and barbering. Some of these had partners and/or apprentices (especially printers and auto repairmen), but many were single shoemakers, seamstresses, watch or radio repairmen, and so on. Plate 4.3 shows shops lining Herbert Macaulay Street in Yaba. Pedestrians must beware of the large open gutter, which collects rubbish as well as rainwater.

In addition, there are large numbers of bars, typing schools and other commercial activities, women trading from their houses and children hawking goods, in an area which is essentially residential. Residents of exclusive residential areas are visited regularly by hawkers, and women selling quick meals are found even on the grounds of the Police College, where their illegality is ignored in the interests of convenience. University porters grow crops on spare land, and young entrepreneurs provide a photocopying service wherever there is a market for it.

Marketwomen

There were at least 30 large and medium markets in Lagos in the late 1960s, of which about a third were on the Island. These markets covered about 100 hectares of land and served most residential areas, though older areas are better provided for than newer ones and there has been pressure to use less of the highly expensive space on Lagos Island for markets (Sada and McNulty 1974, Sada *et al.* 1978). For example, the Ebute Ero market is partly under the Island end of Carter Bridge (see Map 5).

By 1989, many of the old markets, such as Jankara, Oyingbo and Sabo, were in very poor condition. Roofs were disintegrating with rust and rains flooded the footpaths. They are far too small for the demand from traders for space, and are surrounded by the pavement stalls of those who cannot get, or cannot afford, space inside. New markets provide additional space, but many traders find it more convenient to trade in uncontrolled areas. The New Line Market, opposite the Central Mosque on Lagos Island, seems to have started with traders along the walkways, but vacant land inside the plot has also been filled with stalls. There is no roof and conditions are very crowded; access to such a busy area is obviously much sought-after. Makeshift stalls line nearby Breadfruit Street. The Alhaji Issa Williams Street market caters for visitors to the neighbourhood mosque, whereas Ajegunle's Boundary Road market is next to the bus and danfo terminal (see Plates 4.4 and 4.5).

Small markets usually specialize in perishable food, but most also provide non-perishable food, manufactured goods and services. What is available depends partly on size and clientele. Jankara market used to be noted for cloth, but a better selection is now available from small shops, especially along Nnamdi Azikiwe Street. Ebute Ero market has a large area for hardware and auto spare parts. Household goods, home medical remedies and school supplies are found in most sizeable markets. Tailoring, watch

Plate 4.4   Mosque and market, Alhaji Issa Williams Street
Source: Richard Ammann

Plate 4.5   Boundary Market, Ajegunle

and shoe repair, tinsmithing and barbering are sometimes found in markets, but more often are nearby, where space is cheaper.

Most markets are the responsibility of local governments. For example, Ikeja has 1647 stalls and 831 'counter space points' in its six markets and Agege 2668 stalls in 7 markets. Shomolu has 18 markets, with 3889 open stalls and 4901 lock-up stalls. Prices vary with the market; lock-up stalls cost N15–50 and open or temporary stalls N3–10. Markets vary in size, from a 'corner shop' with a few stalls to major markets with over 700 stalls, including specially constructed sheds. Modernization, especially in terms of more lock-up stalls, continues as resources permit. Stalls are also being built at modernized motor parks, which have drains, toilets and water – still far in the future for some of the older markets. The state also runs markets, though it is more concerned with capital-intensive shopping centres and with wholesaling. Since 1984, the Market Development Board has created wholesale markets at Ketu Ikosi, Abule Egba and Okokomaiko and large markets at Alaiyabiagba, Daleko, Mushin and Sura. The state Secretariat at Alausa has its own mini-market (LSMI 1988: 146).

Night markets and Sunday markets are an innovation to provide more space and convenience. Night markets (6–10 pm) were started to get traders off the streets and handle the demand for space without allotting new land for markets. Traders are allowed to use the pavements in designated areas without harassment. Night markets are found in both relatively central areas such as Ebute Metta and new residential areas such as Festac Town. They flourish among crowds of workers returning home: Yaba Bus Stop, Ikeja Bus Stop, Oju Elegba roundabout, Alhaji Masha roundabout. Mushin Local Council opened night markets in Alode, Oshodi, Onitire and Sogunle. However, night markets are not an adequate substitute for larger and more diverse day markets. For example, the residents of Alausa complain that they must go to Ikeja Market for many items, as their night market is not well-patronized (*Lagos Horizon*, 15 August 1989).

Night markets pose two important problems for traders: security and costs. Women need help from their children to carry goods to and from the market, so many young children are out on the streets long after dark. They may even be left to carry on the trade, at a time when robbers are a real threat. The taxing of night traders is as yet unsettled. Traditional elders in Onitire demanded N5 per table per month, but the traders refused, pointing out that only local governments can tax trading (*Lagos Life*, 10 August 1989).

The Ogba Sunday Market began in July 1989 through the efforts of the Better Life for Rural Dwellers Committee, which is headed in each state by the Governor's wife. The official goals are to provide opportunities for rural women to earn more and urban residents to buy food more cheaply. The Lagos State Transport Corporation is to transport sellers from their villages to Ogba, where they can cut out the middlemen/women by selling directly to the public. The greater importance given to providing cheap food for

Lagosians is evident in the stands run by the Lagos State Bulk Purchasing Corporation, Epe Local Government and Lagos State Polytechnic. These sell basic foodstuffs wholesale and retail, with prices as much as 20 per cent off the usual market price. Soap and household equipment (water heaters and toilets) as well as staples are also available. The plan to sell food cheaply has two unintended results. Though Lagos residents who can reach this peripheral market are pleased, the rural women earn less than they should. Second, it is gradually spreading to the regular Ogba market, as women traders are rushing to buy the food so they can sell it next day at standard prices. It remains to be seen how Sunday markets will develop.

While a 'modernization' perspective might lead one to expect that sales of clothing, plastic products, hardware and electronic goods would increasingly take place in large stores rather than in markets, this has only partly occurred in Lagos. Some shopping centres have developed, as at Tafawa Balewa Square on Lagos Island, Falomo in Ikoyi (see Plate 4.6), Oju Elegba in Surulere, Ikeja Plaza and Festac Town. Allen Street, in Ikeja, has the reputation of the most expensive street in the country. There are rumours that drug money went into financing land purchases and the building of department stores here. These centres have replaced central Lagos as a focus for elite shopping.

However, people living near or below the poverty line (a large proportion of the Lagos population) need to get the most for their money, and this can

Plate 4.6 Falomo Shopping Centre, Ikoyi
Source: Richard Ammann

best be done by buying from traders with the lowest overheads and greatest competition. This keeps large numbers of small traders in business rather than replacing them with discount stores and supermarkets. The elites, with cars, can shop anywhere; ordinary people continue to use markets and the traders and small shops that line many streets. In times of shortage, the market is often a better bet than the large shop. Supplies often come through personal relations rather than official orders, and few questions are asked. Thus, markets have continued to compete effectively with large-scale 'modern' commercial enterprises. Their declining share of the local economy is due more to planning decisions than to a drop in popular demand.

The Alaba International Market in Ojo, known as 'little Japan' is an example of the continued viability of markets in Lagos. Established with permission of the Badagry Local Government in 1979, when electronics traders were evicted from nearby Owodi-Ora market, it now covers an area of two football fields and is the largest market for electrical and household goods – new, 'reconditioned' and fakes – in the country. These are available cheap on the 'let the buyer beware' principle. Well organized contacts at the ports and with returnee travellers ensure a steady supply, at prices which undercut local electronics manufacturers. Electricians, welders and painters 'restore' old models for those who cannot afford new ones. The market has its own spare parts section and has attracted at least two banks and several bars. Turnover is about N30 000 on weekdays and N75 000 on Saturdays. Shop space costs N100 to 250 per month (about £20), or one can trade on the pavement for N30–50. The market was closed when rioting traders burnt the police station in May 1990, but it was reopened as soon as repairs could be made; it is too important for permanent closure to be enforced (Nwosu 1989; *West Africa* 1990: 1086).

Used and restored items are also on sale in other markets. The used-clothing seller (sometimes known by the local equivalent of 'the white man has died') is found in many areas, and is increasingly popular since the price of new clothing has risen and more fashionable clothing and shoes are on sale. Empty tins and bottles are reclaimed by scavengers from rubbish tips or collected from houses for resale to traders or companies. Refurbished spare parts from discarded cars, stoves, etc. find ready customers in a situation where 'new' spare parts are almost impossible to find. The scavenging 'trade' has drawn in unemployed young men who have no alternative (*Guardian*, 14 October 1988).

Markets are an important measure of changing styles of living. Television sets and tape cassettes reached the open markets in the 1970s, and nipples for feeding bottles have become increasingly available in spite of health professionals' promotion of continued breast feeding. Due to inflation, there is much less bargaining than there used to be, but markets are still the major shopping centre for those who must buy in small quantities or who want bargains. If there is no nearby market, there are plenty of petty traders to supply daily needs.

Workers and entrepreneurs

Street and House Traders

By no means all trading is done in markets or shops; much is carried on from houses and by itinerant hawkers, aided by the continuing 'go-slow' which makes cars an easy prey for anyone without a permanent place to trade. The police periodically harass street traders, dismantling structures which are blocking the pavements and chasing them away from bus stops and other gathering places. However, this has little effect; they return as soon as the police are out of sight. Many cannot get wage employment; others prefer to be their own boss. The Street Trading and Illegal Markets Prohibition Edict of 1984 has not had much effect, except to lower the income of street traders. Both sellers and buyers can be fined N100 or a month in jail for a first offence, up to N1000 or three months imprisonment for a third offence, but small bribes to the police are sometimes sufficient to forestall this. In 1989, it was reported that street trading was flourishing; holders of market stalls were leaving them because the streets are free and provide more business (*West Africa* 1985: 284; 1989: 89).

Government action against street traders goes back to the War Against Indiscipline in 1984. Local government officials announced their intention to rid their areas of street trading. Police are used to enforce the regulations, and violence has erupted when traders attempted to protect their goods. For example, in a raid on Oshodi Street in 1988, a pregnant woman was killed and thousands of naira of goods were seized by the police. A lame shoemaker was so distraught at the burning of his supplies and equipment at Yaba that he jumped into the fire. (*Punch*, 4 July 1988; *Daily Sketch*, 22 September 1988). It is not difficult to see the programme as class warfare, whereby the poor are being banned from their livelihood by an increasingly wealthy and isolated bureaucracy. The Yoruba see the informal sector as part of their culture, whereas the government wants to organize, control and tax it. The government promises official sites, training and loans, but imposes financial burdens which many traders cannot cope with.

A study of 1148 street traders by the African–American Institute found that three-fifths had been raided; a few had lost their goods as much as four times and 5 per cent had spent three or more days in jail. Fruit and vegetable sellers were especially likely to complain of raids. Only a quarter had goods worth more than N200 (about £14), so they could hardly afford regular losses. Most of them were relatively new to trading and only about one in ten was over 40. Nevertheless, these women made an important contribution to household finances, especially in a time of high inflation. Very few had any other source of income.

Almost anything that can be carried is on sale. As examples, in front of large shops along the Marina one can buy watches, woollen suits, snacks, greeting cards, newspapers and magazines. While waiting 30 minutes or longer at the Ebute Metta end of the Third Mainland Bridge, drivers can buy books, padlocks, flasks, Mars bars, potato crisps, telephones, perfume, car cushions, calculators, kitchenware, matches, soft drinks, ice cream, video tapes, shoes, knapsacks, boxed pen sets, ping-pong paddles, sheets, maps, biscuits, soap and brushes. Even moving traffic is fair game; bargaining can take place on the run. Young people and women, especially, trade because they need the money, but they also fill a need. People whose working day (including transportation) extends from 6 or 7 in the morning to 6 to 8 at night do not want to go far for food or other small purchases. Buying while they wait for a bus or taxi or sit in a traffic jam, or from a trader sitting just outside their workplace is an efficient use of time.

Street trading by children is illegal in Nigeria, but impossible to eradicate because, on the whole, society approves of it. There are cases of child exploitation, but it is seen as an important aspect of socialization for many children, training them for an adult career and improving the standard of living of the poorest urban families. Oloko (1990) divided child trading into four types: selling from one spot, hawking along streets, and going from door to door either in their own neighbourhood or in affluent neighbourhoods. On the positive side, children learn trading skills on the job: distinguishing bona fide customers, encouraging impulse buying, handling competition, rapid calculation and capital accumulation. Many children use their profits for additional food and to pay for school expenses. Such training is especially important for girls, since many women need to support a family when the father disappears or fails to provide. Even those in wage employment may need to supplement a low salary or provide for themselves in enforced early retirement.

The negative aspects include tiredness (especially if they work in the evenings), poor school performance (when children see the syllabus as irrelevant to their needs) and physical danger from traffic accidents or loitering men. Cases of unplanned pregnancy are widely-known, and a few boys become delinquent, spending their cash on smoking or drugs, but neither of these problems is unique to children who trade.

Children are more likely to be involved in hawking if their mothers trade and/or are of low education and income. Children of better-educated or better-off mothers may assist in a market stall or shop, since this is seen as helping them to become disciplined adults. A majority of the school children questioned like hawking. About half worked only 1–2 hours per day and earned less than N10 per day, but profits increased for older children who could be trusted with more expensive items. Older children are also more likely to work beyond their immediate neighbourhood and in the evening, which tends to be the most profitable (Oloko 1990).

Craftsmen

It has been estimated that about 20 per cent of skilled jobs in Lagos are unfilled (McNulty and Adalemo 1988: 227). While in some cases this may be because they require technical training which is not available locally, it is also due to the greater income and/or independence to be obtained working for oneself. Apprenticeship to an informal sector craftsman is the primary way of learning a trade in Lagos, and this tends to be a better preparation for self than for wage employment. During the oil boom, it was difficult for many craftsmen to get apprentices because there were many opportunities to make money more quickly through trading. This has been less of a problem in the 1980s.

While some argue that modern manufacturing will increasingly displace informal sector craftsmanship and that artisans will become merely exploited labourers for major firms, this does not seem to be happening in Nigeria. A few crafts, such as shoemaking, are disappearing because they cannot compete, though shoe repairing has returned to popularity with the recession. Many other crafts are thriving because they produce more variety, more cheaply, than capital-intensive firms. Competition is very keen among the small-scale producers, especially where the apprenticeship system is producing too many new workers (Peil 1979b).

The government's ban on imported garments has encouraged businessmen to set up clothing factories. As a result, tailors are losing out on some lines which can be cheaply mass produced, such as shirts and trousers, but much women's clothing is still produced on an individual basis. Fashion design has become a very attractive field for women; training is offered in many private schools and at the Polytechnic. In spite of massive competition, tailors and seamstresses may earn more in self employment than they could in sweatshop mass production. Increasingly, those who want to get ahead find wholesale buyers for large quantities of the same item rather than waiting for customers to bring their own cloth, as was customary.

Blacksmiths and carpenters profit from the continuing demand from the construction industry and new householders' need for cheap, basic furniture. Most housing in Lagos is built by small-scale firms, which hire craftsmen as they need them. Printers and electricians do well on their own, though the former require more capital investment than most skilled craftsmen. Auto repair is also largely in the hands of small-scale artisans, who are innovative in substituting for expensive imported parts and whose labour costs are far below those of the large firms (Fapohunda 1978: 129; Peil 1981: 104–10).

Services

The service economy developed far in advance of an industrial economy. Services have the stereotype of being cheap to enter, low paid and separated by gender. As technology develops, education spreads and the standard of living rises, this stereotype needs adjusting. There is now a wide range of services available, from the long-established shoe repairing and prostitution to new fields such as computer consultancy and insurance. Services provide a good income for those with capital to invest in equipment or specialized training. Barbers, herbalists, hairdressers, repairmen and domestic workers provide personal services of the traditional type, but private doctors, dentists and lawyers also notify passers-by of their services in most residential areas. Some are organized into formal sector firms, but many are single-person practices.

Some services are becoming more capital-intensive. For example, some shoe repairers have moved from a 'stand' with a few tools along a street (see Plate 4.2) or a small shack in front of a house to a mini-factory with considerable equipment. Inflation makes it necessary to have shoes last as long as possible and customers welcome the ability to change shoes to make them more fashionable. This can drift into making new shoes, becoming a manufacturer rather than just a repairman. So far, very few shoemakers can afford the equipment needed for this transformation (*Guardian Financial Weekly*, 14 August 1989).

Other services require no capital at all, and can thus be used as a last resort. Local newspapers were complaining of professional prostitutes as early as 1882 (cited by Iliffe 1987: 86). Whether a regular profession or just the enjoyment of casual relationships with wealthy men, 'fallen' women are a steady theme in the literature on Lagos (Ekwensi 1961, 1963; Nwapa 1971). There are periodic drives to clear 'good time girls' away, but the demand from elite as well as ordinary men ensures that their services remain available.

Prostitutes may be organized by an older woman or pimp or may be merely women on their own who need the money. They may pick up clients in hotels and bars or work from home. For example, Goriola Street in Ajegunle has a reputation for having large numbers of prostitutes. Some of these are looking for a husband; others merely seek to survive in a city where there are few jobs open to uneducated women who lack capital. Thomas (1985) interviewed 100 prostitutes in Surulere, between Agege Motor Road and Oju Elegba Road/City Way. Only two-fifths were Nigerian, mainly from Bendel, Imo and Anambra States; the aliens were mostly Ghanaians or Togolese and thus subject to deportation. (It was estimated that there were 5000 Ghanaian prostitutes in Nigeria in 1988, mostly in Lagos). Half of Thomas' interviewees were divorced and nearly three-quarters had children. Money was the chief motivating factor; though their average income was less than half the minimum wage, most earned more than previously and would find it hard to stop for this reason. Many women 'befriend' and maintain a household for men in exchange for support or occasionally provide sex for boyfriends or employers in return for gifts.

Women are also moving into new fields. *Lagos Horizon* (22 August 1989) featured Bukola Sanni, a woman battery charger. Although she had completed the West African School Certificate, her mother advised her to learn a trade which was less crowded than hairdressing and fashion designing. After two and a half years training, she is established at a large petrol station in Ketu and doing well. She expects to continue the job after marriage, and her ultimate plan is to have a battery factory. Women are also moving into printing and other skills which require dexterity rather than strength.

The unemployed

With Lagos' position as a prime target for migrating school leavers, continuing problems of unemployment and underemployment are hardly surprising. However, the proportion without work is lower than expected because of the propensity of those who cannot find wage employment to take up some entrepreneurial activity. Yesufu (1968) found about 7 per cent unemployment in Lagos; half had never worked before and most of the rest had only had one previous job. Unemployment was reported to be 8 per cent in metropolitan Lagos in 1976 and 7.2 per cent in 1989, but these figures are likely to underestimate the problem. Most of the unemployed are unknown to the government; few people register with the Employment Exchange because access to jobs in Lagos is far more likely to be through personal contacts than through the Exchange (Yesufu 1968; *Master Plan* 1980: 79; FOS 1989b).

While there is considerable turnover of unemployed people, there is also much long-term unemployment; two-thirds of those located in Yesufu's survey had been out of work for more than six months and nearly half had been searching for over a year. These had refused to return home; many others try to find work in Lagos and leave when they are unsuccessful. The long-term unemployed tend to be well into their twenties, men who have settled in Lagos and are thus willing to hang on until they can find work. They are often relatively well-educated, and thus see Lagos as the best possibility for finding the jobs they seek. Those with little education quickly turn to self employment.

Table 4.3 presents the most detailed statistics available, the result of a large survey of Lagos State. It is clear that unemployment declines rapidly from about age 25 and that it is higher for men than for women under 20 –

Table 4.3 Percentage unemployed, by age and sex, 1976

| | Lagos Division | | Ikeia Division | |
	Male	Female	Male	Female
15–19	29	22	25	19
20–24	29	32	27	33
25–29	14	15	18	26
30–34	7	10	6	9
35–39	4	7	5	2
40–44	3	7	2	2
45–49	3	2	4	1
50–54	2	2	5	1
55+	6	1	4	1
10–14, DK	3	2	4	6
Total	100	100	100	100

Source: Lagos State, *Digest of Statistics* 1987, Tables 1.14 and 1.15.

largely because young women withdraw temporarily from the labour force to have their first children. Women in their 30s and 40s who return to the labour force face more unemployment than men, who have settled into a job by that time. Women tend to retire from the labour force in their late 50s, when the oldest child can support them and they can help out at home while daughters or daughters-in-law work, whereas elderly men may face renewed unemployment.

While work was relatively easy to find in the late 1970s because of the oil boom, unemployment rose in the 1980s because the large drop in oil income meant that both the government and private companies had to lay off large numbers of workers. The newspapers were full of gloomy headlines: '9000 laid off' and '7000 employees sent on leave' (the Nigerian Bottling Company had no import licence for raw materials). All state employees with 35 years service were retired in 1989, which put many still-healthy older men out of work. At the same time, it is clear that the gloomy forecasts of the *Master Plan*, that unemployment would increase from 30 per cent of the labour force in 1978 to 41 per cent in 1995, are unlikely to come true. It has never been as high as 30 per cent, and the informal sector provides an outlet (*Master Plan* 1980, Fig. 11–13; *West Africa* 1985: 703; 1989: 164).

However, an increasing problem is that unemployment does not just hit those with little education. Over twenty thousand graduates were completing their year with the National Youth Service Corps in August 1989, at a time when few employers were interested in them. At a time of recession, even those with a masters degree in business administration have problems finding employment. This leads some of them to set up their own businesses, but many are resentful that the jobs for which they have struggled so long are unavailable. A man who had returned to Lagos after seven years studying business administration in Sweden committed suicide after a year of searching for a job (*Guardian Financial Weekly*, 14 August 1989; *Lagos Life*, 10 August 1989).

Summary

Commerce and industry are at least as important to Lagos' livelihood as government, which is why the move to Abuja will not affect it unduly. Multinational corporations and large local manufacturers both find Lagos the obvious place to do business. A few major banks may be based in the North or East, but without a Lagos branch much business would be lost. This is partly necessary for obtaining a share in government largesse, but external dealings through the port and airport are also essential to the success of many businesses. Though a 100 per cent increase in fares has made it difficult, women traders also profit from buying trips to London.

Most of the nation's 'Achievers of Repute' live in the capital at least part of the time; they use its clubs for wheeling and dealing, and avoid the inconvenience of distance in a country where postal and telephone services leave a lot to be desired. Age is neither an asset nor an impediment for entrepreneurship in Lagos. Though it remains difficult for women to reach the top, some have done so and more are on the way: Mrs Grace Ogunnusi is President of the Association of Nigerian Exporters. Some men move up as managers of large enterprises; others succeed through their own enterprises – serving as models for thousands of aspiring entrepreneurs. Large numbers of Nigerian managers and technicians are now available to replace departing expatriates. A major problem is an unwillingness to wait for promotion.

Public corporations have not been very successful, as Chapter 8 will show more fully. The port exhibits typical problems of bureaucracy and inefficiency, partly through the inadequacies of its own management and labour force, but also because of government interference and endemic corruption in the society. As with so many other aspects of Lagos life, the port operates on personalist principles, which complicate the running of a major business.

While government employees play a prominent role through the power they exercise and their wages and conditions, which serve as models for industrial bargaining, they are outnumbered by both private employees and the self employed. Lagos is the centre of trade unionism in Nigeria, though as we shall see in Chapter 5 its workers are not well paid in relation to the cost of living. Labour leaders are similar to financiers and industrialists in their attachment to government power; it will be interesting to see how many move with the government to Abuja even though this cuts them off from the majority of their followers. Factionalism has made it difficult for unions to attain the strength which comes with size, and the popularity of self employment means that most workers do not put much faith in progress through unionism.

Self employment is seen as the real road to progress, even though for many (especially women) it only provides a rough survival in the city. Young and old, rich and poor, are ready to 'have a go' at buying and selling, contracting and manipulating people and resources. Many with regular wage employment operate a small business on the side, to increase their income or prepare for full-time working for themselves. This tendency goes back to the city's origins and seems likely to continue indefinitely. It is one reason why dependency theory is only acceptable to the intellectual elites – too many people are busy making their own decisions. They are doubtless affected by the world economy, but government policy and local corruption have much more to do with what happens in Lagos, who succeeds and who survives.

The present government is hard on women traders, preferring a 'clean' environment to the continuance of their necessary activities. Traders and hawkers avoid this pressure as best they can, protest whenever this seems likely to be worthwhile, and express their political opinions when elections occur. If all trading were removed from the streets, Lagos might temporarily resemble a European city, but it would soon close down – its people unfed, services unobtainable and the mass of the population departing for another city where they could make a living.

Craftsmen have already been removed from the streets in several Nigerian cities, to the detriment of those who need their services. Their small businesses are being encouraged in Lagos in an attempt to cut down unemployment. On the whole, these craftsmen can compete with the formal sector by offering cheaper goods and filling gaps in the market. Many combine wage and self employment, in the Lagos tradition. Unemployment continues to get the headlines, but does not appear to have increased as much as the pessimists predict. Many people have lost their jobs in the recession of the 1980s, but they are inventive in finding alternative sources of income.

The next chapter examines family resources and the government provision of education and health which, like manufacturing and government jobs, are more available in Lagos than elsewhere in the country.

5
Families and basic needs

C.M. Okunlola is a self-employed Yoruba tailor aged 40. He was born and completed primary school in Abeokuta and moved to Lagos in 1965. He rented a room in various houses, but needed more space and managed to acquire his own house in Ajegunle in 1972. This has five rooms and two shops, one of which is used for his business. Four rooms are shared with his wife (a petty trader), four daughters, an unemployed nephew, his brother's wife, a young niece of his wife, two children of distant relations and two unrelated housemaids. The two oldest children are in primary school; the housemaids never attended school. He has three brothers in Lagos whom he visits daily. His parents came to visit him recently, bringing farm crops; he entertained them during their stay and gave them money. He visits home every month, bringing cash and provisions. For a recent child-naming ceremony, he invited his brothers, four kinsmen from home and 40 friends, mostly also from Abeokuta. Most of his spare time is spent visiting close friends (known since childhood) and relaxing at home with the family, but he belongs to an extended family association, the Egba Association, a Muslim brotherhood and an esusu (savings society). He plans to return home in another ten years, since he can continue tailoring there (1972 interviews).

Family and kinship link all sectors of society, since moral norms strongly enforce maintenance of these ties. The family is the prime source of welfare, since little is provided formally by the state. Few people get pensions and most young people expect to help support elderly parents or relatives. Capital cities are always expensive, and recent rises in the cost of living in Lagos have put many families in jeopardy. The government's main contribution to basic needs of residents are in the fields of education and health. Education is particularly important as an enabling mechanism, offering the hope of stable and sometimes lucrative employment. While the Lagos State government is relatively liberal in funding education and medical care, families still have costs which not all can pay. The wealthy tend to use private schools and medical services; those who cannot afford these must settle for overcrowded and under-resourced government services.

Households

Households are the basic unit of society. The General Household Survey (FOS 1986) defined households as persons who eat their principal meals together and usually live under the same roof. Household composition is often more complex in Lagos than in Britain. While a few people live alone, most share accommodation with family and/or non-family members. Some large family houses in older neighbourhoods provide space for extended family members (siblings, cousins, etc., of varying generations) to live under the same roof; on newer estates people of moderate wealth can sometimes acquire enough room to have three generations sharing the same household, and temporary accommodation with relatives is often essential for the poor. Divorce, polygyny, fostering and accommodation of domestic servants or apprentices (relatives or employees) also lead to variety in household composition. Separation of partners leaves many single-parent families, and polygyny may mean that two or more wives and their children share accommodation.

Size and Composition

The General Household Survey (FOS 1986) found 3.5 persons per household in urban areas of Lagos State, compared to 4.8 for urban areas of the country as a whole and 3.4 for the three neighbouring states with largely Yoruba populations. Monthly household income was N244, 30 per cent above the national average, but below that of several other states. Lagos State has the lowest proportion of recorded household enterprises and owner-occupiers in the country, but its houses are relatively well supplied with amenities (see Chapter 7).

Morgan's 1967 survey of Lagos found an average of 3.8 persons per household. Half were family households headed by the husband (averaging 5.5 persons each); 21 per cent each were single or kinship households and 7 per cent were non-family households (usually two or more friends sharing a room). Overall, 11 per cent of the people in the sample were adults living without a family – a large proportion for such a family-oriented society. Twelve per cent of households had ten or more persons; these tend to be indigenous or long-established families living in their own houses. A quarter of urban households in Lagos State in 1984 included relatives, with or without the nuclear family of spouses and children (Morgan and Kannisto 1973: 27; FOS 1986: 37).

Children make the largest contribution to household size; the mean live births to women in Lagos State increases from 1.6 at age 20–24 to 6.2 at 45-plus. Urban women have fewer children overall than rural women, largely because fewer city women have more than four. Both traditional and modern means of contraception are used three times as often by city as by rural women. While better-educated women tend to want fewer children than the uneducated, the number of living children is not much lower because city women have better health and nutrition and are more likely to give birth in a hospital (Lucas 1974; National Population Bureau 1986; Lesthaeghe *et al.* 1989).

The number of dependants in the household is directly related to socioeconomic status. More income buys more space, and relatives take advantage of space not needed for children. Ohadike (1968: 83) found that husbands who were professionals or administrators had four times as many dependants in their households as unskilled manual workers. Economically advantaged households where the wife worked were the most likely to have domestic servants.

Many of the people who live alone are young, not yet married, but others are old people who have no relatives to accommodate them. Two cases from a study in Shomolu illustrate some of the problems which old people on their own face: Alhaji Ola was a practising Muslim healer. He and his wife had separated, according to Yoruba custom, because they were both old. He saw his children regularly, but lived on his own. Domestic tasks such as cooking were a problem; he hoped to save enough to marry a young wife who would care for him. Mrs Adekunle had inherited a house from her mother. When she retired from trading, she lived on rents from her six tenants. She had no children or siblings, and had alienated both the tenants and neighbours. She complained of loneliness and rheumatism, but her personality made it difficult to improve her social situation (Bamisaiye and DiDomenico 1983).

Marriage, Divorce and Polygyny

There are many marriages where the partners remain faithful over many years, but also many breakups due to quarrels over money, infertility, the influence of relatives or differing expectations. The fragility of marriage in Lagos is partly an inheritance of traditional customs and partly a response to changing conditions. Women expect to be self-reliant, and many postpone marriage because 'sugar daddies' are more satisfactory than husbands. Formal ceremonies (traditional or·modern) are socially approved of but expensive; 'befriending' is an acceptable substitute, and the prevalence of polygyny make it relatively easy to change one spouse for another. In addition, it is customary for partners to separate in old age, each turning to relatives or children for support.

Expectations of marriage differ with gender, income, education and cultural background. Stimulated by education, women's magazines and women's pages in the newspapers, the wife often wants a far more egalitarian relationship than her husband, and she may be too tired after a long day at work to provide the services he takes for granted. She may remain with an elite husband because he provides a higher standard of living than she could attain on her salary or because the children would be his should a divorce occur, but overall marital ties are not very strong. Where women are virtually self-supporting, they feel free to leave a husband who cannot maintain them.

Relatively few cases of divorce go through the Lagos Magistrate's Courts, since formal dissolution is not required unless the parties had an officially recognized marriage – by Ordinance. Nevertheless, it appears that the numbers are rising. Courts in Ikeja, Mushin and Yaba had 843 divorce cases between 1980 and 1988, of which 121 were in 1988. The major reason given for divorce was adultery (of women) or taking a second wife (by men). Thus, although polygyny is widely accepted by Yoruba men, many women are unwilling to put up with it and many men are unwilling that their wives should 'play around' (George 1989).

The incidence of polygyny is low in Lagos, but statistics may be somewhat misleading, since men whose social milieu disapproves (well-educated, Christian elites) may support women outside of marriage or practise serial monogamy (a series of wives) instead. It is also difficult to measure because many such wives have separate households; some remain at home in the village or live in another town where the husband does business. Only 1.4 per cent of ever-married women in the Fertility Survey were living in polygynous households; the ECA study (with a more affluent sample) reported that 6 per cent of currently married men had two wives in the household and 1 per cent had three or more (National Population Bureau 1986: 12; ECA 1980: 39). Polygyny increases with age, regardless of a man's education. Men who grew up in a city are as likely to be polygynous as those who grew up in a village, partly because better jobs give them enough money to support more than one wife. Many affluent businessmen see polygyny as one of the perquisites of success.

Domestic Servants

Women in wage employment need help with child care and domestic tasks; some rely on their mothers or older children to help with the younger ones, but servants are a useful addition to the household. They are present in about 6 per cent of Lagos households, though they are sometimes identified as kin. The availability of servants increases somewhat with household size, but income is the prime criterion. While the rich may have several – cook, gardener, watchman, nursemaid – poor families may have a young relative who helps out around the house in exchange for accommodation and an introduction to city life. A study of staff families on the University of Lagos campus found that 75 per cent had household help. Most women preferred Nigerian paid help rather than aliens or relatives. Three-fifths of the domestic servants were under 15 and 65 per cent were male; only 40 per cent got a salary, but 70 per cent were getting some schooling (Obuji 1987).

Before the oil boom, servants were cheap; in 1974 the average wage was N4.40 per month. The expansion of education has made it much more difficult to find and keep young servants and raised wages considerably. The arrival of Ghanaians and Togolese during the 1970s was a boon to housewives, since they were willing to work for lower wages than Nigerians. When these aliens were expelled in 1983, the wages demanded by local domestics rose immediately. Experienced servants demanded N180, 50 per cent above the official minimum wage, plus free accommodation and meals (ECA 1980: 81; Fapohunda and Ojo 1985; Iroh 1985).

Through custom or necessity, servants are exploited; conditions are often hard and hours are long – many get no regular time off. Problems on both sides of a difficult relationship mean that turnover is high. Women use networks of relatives and friends to find new domestics, since their free access to the house requires as much guarantee as possible; nevertheless, there are many complaints about stealing, collusion with thieves and general irresponsibility. Male domestic servants may be somewhat more committed to the job than females; they tend to be older and have taken up this work because the only alternative is unskilled labour, though some young boys are sent by rural relatives so that they can go to school. Housegirls/nursemaids, on the other hand, tend to be filling in time between school and marriage or hoping to save enough to go into trading.

Family contacts

Common accommodation is only a small part of the attachment of Lagos residents to their extended families. The urban household is often seen as merely an extension of the rural household, and people who cannot share the same roof still manage to see each other or maintain contacts through gifts. Visiting relatives in the city depends on propinquity. Those who live in another part of the metropolis may only be visited occasionally because of the time and cost of crossing the city, but those who live nearby are usually seen often, daily if possible. Urban life differs from rural life in that urbanites have more control over the frequency of contacts with relatives. Both migrants and indigenes can choose to live close to some kin and further from others, to see some often and avoid others with whom they do not get along. Men are more mobile than women, so it is easier for them to maintain contacts with a wide circle of relatives.

There is also massive movement out of Lagos for holidays, especially at Christmas, to visit those at home; many whose hometowns are nearby visit on weekends at least once a month. Those with elderly parents are particularly likely to make frequent visits. People coming to the city for trade, schooling or medical care call on relatives as a matter of course, sometimes staying with them for weeks or even months. Mothers also come to help out when a new baby is born, or the daughter may go home for the birth.

The postal service is not very reliable, but travellers carry gifts and messages from those who cannot make the trip. Most migrants send home money at least once a year, and gifts of items available in the city are expected. These contacts are important for inheritance and hometown politics; urban success pays for land disputes and contests over who will be the next chief of the village. Most migrants intend to return home eventually, and maintaining contacts ensures that there will be a place when he or she decides to retire (Peil *et al.* 1988).

Cost of living

Lagos is among the world's most expensive cities, yet a majority of Lagosians are poor by both local and international standards. Rising costs are a major problem, even in households with several earners; real wages dropped for all income groups between 1976 and 1982, though more for middle and upper income employees than for labourers. In 1977, at least a fifth of Lagos employees were on government pay Level 1 and about half at Levels 1–3 (under N1200 per year). The average unskilled worker in Nigeria's private sector got only N2000 per year in 1982 and skilled and lower clerical workers got only N3000; in contrast, senior staff earned N14,000 and chief executives N42,000. Wages in Lagos were somewhat higher than these averages, but not much higher at the bottom. Both the Army and the civil service had pay cuts in 1985, and widespread redundancies in the civil service and private firms have made jobs at all levels insecure (ECA 1980: 113; Fashoyin 1986: 129–38).

With 1960 as zero, the Cost of Living Index at the end of 1971 was 181. In comparison, with 1975 as zero, the Index had risen to 1107 by the end of 1989 (see Table 5.1). The price of basic foods and household items such as soap and toothpaste rose very rapidly in 1989, as the exchange value of the naira fell. Cost of living statistics are available only for the whole country, rural and urban; rises have probably been higher in Lagos than for smaller cities which are closer to their sources of foodstuffs and where housing is in somewhat less demand, though imported items are probably cheaper in Lagos.

In 1971, the average Lagos household spent at least two-fifths of its income on food and at least a seventh on rent; a union claim for higher wages in 1979 estimated that a family of six needed N214 per month, of which half was spent on food and over a quarter on accommodation (Peil 1973: 13; Fashoyin 1986: 124).

High demand and short supplies raised prices of basic foods in 1988; imports of rice and wheat were forbidden and competition increased for the limited supplies of local food. Food price rises have been very similar for all income groups, though the rise in staples (the most important source of food for poor households and a disproportionate contributor to inflation in food prices) has been greatest for high income households. Prices are consistently cheaper in Mushin and Iddo markets than in the major supermarkets. However, market and chopbar (cheap restaurant) prices rapidly reflect

Families and basic needs

Table 5.1 Urban Consumer Price Indices, by Income, 1982–9 (1975=100)

Year	Total	Food	Accommodation	Clothing	Transport	Other Services
Low income, wage						
1982	275	311	232	223	199	265
1986	507	571	377	538	339	492
1988	704	902	400	711	543	697
Low income, self employed						
1982	291	325	233	241	212	250
1986	504	620	386	532	341	487
1988	765	930	441	707	387	565
Medium income						
1982	261	300	231	193	222	295
1986	527	569	435	507	350	527
1988	717	951	463	611	396	556
Upper income						
1982	266	280	253	248	224	324
1986	578	535	404	548	437	578
1988	704	902	400	711	543	697
1989, all	1107	1311	552	967	548	713

Source: FOS 1988; 1989b.

changes in income, supply and demand – food sellers ensure their share by raising food prices whenever there are wage rises. Plate 5.1 shows a small chopbar where workers can get basic meals. Note the rubbish in the unpaved street.

The official minimum wage was N150 per month in 1989; the government resisted pressure for a large rise, but many workers, (especially the self-employed and employees in small firms) did not earn that much. N150 would buy a half tin of local rice, a tin of garri (dried casava), a tin of powered milk, a litre of groundnut oil, two small loaves of bread and six eggs for the month – with nothing left for fruit or vegetables, snacks, rent, transport, clothing or other needs.

The contribution of accommodation to the cost of living is difficult to measure in Lagos because so many people do not pay 'normal' rent. This includes those living free in family houses; those whose rent is subsidized (e.g., higher civil servants, employees of large companies or the university and members of the armed forces); those who are repaying loans or mortgages; and domestic servants whose accommodation is provided.

Rents in low income areas rose about 100 per cent between 1968 and 1972, when a single room cost N10–20 per month (HRRU 1974: 24–5). The rise during the 1970s was slower than for other prices; it is more difficult for landlords to raise rents than for traders to raise food prices (see Chapter 7). By 1977, only families earning over N4100 paid, on average,

Plate 5.1 Restaurant on Ohuntan Street, Ajegunle

more than N20 per month rent, though some who could have paid more were unable to find a suitable place. About a third of householders earning N2532–4100 spent more than N20 per month (ECA 1980: 120). Rents rose less than other items in the 1986–9 period. Nevertheless, many households are spending more than 25 per cent of their income to rent a single room. Self employed household heads with low incomes spend more on both food and accommodation than those in wage employment, but less on transport and services. Their housing must often accommodate business premises, insofar as they have any.

Clothing costs have risen rapidly for all three income groups. Clothing has an important role in social life; both men and women may spend considerable sums on colourful prints, embroidery and lace if they can afford to. Most people have both Nigerian and 'Western' wardrobes. The frequent washing necessary in the Lagos climate wears out clothes rapidly, but new clothing is also part of communal activities such as weddings and funerals. An inability to purchase proper clothing can force a withdrawal from friends and contacts.

Increases in mass transportation charges hit the poor particularly hard; wage employment often involves long bus journeys or walking to save money. The government tries to control fares, but transportation is largely in private hands and petrol and spare parts must be paid for (see Chapter 8). The cost of other services appears to be rising more rapidly for the poor than for those with higher incomes. Most families have little left for school fees, medical care or other emergencies. Any savings tend to be invested in business; even long-term wage workers are looking for opportunities to expand their incomes.

Education, health and welfare

Government is the main provider of schools and health care; they are a major charge on the exchequer and almost the total of its welfare provision. The early history of these services was discussed in Chapter 1. Lagos attracts clients from a wide area. While basic needs for education and health are reasonably well catered for compared to the rest of Nigeria, the widespread recourse to private service indicates that what is provided is well short of the demand.

Teachers and pupils

By independence in 1960, Lagos city had 112 primary schools and 20 secondary schools, catering for 8182 pupils; about a fifth more were attending school in the wider metropolitan area. A teachers' training college, Trade Centre and Yaba College of Technology completed local provision until the University of Lagos was founded in 1962, at the same time as Ahmadu Bello University in the north, and after the Universities of Ibadan and Nigeria (at Nsukka, in the east). Lagos State University was founded in 1983 near Badagry, but draws most of its students from the metropolis (Williams and Walsh 1967: 136–7, 150; Fafunwa 1974: 94–9).

The growth of education in Lagos was slowed by the distrust of Muslim indigenes. Saros and Brazilians tended to be Christian and saw education in English as important for advancement, but Muslim parents felt that Western education was dangerous because it would draw children away from Islam. Literacy was also unnecessary for success as a trader or fisherman. The takeup was therefore much greater among migrants to the city than among the host population. However, the introduction of national politics and the struggle for statehood taught the indigenes that Western education was essential for the autonomy they sought. Since almost all of the migrants coming to Lagos have been to school, adult literacy is higher than elsewhere in the country; in 1985, it was 94 per cent for men and 79 per cent for women (FOS 1986: 41).

Private secondary schools have long been a feature of Lagos; among his other enterprises, Nnamdi Azikiwe ran Lagos City College before he became a full-time politician. In an attempt to raise standards, the military government took over voluntary agency and private secondary schools and training colleges in 1975. This was largely justified because so many schools had become commercial operations which provided little education for their numerous and hopeful clients. The shift system which was introduced at about that time was very unpopular; Lagos schools which ran three shifts

(7:30 – 11 am, 11:30 – 3 pm and 3–6:30 pm) were manifestly inadequate for their task. Overcrowding was worst in rapidly growing low income areas such as Mushin; parents in elite neighbourhoods could afford private schooling for their children.

Governor Lateef Jakande won considerable favour with the electorate by building more schools and promising to make both primary and secondary education fee-free and compulsory. Hostel charges were abolished and boarding schools were phased out. Anyone of state origin who obtained admission to a university would have his/her fees paid by the state. The expansion which resulted is evident in Table 5.1: 11 156 classrooms were built in 1980. The demand was so great that only children whose parents could prove that they had paid taxes in Lagos State were allowed to register. Some migrants' children whose parents lacked tax certificates were sent home, where the effective charge was lower. To register a child for a Lagos State primary school in 1989, parents must have been resident in the state for 12 months and have paid the N20 special levy. The requirement of the child's birth certificate is a powerful incentive to register all births. Nearly all Lagos children get at least primary schooling and the proportion in secondary school is the highest in the Federation.

In 1989, the Ministry of Education recorded 877 government primary schools with 15 430 teachers in the metropolitan area; there were 342 secondary schools with 11 956 teachers. Though local councils are officially responsible for education within their borders and are encouraged to find more of their own costs, the federal government pays 65 per cent of the cost of primary schooling. The Lagos State Schools Management Board spent N77.4 m in 1980 and N164.0 m in 1987; about 84 per cent goes for salaries. School boards have been appointed for all secondary schools, including representatives of parents, teachers, the government and the local community. These are to be responsible for raising additional funds for the school and keeping an eye on how resources are used, the maintenance of discipline and academic standards (LSG 1987: 28; *Lagos Horizon* 22 August 1989).

Table 5.2 shows a nearly balanced sex ratio for primary and secondary schools – there are about as many girls as boys at these levels. This was characteristic of primary schools in 1973, but a much higher proportion of both boys and girls now goes on to secondary school. The proportion of girls in secondary schools is remarkably similar in various parts of the state; this confirms that education for girls is widely accepted even in heavily Muslim areas. Teaching in primary schools has become a largely female occupation (sex ratio 41), and even secondary schools have more women teachers than men (sex ration 96), which reflects the better-paying alternatives open to men (LSG 1989c).

Although most children now go to school, there is still a problem with adult illiteracy and with people who want to get more schooling than they achieved as a child. Local government run adult education programmes, though more for their rural than for their urban populations. In addition,

Families and basic needs

Table 5.2 Education in Lagos, 1961–9, numbers and sex ratios

	Primary Number	SR	Secondary Number	SR	Vocational Number	Teacher Training Number	University Number	SR
1958[a]	73 400		5230				0	
1963[b]	143 552		14 631		2234	1240	214	418
1973–4	279 583	105	23 737	149		591	3400	504
1987–9	748 000	100	313 000	108	4292	3181	19 915	283

Sources: Williams and Walsh 1968: 136–7, 150; LSG 1973, 1989c; *Commonwealth Universities Yearbook* 1965, 1975, 1989.

[a] Includes local authority and private schools, aided and unaided. The numbers assume that 25 per cent of primary pupils and 14 per cent of secondary pupils lived elsewhere in the metropolitan area.
[b] This includes enrollment in Ikeja Division plus 20 per cent of enrollment in Badagry Division. Private schools in the City had 93 051 in primary and 6448 in secondary schools (mostly government-aided).
[c] Primary and secondary are 1989, city; the rest are 1987, state. University 1987 includes the Lagos State Polytechnic and Lagos State University as well as the University of Lagos. The sex ratio excludes the polytechnic, for which data are not available.

the Continuing Education Board runs part-time post-primary courses; these had about 16 000 students in 1987. Special schools for the blind, deaf and physically handicapped catered for 1277 primary pupils in 1987 (FOS 1987).

The private primary sector is widespread and uncontrolled. There are about 260 approved private primary and nursery schools and about 8000 which are not approved. These have at least 23 000 pupils (FOS 1987). Nursery schools are important for working mothers who need someone to look after younger children. At the primary level, there is considerable dissatisfaction with the public sector. Parents want to get their children into the best secondary schools, and this requires better teaching and resources than many government primary schools can provide. Some private schools are purpose-built institutions in elite suburbs, with playing fields, swimming pools, laboratories and libraries; fees are high and children may be collected by school buses. Others are small establishments linked to private homes or are in crowded, noisy accommodation in slums.

Ownership of private schools may be in the hands of institutions such as the university or the army; some are linked to embassies (American, Dutch, French, German, Indian, Italian, Lebanese) and others are run by private entrepreneurs who find education a lucrative business. The best do very well by their pupils; the worst may offer little more than false hopes. Costs vary with what is provided. Nursery school fees are often over N1000 per year, including meals – a considerable drain on the family budget and making pre-school children more expensive for many parents than older ones (Fapohunda and Ojo 1985: 84).

The embassy-linked schools attract a wide range of pupils and staff – both Nigerian and expatriate; many have a waiting list. Some provide only kindergarten and primary classes, but others extend into secondary. For example, the American International School on Victoria Island, which covers the US curriculum through ninth grade, has only about 20 per cent Americans among its 350 pupils. Teachers imported from Tacoma, Washington live at the school and are paid American salaries. Local teachers, Nigerians or American wives of Nigerians, receive a lower salary, though it is equivalent to a Lagos University professor. The Lebanese School in Yaba has 600 students of 19 nationalities; 40 per cent are Lebanese, and forms 1 and 2 in Arabic are provided as well as an English-language primary curriculum. The French, German and Italian schools cover the secondary as well as primary curriculum in their own languages, preparing pupils for universities at home. British children usually attend St Saviour's School in Ikoyi or Grange School in Ikeja; both also have large numbers of Nigerian pupils (Cox and Anderssen 1984: 25–8).

Only nine private secondary schools are recognized by the State Ministry of Education. These tend to have diplomatic or other elite links, continuing from selective private primary schools. The International School is a notable case. Governor Jakande wanted to bring the University Staff (primary) School into the public sector in 1979; the parents refused because it would have meant that teachers could be transferred at will and standards would inevitably decline. The government then announced that only children from government primary schools could enter state secondary schools. Children from private primary schools would have to find a place at a Federal Government College, the Army School, or a private (fee-paying) secondary school. The University Staff School remained private and selective; parents built the International School to maintain access to high-quality secondary schooling. University staff contributed their skills (i.e., drawing plans, providing legal and educational advice) and their children's fees are subsidized. The school is very popular, with 800 students and a new technical wing. The large site near the University has plenty of room for expansion.

The goal of primary schooling is passing the National Common Entrance Examination (NCEE) well enough to earn a place at a good secondary school, as this is essential for good School Certificate results five years later. The most prestigious schools, including Federal Government Colleges, select pupils with the best NCEE results. The level of competition is evident in the scores needed on the NCEE. In 1989, the highest scores were required in Bendel State (543 for boys and 535 for girls) and the lowest in Abuja (394 for boys and 368 for girls). Lagos was eighth of the 23 states, requiring 523 for boys and 519 for girls to pass. In many schools a majority of pupils 'fail'; this fuels the demand for more secondary schools. Even in a state where secondary schooling is free, large numbers of children who could profit from it cannot find a place.

As the output of the schools and universities rises faster than the number

Plate 5.2 Commercial school, Ajegunle

of jobs, the road to success is increasingly paved with certificates. Job advertisements usually specify how much education is required of applicants. Civil service categories are set out according to the amount of education required for the job. Management applicants may be expected to have an MBA as well as a good first degree. Increasingly, any wage employment requires secondary schooling and even apprentices are expected to have completed primary school. While a few self-made successful businessmen are relatively uneducated, the young ones are often graduates. For those who cannot continue formal education, private commercial schools promise access to clerical jobs. Plate 5.2 shows one of the smallest.

Doctors and patients

Health care is delivered by a wide variety of agents. Federal and state government ministries disperse health funds, while local councils have departments for health services. There are special government services for schools, child welfare, maternity, immunization and environmental sanitation. The Lagos University Teaching Hospital (LUTH) Medical School, Dental School and Institute of Child Health also provide a wide variety of services. NGOs such as the World Health Organization, UNICF and UNESCO promote research, inoculation programmes, etc. The armed forces and other large-scale employers provide in-house or on-call facilities. Voluntary associations, especially churches, offer Western or traditional treatment. While a majority of medical personnel are employed by the government, there are also a large number of private doctors (often with their own hospitals or clinics), dentists, pharmacists and traditional healers. In 1979, Lagos State had 924 doctors and 10 240 hospital beds, 25 per cent and 19 per cent respectively of the national totals (Onokerhoraye 1984: 123–6).

In 1984, Lagos State had eight government general hospitals (including LUTH, army and prison hospitals) and six specialist hospitals, for maternity, children, orthopedics, infectious diseases, psychiatric and tuberculosis cases. LUTH is the largest, with 720 beds. Five of the general hospitals and all of the specialist ones are in the metropolitan area. Lagos Island is particularly well served, with a general and a children's hospital and the Lagos Island Maternity, which is reputed to produce more babies than any other hospital in Africa. This concentration poses problems for patients, since only a small proportion live within a convenient distance of these hospitals and a traffic 'go-slow' can delay arrival (FOS 1985: 98).

General hospitals in Ikeja, Shomolu and Yaba and LUTH, in Surulere, are closer to the mass of the population. The 81 maternity homes, 33 maternal health centres and 103 other clinics and health centres are widely spread through both rural and urban areas of the state. Private hospitals are profitable in Lagos, especially for maternity cases, and their number is growing rapidly in all areas. Shomolu Local Government estimated that they had 150 private hospitals in 1989, up from 78 in 1985. Private hospitals provided 25 per cent of the state's 5229 hospital beds in 1985; 43 per cent were under federal control (including LUTH), 28 per cent under the State Health Management Board and 3 per cent under local government (FOS 1985: 98–102).

Government hospitals admitted 28 787 patients in 1988, of which 31 per cent were at the Maternity; the six health centres admitted 5367, many of them also maternity cases. There were 140 200 live births registered in metropolitan Lagos in 1987, of which about 78 per cent took place at small private hospitals and maternity clinics, 10 per cent in government institutions (5 per cent at Island Maternity) and about 12 per cent at home. The number of births has dropped in recent years, though perhaps this is as much due to the poor economic situation – inflation and unemployment – as to the acceptance of the principle of birth control. Only 13 per cent of women reported using modern methods of contraception in 1981–2, and use is often irregular (National Population Bureau 1986: 29).

The major contribution of both hospitals and health centres is in treating out-patients. Free medical care in government hospitals and clinics was inaugurated in 1979 and ended in 1988; poverty is so great that the numbers using them dropped more than 50 per cent almost immediately and remained at the lower level. Nevertheless, Ikeja and Lagos Island general hospitals had 21–35 000 out-patients each per month in 1989; daily attendance may be over 3000. The busiest health centres (at Apapa, Ajegunle, Ebute Metta, Isolo and Surulere) see 8–14 000 out-patients each month, averaging 3–400 per day.

These units have only 30–44 beds and 17–26 cots each, except the Ajeromi (Ajegunle) Health Centre, which has none. No deliveries can be done there, though it is the only government health facility for an area with over one million people. The clinic at the Catholic mission, not far from the government health centre, is very busy; doctors from LUTH volunteer their time to help out. There are also numerous private hospitals, maternity homes, and pharmacies in the area, which help to make up for government neglect (LSG 1987: 96–103; LSG 1989c: 40–3).

The major reasons for being admitted to hospital are complications of pregnancy or childbirth (50 per cent) and infectious or parasitic diseases (16 per cent). Infectious and parasitic diseases are also the largest problem of out-patients (35 per cent, mainly malaria, diarrhoea and measles), followed by 'ill-defined conditions' (16 per cent), digestive diseases (9 per cent) and respiratory problems (7 per cent). Given the frequency of traffic accidents, it is interesting that 1749 cases of 'injury and poisoning' were admitted in 1987, of which 231 died; pedestrians are more at risk than those in vehicles, and most traffic victims are not admitted to hospital. While 251 494 out-patients sought treatment for malaria, only 976 were admitted and 32 died. This represents only a small part of the malaria suffered by the Lagos population. Most people buy anti-malaria drugs without prescriptions from pharmacies and treat it at home; only very serious cases reach the hospitals (LSG 1987: 105–8; LSG 1989c: 40–1).

Families that cannot afford to use private doctors and dentists often rely on the large paramedical sector. Many seek advice from a pharmacy or traditional healer, since the wait at a hospital or health centre may be long and the doctor or nurse is sure to be very busy. There are said to be 10 000 'quack doctors' in Lagos, and fake drugs are a major problem. Both pharmacies and religious healers promise quick cures for major and minor illness; many trained and untrained pharmacists provide 'consultations' and injections at the back of the shop. Many people have little faith in or cannot afford western medicines. Treatment is often delayed by people who believe that sickness is destiny; illnesses which do not respond to treatment are believed to have a supernatural cause, which requires alternative treatment, perhaps back in the village.

Lagos began a mass Early Primary Immunization (EPI) campaign in 1986 to ensure that all children are protected against diphtheria, polio, tuberculosis, and tetanus. Local councils advertise widely to attract parents to primary health care clinics, mobile clinics and schools, providing free inoculations throughout the area for a month each year. Numbers are down somewhat from the first year, when there was considerable catching up to do, but the programme continues to be successful. Shomolu local government immunized 57 000 children against diphtheria and polio in 1988 and mainland local government immunized 96 000. Cholera and yellow fever inoculations are also available at special sites.

The Dental School was the first in tropical Africa. There has been considerable improvement in dental provision in recent years, as its graduates set up in private practice all over the city. There is considerable difference in the level of service between the LUTH clinics, with consultants on call; the government dental service, which sees 3–4000 patients per month; a private office above a bank on the Marina with expatriate dentists and a secure electricity supply; and the small office of a private dentist in Ajegunle. Nevertheless, the general public now has some access to care.

Institutional welfare

Government welfare is very limited; most assistance is provided by families. However, institutions for destitutes, motherless babies and the elderly are run by the Ministry of Youths, Sports and Social Development. There are also government programmes to promote the welfare of seamen and prisoners (Ola Daniel 1975: 192–4; LSG 1987: 126; LSMI 1988: 203).

The Rehabilitation and Training Centre was founded to clear the streets of beggars and destitutes. It originated from a camp for beggars opened in 1972 at Gbadada Estate. It caters for the blind, cripples and lepers, but the majority of inmates are 'mentally ill able-bodied beggars'. Most inmates are 'raided' into the centre, and escape when they can. The centre was full during the All-African Games of 1973 and the African Festival of Arts and Culture in 1977; numbers then dropped, but rose again during the 1980s as the economy declined. There were only 237 inmates at the beginning of 1983, but 1002 at the beginning of 1987. During this period, it catered for up to 5445 inmates per year, of which a majority (presumably most of the beggars) absconded. Medical care and some vocational training are available, but without capital and follow-up services most of these men are likely to continue begging, an acceptable occupation for Muslims. Begging has increased with the recession; beggars now solicit at fashionable parties as well as in street traffic.

The Motherless Babies Home was established as a charitable venture and taken over by the state in 1977. A new building is being completed at Marina. From 40 to 85 babies are admitted each year, of which up to 20 die. This is partly because abandoned babies have not been properly cared for, but the Home also has problems maintaining proper standards with a low-paid staff. Nigerian families generally welcome new arrivals, and fostering by relatives is a widespread custom. These abandoned babies are only a small proportion of children born in Lagos whose mothers are unable to care for them, but 'baby dumping' seems to be much less common than in Harare. The majority of children at the home are released for adoption, but a few are claimed by relatives and a few fostered.

The state also issues certificates to day care centres conforming to prescribed standards. There is a huge demand for day care by working mothers, but most 'nurseries' care for only a few children, with minimum equipment; only a small proportion of carers are certificated. Young children being 'minded' in crowded residential areas often have little space to play; there are only nine public playgrounds in the state.

Most elderly people follow the traditional pattern, returning home in old age, but the increasing numbers of people surviving to old age and widespread migration mean that there may be no one left in the village to care for the elderly. Old women are increasingly moving to the city to live with their migrant children. They have an important role in taking care of the young children while both parents work, but crowded housing and conflict with daughters-in-law may make grandmother less welcome. So far, there is very little alternative, in Lagos or elsewhere in the country (Peil *et al.* 1989).

The Old People's Home in Yaba was founded in 1928 by the Catholic Mission and taken over by the state government in 1981. Twenty to thirty destitute elderly, all migrants, are housed in one-storey blocks of rooms. A few are claimed by relations, but most have no living relative to whom they can go and remain at the home for many years, until they die. There is need for more places, but building has been stalled by lack of funds. A matron and cook are in charge; those who are able, help with sweeping, etc. A major problem is lack of income; residents are not allowed to trade, which would at least provide pocket money, and have little to do all day.

Another old people's home, for 12 people, was founded in 1986 at the Catholic parish in Mushin. Most of the inmates are women, who are encouraged to help with domestic tasks. Like the government Home only destitutes are accepted, though they may not be completely without relatives. One old lady owned her house, but was made to sleep in the hallway and not looked after by kin who wanted the house for themselves. There is a growing interest among the elites in providing care for their elderly parents which is near enough for frequent visiting but outside the family home; so far they have no alternative to family care. Among the mass of the population, women with no living children are most at risk. They try to find some relative who will at least house them; in a few cases, they are looked after by neighbours or fellow church members.

There are several community centres run by the government and by churches. The former mostly provide recreational facilities, while the latter may offer a range of services – clinic, employment advice, sports, play activities for children, literacy classes, vocational training for women, etc. These are financed through voluntary donations from the business and expatriate community as well as from parish funds. Sports will be discussed in Chapter 6.

Summary

The family is the core of society. The struggle for success is a family as well as an individual activity, and except for young people recreation is largely resting at home with one's family. There are a few people, mainly elderly women or long-distance migrants, who have no family members in Lagos. But the majority have someone to whom they can turn, and most of those who do not develop ties with people from the same hometown or religion. Thus, even people who live alone have links of blood, marriage or affinity which provide some security. These links cross factors of income, education and occupation, to bring together people who might otherwise be in conflict. Crowded households often accommodate people who have a range of social statuses in the wider society.

Household size and composition change over relatively short periods, as visitors arrive, marriages break down or people find new jobs, die or return home. Fertility rates remain high because children are valued, though urban costs promote the limited acceptance of birth control. The rising cost of living may encourage smaller households insofar as support is required, but values change slowly, hospitality is expected and rent can be shared. Inflation may also increase contacts with rural relatives, as a cheap source of basic provisions.

Education for all is seen as fundamental in Lagos, which has the resources to provide for its citizens and a strong political demand for schools. Private schools also flourish, since the government cannot satisfy the demand. The same is true for health care, where there is far less provision than the public needs, some of it at a higher price than the poor can afford. Private facilities, of widely varying quality, thrive on the public need for their services. The government is not able to provide much other welfare service; families are expected to take care of paupers, widows and orphans, the handicapped and infirm. There is plenty of evidence that more welfare services are needed, but also that a great deal of support is being given by a wide sector of the Lagos population.

The next chapter will examine the social life of rich and poor and the relationships between them. Separation is fostered by income, education and access to housing and other resources, but contacts are encouraged by business, politics and the strength of family and hometown ties.

6
Rich and poor

Olufela Anikulapo-Kuti (1938–) was born into the elite Ransome-Kuti family in Abeokuta. (He changed his name a few years ago to be rid of 'colonial mentality'.) His paternal grandfather was a Brazilian returnee and missionary, his father was Headmaster of Rbeokuta Grammar School and his mother a teacher and activist for women's rights. His two brothers are doctors and his sister a nurse: Olikoye Ransome-Kuti is a professor at LUTH and Minister of Health; Beko Ransome-Kuti was Chairman of the Nigerian Medical Association until his detention for leading the doctors' opposition to the government; he later led the Committee for the Defence of Human Rights. Undisciplined since childhood, Fela was sent to Britain to study medicine, but family support was cut off when he switched to Trinity College of Music in Dublin. He formed his first band and married in London, returning to Nigeria in 1962. He found work for the Nigerian Broadcasting Corporation 'terrible' and began experimenting with what was to become Afrobeat.

A full-time musician since 1967, he learned to combine politics and music during a tour of the USA in 1969. In 1970 he founded the Kalakuta Republic, a communal compound where music, sex and drugs offered a freedom not available in ordinary life. The early 1970s were very successful musically, but the military government did not take kindly to his anti-authoritarian stance and the police took increasing notice of his 'illegal activities'. Songs about government corruption and Fela's 'distracting' participants in the Festival of African Arts and Culture led to 'unknown soldiers' burning his house and destroying all his possessions. His mother was thrown from a window during this violent attack. The government took the land, without compensation, for a secondary school. The production of highly popular music and his irregular lifestyle continued, as did the suspicion of insecure governments. He was arrested in 1984 and jailed for dealing in foreign currency as he was about to take off for an American tour and jailed again in 1986. A scheduled concert for 20 000 students in 1989 was obstructed by over 1000 police in what he calls 'Operation stop Fela'. His new Shrine, in Ikeja, is a popular nightspot, with girls and Indian hemp easy to get. Money may be short, but his contribution to the development of African music and his *yabis* – political jibes on corruption and injustice – ensures his place in

Lagos society. His children grew up in Lagos with their mothers; his eldest son, Femi, is a saxophonist with his own group (Udenwa 1988; Anikulapo-Kuti 1989).

Both poverty and wealth are very much in evidence in Lagos; a prime reason for living there is to move from one to the other; several of the ways of doing this have been discussed in earlier chapters. Most people know someone, at least distantly, who has moved up or down the ladder of success, sometimes quite a long way. The focus of this chapter is the social life of rich and poor, the differences and similarities which go to make up daily experience.

Poverty was often noted by early visitors to Lagos: damp, dirt and disease were the lot of fishermen and manual labourers in the 1890s. Elderly Hausa beggars, women petty traders, unemployed migrants and child labourers imported from the hinterland had difficulty surviving in Victorian Lagos, which lacked an alms house or network of formal welfare organizations. Many of the same conditions characterize today's poor – youth or old age, illness, unemployment, inexperience and lack of a kinship network are closely related to inadequate resources for survival (Iliffe 1987: 164–71).

Religion is a more visible phenomenon and a more basic part of daily life in Lagos than in most Euro-American cities. Religious and social affiliation are partly shaped by ethnicity or place of origin and partly by the insecurities of a society undergoing rapid change. Religion affects social life through associations and friendship networks. Most people in Lagos belong to at least one association, often related to their hometown, religion or need to save for emergencies. Few participate in sport, but football matches draw large crowds. Most recreation is informal, with family and friends, though there is commercial recreation for those who can afford it. Crime affects all levels of society, and the social life of the city is partly conditioned by anxiety to avoid armed robbers. The police are not much help, due to poor resources and inadequate professionalism.

Clerics and Followers

Religion has played an important role in Lagos history and continues to be a basic element in everyday life. Early struggles between local chiefs and outside parties – the British and Yoruba groups hoping to monopolize trade – often included a religious factor because missionaries of Islam and Christianity went to different areas. Early Christians worked out of Badagry and Abeokuta, whereas wandering traders from Nupe brought Islam and their traditional religion to the coast. Christianity was treated with suspicion because many pastors were seen as allied to the British, whereas malams (Muslim clergy) became part of the local community. Christians and Muslims have cooperated politically at least as much as they have opposed each other, perhaps because internal factionalism has been more important than external divisions. The Rev. M.S. Cole translated the Qur'an into English, though there were very few conversions from one world religion to the other. Social life tends to be separate, partly because of class alliances (Osuntokun 1987).

In the early days, a majority of Lagos' population was Muslim, but migrants have tended to be Christian. In 1977, 30 per cent of the population were traditional Muslims and 8 per cent Ahmadiyya Muslims; three-fifths were Christians, about equally divided between Catholics, 'established' Protestants and local churches, including Aladura (praying) and healing sects; and only 2 per cent claimed to be followers of traditional religion or of none. Most 'mainstream' Protestants are Anglicans, Baptists and Methodists because their missionaries were most active in the areas from which most migrants come to Lagos (Ohadike 1968: 78; ECA 1980: 25).

Members of the main religious groups are found all over the city, but there is some clustering because affiliation is related to income and ethnicity. A large majority of the indigenes on the Island and northerners in low income areas such as Agege and Ajegunle are Muslims. Many small separatist churches are also found in low income areas. 'Mainstream' Protestants are best represented in high income areas such as Apapa and Ikoyi. The increasing participation of Muslims in state education and their success in business has blurred these areal boundaries considerably.

The Muslim community has historically been poorer than the Christians because Muslims shunned western education and worked mainly as traders, fishermen and labourers. Christians, with 'modern' education, were more available for clerical and professional jobs throughout the colonial period. However, in recent years more Muslims ·have taken up educational opportunities and moved into the civil service and the University as well as creating larger businesses. State and local government officials are now more representative of the population; Muslims in wage employment get time off for prayer on Fridays. Many new mosques have been built in recent years, partly with money from abroad, but also to demonstrate the importance of Islam in Nigerian life. There are at least nine mosques on Lagos Island. The oldest still in use is the Shitta Mosque, built 1891–4. The Central Mosque, completed in 1913, was replaced in 1988 with a very impressive, gold-topped building.

Muslims' capacity for division is similar to that of Christians, though worked out in different ways and with fewer parties. Conflicts often centre on control over the central mosque, because this is the prime leadership role in the community and Islam is democratic to the extent that local groups rather than outsiders decide who should fill leadership roles. The Lagos Muslim community suffered internal conflict between the Lemomu (imam) and Jamat parties for over 30 years, from 1915 to 1947 (Danmole 1987). The major protagonists were the Chief Imam, Ibrahim, who tended to support British colonialism as bettering the lives of his people, and Adamu Animshaun, whose Jamat party was composed largely of local rather than northern Muslims and opposed to anything British.

The conflict started with the administration's attempt to inaugurate a water rate, which was opposed by Jamat and a majority of the people as additional taxation. The Jamat party also attacked the Chief Imam as not exercising sufficient supervision over donations to the mosque and being too strict in his interpretation of Islam. When Jamat attempts to depose Imam Ibrahim and impose a constitution for the mosque were unsuccessful, members of the two parties engaged in considerable violence, locking each other out of the mosque and fighting in the streets. There were also battles with the Ahmaddiyya Muslims, a modern sect. The deposition of *Oba* Esugbayi (not a Muslim) in 1925 was partly because he favoured Jamat. The parties went to court over the succession to Imam Ibrahim, and Jamat's candidate won; Lemomu appointed their own Chief Imam and ceased to participate in Central Mosque activities. The constitution was finally adopted in 1938. Peace talks in 1937 and joint prayer at the onset of war in 1940 brought the two parties closer together; Ibrahim's son was selected as Chief Imam in 1947.

The Anglicans (often known as CMS – Church Missionary Society) and Methodists arrived in Lagos by the middle of the nineteenth century; churches were soon followed by schools as a way of attracting converts. Anglicans had the advantage of British support throughout the colonial period. They have had Nigerian pastors since 1875; some of these joined with Muslims as early advocates of independence (Ohadike 1968). The Archbishop of Lagos, the Rev. Joseph Abiodun Adeliloye, is in charge of 96 churches, 130 priests and about 160 000 members. Christ Church Cathedral, on the Marina, was built between 1925 and 1947, replacing an older church. The centre appoints and pays priests and helps them build new churches. New areas get attention as soon as possible, since having a priest and a building, however simple, attracts both migrant Anglicans and new members. Parishes which were 'missions' of the Cathedral in the 1950s now have 'mission' churches of their own.

The Catholic mission in Lagos was formalized as part of the Vicarate of Dahomey in 1870; after several reorganizations, it became the Archdiocese of Lagos in 1950. The Cathedral, on Catholic Mission Street, is opposite Lagos City Hall. The Archdiocese covers part of Ogun State as well as all of Lagos State; it has about a million members, 74 priests and 72 sisters. While the top of the hierarchy was Nigerianized with the appointment of His Grace Most Rev. Dr A.O. Okogie as Archbishop in 1973, about half of the priests are Europeans. There are 24 churches in Lagos itself, some of them catering to as many as 10 000 parishioners on a Sunday and running outstations in schools or chapels. The church runs 3 clinics, 3 community centres, 7 private schools and a school for the blind supported by the state government.

Separatist churches include local foundations and imports from abroad (especially the USA). There are many of these small churches in poorer areas of the city (see Plate 6.1); many people prefer a face-to-face community to a large institution. As a church grows, it often splits to form new branches or

Plate 6.1   Pentecostal church on Achakpo Street, Ajegunle

new churches. Charismatic individuals are also free to form their own churches, which are often ephemeral. Some of these churches are commercialized; the Holy Ghost Church of God in Yaba has a fund drive for N1.5 m. However, Lagos separatists generally lack the cash and entrepreneurship which has made some sects so prosperous in Nairobi. Many Nigerian Christians are flexible, attending whatever church is convenient and sometimes participating in both Protestant and separatist services. Traditional rites are widely performed as well. In their own terms, life is insecure and supernatural help is welcome, from whatever quarter it comes.

The first recorded schism in Lagos was the formation of the Native Baptist Church in 1888; the United Native African Church separated from the Anglicans in 1891. Both of these introduced African music and religious ideas into the liturgy, which made it more understandable to local people (Osuntokun 1987: 135). The Cherubim and Seraphim Church, the largest and best known of the Aladura churches, was founded in 1925 as a result of a vision by a young Anglican girl on Lagos Island. It spread from there throughout Yoruba country and eventually to Ghana, Sierra Leone and England (Peel 1968). The Cherubim and Seraphim have been institutionalized to the extent of running a Theological Seminary and Bible School in Lagos.

In hard times, spiritual churches attract relatively well-educated young people who find that Lagos does not live up to their expectations. They prefer the African-oriented liturgy, intense social interaction (meetings at least three times a week) and the lack of social stratification (everyone wearing white robes and barefoot) to the impersonality and European culture of world Christianity.

Over-enthusiasm for spreading the good word led the government to ban religious preaching on vehicles and in residential premises in 1985. All religious organizations were required to register. The Religious Organizations Edict was impossible to enforce and was repealed six months later, though Ghana tried the same thing in 1989. The government continues to be interested in religious propagation, insofar as it may lead to public disorder. So far, the militant fundamentalist Islam which has erupted violently several times in northern Nigeria has been muted in Lagos, where accommodation and tolerance have been seen as more useful than opposition. (*West Africa* 1985: 2233; 1986: 539).

Social activities

Lagos social life is experienced in widely differing ways by people at various income levels. Conspicuous consumption can be a political problem, as how money is acquired and spent affects people's attitudes toward their leaders, their willingness to cooperate with the system or their reaction to attempts to overthrow it. Overall, the intense economic and political activity discussed in Chapters 3 and 4 reflects the widespread attitude that there is a cake to be divided and that individuals and families are willing to fight for at least their share. Though most of the population are poor, they are not apathetic; the hopes of riches and social contacts, however rare, with those who have them contribute a dynamism to the city. These contacts may be as members of associations, participators or spectators at sporting events, or (most common) in social events sponsored by 'big men' or informal recreation with family or friends.

Members

The state government divides voluntary associations into four categories: youth, welfare, philanthropic and social (LSMI 1988). Many of the 30 youth organizations are umbrella bodies with numerous branches: Boy Scouts and Girl Guides, Federation of Boys and Girls Clubs, Nigerian Security and Civil Defence, St John's Ambulance Brigade, Red Cross Society, Voluntary Workcamps Association. Many are based on religion: the Islamic Youth League and Ahmadiyya Youth Association, Methodist and Catholic Youth Associations, Boys and Girls Brigades. The YMCA and YWCA were introduced in 1906, but remain fairly small (about 900 each), whereas the Scouts (1958) have 21 000 members and the Sheriff Guards (1965, for Qur'ânic study) have 19 500. The Muslim Students Society (also 1965) is the largest of all, with 78 900 members. It is active in the universities as well as with younger students.

The seven welfare organizations are small. They are concerned with women and children, the blind, mentally handicapped children, prisoners, ex-servicemen and animal welfare. It is notable that the Nigerian Legion, concerned with the welfare of ex-servicemen and their families, was not founded until 1962, long after the war in which most members served.

Philanthropic organizations include several international associations: Rotary Club, Lions and Lionesses, Inner Wheel International, Jaycees International and Soroptimists. There are numerous branches of these throughout the city and notices recording their more public donations – protective stands for traffic policemen, a small park on Lagos Island, statues. They have regular meetings and provide assistance for welfare projects – community centres, clinics, scholarships, etc. Most of the members are Nigerian, but expatriates may join a local branch while they are in the city. The African-American Institute focuses mainly on scholarships and advice for Nigerians who want to study in the USA, but it also funds local projects, such as the study of market women discussed in Chapter 4.

Private philanthropy is sometimes officially recognized. Mrs O.O. Ramos, a social worker, became a local hero on 28 June 1989. A downpour flooded roads, greatly slowing the return home of thousands of commuters; some were on the road until after midnight. The street in front of Mrs Ramos' house in Yaba was solidly blocked and her husband, a Lagosian accountant, called to say that he could not get home. When a woman came to the door to ask for milk for her infant, Mrs Ramos took her in, and provided meals and access to the telephone for many other complete strangers. The Rotary Club gave her an award for 'work for humanity' (*Lagos Horizon* 29 August 1989).

There are about twenty social clubs providing sports and recreational activities for the elites. The most exclusive is the Metropolitan Club, where male-only membership is by personal invitation; its rules require a balance between Nigerians and foreigners and its Tuesday luncheon is a must for top businessmen. The Lagos Lawn Tennis Club is the oldest; it was founded in 1895. The Yoruba Tennis Club was founded in 1926 to counter the LLTC's racial exclusion. Other specialist clubs include the Lagos Yacht Club, Motor Boat Club, Apapa Boat Club, Polo Club, Saddle Club and Ikeja Golf Club. Fees are high – N250–2000 to join and N150–1300 yearly subscription, but there are usually waiting lists. These clubs are popular with expatriates, who can afford the fees and who want a safe place to exercise and socialize, but they are also popular with wealthy Nigerians, since the bars and luncheon tables are an important place to do business. The Ikoyi Club, the largest and with the widest range of activities, is run by Nigerians in colonial style. There are also clubs specifically for businessmen, such as the American Business Association, open to executives employed by US firms, or the Full Gospel Fellowship and Business Association, which combines religious and commercial interests.

A small study of the Island Club, the Yoruba Tennis Club and the Eko

Club in 1987 reported their sizes as 5000 plus, 500 plus and 253 respectively. Although families could participate, husbands, as official members, made the most use of club facilities. Most of the members were over 40; half were businessmen, a quarter were professionals, and the rest were about evenly divided between managers in the private sector and civil servants or diplomats. Most had belonged for more than six years and about a third belonged to other clubs. They had joined for leisure, fellowship or business, in that order, but nearly two-fifths said they made business contacts through the club. No one mentioned politics, but this certainly plays a large role in conversation. They paid N250–1000 in fees and levies, but most were satisfied with what they got (Onenekan 1987).

Many small associations all over Lagos unite people of common background, religion or occupation, those who want an opportunity to save or who seek informal social activities. Only about a quarter of men and a third of women in Lagos do not belong to such an organization and many belong to more than one (Barnes and Peil 1977). The most popular are based on primary ties – membership is confined to people of the same extended family, hometown or ethnic subgroup. Extended family meetings on a weekend once a month can be large affairs, with hired chairs and refreshments. Ethnic associations were very popular and sometimes politically powerful immediately before and after independence, but their potential for conflict made it necessary for the government to ban them. Small organizations, of people with lower-level ties, are more likely to have a positive effect, providing support for village development and help to individuals when trouble comes. Insofar as they emphasize links with home, they encourage people to be less concerned with conditions and politics in Lagos, leaving this to the indigenes.

Most churches have numerous societies, segregated by sex, age or interest to maximize participation (see Plate 6.2). Singing and bible study are particularly popular. One large parish had 33 associations: 11 for women, 10 for various ethnic groups (including Togolese and Ghanaians), 2 each for youth and men, and 8 others. Women's or young people's organizations in the major churches are often linked to larger bodies, as are Muslim youth groups.

In addition to trade unions, occupational organizations include craftsmen's guilds, factory or civil service football teams, staff associations and market women's groups. Savings societies are a useful resource for the poor, helping them accumulate capital, pay school fees, etc. The major requirement is trust between the members, since all must continue to contribute until the cycle ends to ensure that everyone gets an equal return. The well-off may prefer banks because they pay interest, but the poor find savings societies less intimidating and more flexible. Some give low interest loans, a considerable improvement on the 25 per cent per month charged by moneylenders. Finally, recreation societies are especially popular among the young, though in Lagos the availability of commercial recreation makes it unnecessary to form a club for this purpose.

Plate 6.2 Women's Society members celebrating
Source: William L. Reilly, S.J.

Expatriate wives have numerous associations – British, American, Indian, French and the International Women's Societies. These provide information and assistance to newcomers and a chance to socialize. Nigerwives was formed in 1979 to build informal networks among wives of Nigerians. Initially, most were British, Irish, American or West Indian, but in recent years the spread of Nigerian students abroad has brought increasing numbers of wives from Asia and Eastern Europe. Nigerwives help them to cope with cultural misunderstandings and daily inconveniences, inform them of their rights, work to eliminate discrimination against those who choose not to adopt Nigerian citizenship, and support wives whose husbands die or take another wife. Nigerwives has 600 members in 27 branches, of which Lagos is the largest. Monthly meetings and a newsletter keep members in touch, but they can also be called on whenever the need arises. Recently, a group of husbands formed Friends of Nigerwives, which helps husbands with problems which frequently arise in intercultural marriages.

There are also special interest groups, such as the Lagos Horticultural Society, Nigerian Conservation Foundation, Nigerian Field Society, Nigerian Book Club, Ikoyi Singers and Nigeria Britain Association. Neighbourhood groups, such as the Harmony Boys Club (motto: incomprehensibility) and the Isale Eko Association tend to flourish in long-established areas. The latter has maintained a public toilet and represented local needs to the government since 1956. The African Brotherhood Lodge in Yaba was founded in 1938; social activities maintain such organizations as their other functions change.

Sportsmen and women

Many traditional sports and games, such as wrestling and *ayo* (a game with seeds or small stones widely played in Africa), are still popular in Lagos. These are mostly played casually, by friends, though they are sometimes included in sports festivals. Imported sports are under the direction of the Lagos State Sports Council, which was established in 1962 to organize football and athletic events. The Rowe Park Sports Centre, opened in 1970, remains its headquarters. A Lagos State Ministry of Sport and Social Development was established in 1973. It coordinates associations for various sports, helps to organize sports festivals and training for coaches and promotes development in schools, the building of stadia, etc.

Football was introduced in the early 1930s; works and neighbourhood groups began organized league competition in 1936. Government departments, private companies and schools at all levels have teams which compete for various cups; Nigeria's Green Eagles and Golden Eaglets international teams also operate from Lagos. A measure of the popularity of football is the overcrowding at major matches, with the associated threat of violence from excited fans.

The first stadium, built in 1930, was renamed King George V Stadium in 1936 in honour of the coronation. It became Lagos City Stadium 1963–73, then was pulled down. Onikan Stadium was opened on the same site in 1982, for football and cultural events. The National Stadium in Surulere was built in 1976 to hold 80 000 people, but has occasionally held 100 000. After 12 fans and an international soccer star died in August 1989, it was closed and scaled·down to 70 000 fans. Teslim Balogun Stadium is being built in the same area. It will hold 30 000 spectators and have athletic tracks, facilities for tennis and squash, an Olympic-size swimming pool and an indoor sports hall. These and other stadia at Agege and Ikeja are the major source of revenue for the Sports Council. Agege Stadium is being renovated to handle Division III and IV matches and a New Golden Eaglets Stadium will be built at Ikeja. (LSMI 1988: 295–300). Some large employers provide sports facilities, such as the UAC Sports Ground, the Union Bank Sports Centre, and fields near the Police College. The Racecourse, at Tafawa Balewa Square, is only rarely used for racing.

Sports are frequently learned at school; elite schools, with extensive playing fields and money for equipment, provide much more training, for more sports, than ordinary schools. This is particularly important for tennis, squash, judo and swimming. There are only two public swimming pools, at Rowe Park and Onikan (Marina). Boys and girls' clubs competing in various sports also require adults with time to supervise and children with

Plate 6.3   Pingpong, Ajegunle

time to train. Since public facilities are very limited, adult access to many sports is mainly for those who can afford membership in private clubs. On the other hand, football can be played in any open space and pingpong is cheap to play; the only manufactured item needed is a ball (see Plates 6.3 and 8.1). Pingpong was introduced by Chief J.N. Farnsworth in 1949; his energy helped to promote the game, train coaches and organize numerous clubs for youngsters. The higher level of resources and the early start of most sports there gives Lagos an advantage over the rest of the country. A majority of Nigerian teams for international basketball, hockey and wrestling events are from Lagos; local contenders also do very well in national sports competitions (LSMI 1988: 285–95).

Recreation

Entertainment is provided by officially-sponsored institutions and events; commercial facilities such as restaurants, bars, nightclubs, cinemas and theatres; and informal activities inside and outside people's homes. Music and dance are very popular in Lagos, whether they are provided over the radio or television, by nightclubs or bars, or in an open space on a weekend as part of a wedding or family gathering.

The National Museum, Onikan, is one of the great museums of Africa. While it used to be crammed with items from all over the country, helping to teach Nigerians about the wealth of local art produced by their numerous ethnic groups, it is now more oriented towards foreign tourists, focusing on far fewer items of international standard. It has a small restaurant and craftsmen's huts so that tourists can see how things are made. Either version of what a museum should be demonstrates the wealth of Nigerian art.

The National Library, on Broad Street, the City Library and a few branch libraries are supplemented by libraries run by the British Council and the US Information Service, both also on Lagos Island. These are particularly attractive to students whose school libraries are grossly inadequate. The oldest bookshop, near the National Library, is run by CMS, but sells textbooks and fiction as well as religious literature. Several new bookshops have opened in recent years in various parts of the city, responding to a great increase in the number of educated adults and locally published books; many small general shops also sell texts, periodicals and novels. While most books on sale are paperback, the publication of *Lagos State Life and Culture*, in full colour and coffee-table format, is a notable exception (Sonuga 1987).

The National Theatre and National Gallery of Modern Art, overlooking Eko Bridge, was built for the 1977 Festival of Black and African Arts and Culture (FESTAC). It has a VIP complex, halls for 5000 and 1200, two cinemas for 800 each and stage and orchestra platforms which can be removed for sports. Unfortunately, the National Theatre is seldom used and is disintegrating. More live drama comes from the State Cultural Standing Troupe; the Pec Reperatory Theatre, a professional company at the J.K. Randle Theatre opposite the National Museum; and the Festival Players, an amateur group in Ikoyi.

The state also keeps an eye on traditional festivals, such as Eyo, Igunnu and regattas in honour of Olokun, goddess of the sea. The Adamu-Orisa Play or Eyo Festival is associated with a death in the Lagos royal family. Olokun and Awosi festivals ask for good fishing, peace and development. Ogun and Egungun festivals are common to Yoruba in many areas. Igunnuko masquerades, which came from Nupe, are celebrated in Oshodi (Gbadamosi 1975: 174–6; LSMI 1988: 265–75).

The first motion picture was shown in Lagos in 1903. Cinemas were popular in the 1960s, but are now in decline. Cinema owners suffer from high taxes, ticket fraud and the cost of maintenance. Television has provided competition, but the threat of armed robbers at night has been responsible for the major drop in attendance in recent years. Distribution was largely in the hands of Indians or Lebanese until indigenization in 1972; they still have considerable influence. It is hard to get films, so the same ones are used over and over, for up to seven years. Since they are changed daily, advertising is of little use. There were 43 cinemas open in 1983, most charging about N1 and showing mainly Indian films – audiences like plenty of action. The National Theatre has the largest and most expensive cinema; it seldom shows local films (presumably supply is a problem), though they attract good crowds. Some embassies show films, including Nigerian productions, to selected audiences or loan them out to schools (Balogun 1987).

Rich and poor

Radio and television play an increasing part in daily life; aerials are blossoming even in slums, where the set may have to be attached to the ceiling because of crowding at floor level. These are important for spreading national news and government information to the mass of the population. Local Yoruba plays attract large audiences, but travelling theatre groups find they can make far more money from television than from live performances (Barber 1987).

As elsewhere in the world, commercial recreation in Lagos differs considerably depending on one's income. Hotels are less important for accommodating travellers than for providing the venue for social occasions celebrated by the elites: birthday parties, weddings, appointment as head of a company or 50 years in business, appeal funds, induction of club president, etc. Hotels also provide many of the expensive restaurants and bars. Independent restaurants tend to be located in Ikoyi, Lagos Island, Victoria Island, Apapa or Ikeja – where the elites live. Nigerian food is seldom available, except at the Lagos University Guesthouse or the Museum; Chinese and Indian restaurants are most common.

Poor people get snacks from street venders and meals from chopbars – which serve cheap local food and drink. Buying cooked food is common in Lagos because Yoruba cooking takes considerable time. If the wife is a busy trader, it pays to buy meals from other women. Meals are usually not social occasions, as a European trip to a restaurant would be; a group of workers might chat while they eat, but many people eat alone, even in their own homes. A meal taken as part of a celebration is quite different, since the main purpose is social. It is usually provided by women in the family hosting the party rather than by a commercial enterprise. Given the shortage of space, such events often take place in the street; neighbours and passersby listen to the music and even join in the dancing.

Waterman (1988) shows how popular music developed in Lagos as an expression of changing social identity and experience. *Asiko, sakarà* and palmwine music drew inspiration from the traditional music of the many peoples migrating to Lagos, but also from international imports. At the turn of the century, satirical songs (*kérikéri*), emulating the praise singing popular in village markets, were used to show the Yoruba's scorn for strangers and deviants. The colonial authorities eventually banned them, but new forms took their place. Elite music at this period was largely of European import; R.A. Coker (1871) and Ekundayo Phillips (1911), the first Lagosian musicians trained in Europe, concentrated on oratorios and organ music for churches. Popular music was quite different. *Sakarà* was praise singing with dance, performed by Muslims, a syncretic form drawing on Muslim and Yoruba music. *Asiko* was a Christian form of *Sakarà*, part of the rise in syncretic Christianity and especially popular at celebrations such as weddings and baptisms. The first recording of popular music was made in 1930.

Expansion of the migrant wage-earning population provided a clientele for popular musicians, who developed palmwine music to express their interests. The first palmwine musician to record commercially was Irewolede Denge, an Ijebu Yoruba. This form was influenced by immigrants from all along the coast, as highlife was later. By this time, orchestras and concert parties were beginning to form. These provided more complex entertainment for larger groups, but continued to use local proverbs and idioms to express the aspirations and achievements of their listeners. The music helped to give meaning to experience and to shape social and political ideas. The music scene is now far more complex, with competing forms and higher-paid performers, but there is still much popular music on the streets.

Nightclubs operate at several income levels, drawing on local as well as imported music. Popular clubs and bars are scattered throughout the city. Some have live music only once a week; others operate from early evening until well into the next morning. The most popular is Fela Anikulapo-Kuti's Shrine in Ikeja; his biography forms the introduction to this chapter. Sunny Ade also has his own club in Yaba, which specializes in juju and highlife. Juju music was originally performed by a tambourine drum, but has become sophisticated and electronic. Highlife combines local, brass, samba and western music to comment on problems of daily life. A wide range of popular music – fuji, reggae, funk, jazz – is available; some individuals and groups remain popular for a long time. Drumming is an important feature of informal music in residential areas (Ekwensi 1963; Aig-Imoukhuede 1975).

There are several strands to art in Lagos. Some date back to traditional skills – it was an important centre for weaving, cloth dyeing and carving in the 1850s and such work is still on sale today. However, the interests of modern clients and the availability of academic training have pulled artists in new directions, especially painting. Many Nigerian artists come to Lagos because this is the best place to sell their output, either through small galleries, expatriate links (including the Italian Cultural Institute and Goethe Institute), to businesses wanting to decorate their office buildings, or on doorsteps or Bar Beach. Notable Lagos-based painters include Ajayi, Emokpae, Grillo and Okeke, Onobrakpeye and Kola Oshinowo; they often combine traditional motifs with contemporary fashions and techniques. Fred Archibong has become known as a 'corporate sculptor'. He was trained in the USA, and gets numerous commissions for corporate and government buildings. Unfortunately, the local market for art is still small, so local artists need sales abroad if they are to prosper (Aig-Imoukhuede 1975; *Business*, II: 3, 1989).

Elites

It is difficult to specify precisely who belongs to the elites, since there are now many – political, military, intellectual, professional, business, leisure, etc. Many of the top people see a good deal of each other; they have kinship ties, knew each other at school or university and have common political interests. Politicians, musicians and football heroes are the most transient. Former politicians may remain among the elites insofar as they have made enough money to support an elite lifestyle and are not currently in prison.

The military, centred on Dodan Barracks in Obalende, have furnished national leadership during much of Nigeria's existence; it is difficult to accept that they will completely 'return to the barracks' when the politicians run the country again in 1992. Generals are public figures in a way that would not happen with a less politicized army (Luckham 1971; Campbell 1990). The fact that many Nigerian generals retire into successful entrepreneurship suggests both that contacts with the rest of Nigerian society are strong and that there are many opportunities for top military men to acquire the necessary capital.

Lawyers and judges may become well known for upholding the government or attacking it. For example, Gani Fawehinmi sued the government in an attempt to get investigations of questionable activities such as the murder of the journalist Dele Giwa and the death of the Dawodu brothers (see below). He has spent considerable time in jail for contempt of court, but continues to be a legal gadfly. On the whole, doctors attract less attention unless they strike for better conditions, but Prof. O. Ransom-Kuti's tenure as Minister of Health has provided a platform for improving the health of ordinary Nigerians.

University personnel, especially professors, have more influence than is the case in countries where there are more of them. They may accept federal or state office (as I.S. Aidu, J.M. Aminu, A. Gandonu and O. Ransom-Kuti did) or run for Parliament, though like civil servants they must now resign their job to enter politics. They are called on to speak on public issues and their contributions are reported in the press. Intellectuals include novelists such as Chinua Achebe, Cyprian Ekwensi and Wole Soyinka, who write and speak about cultural change and political issues. Though they may spend little time in Lagos, they are often close observers of what goes on there.

The activities of all these people are copiously reported in the daily, weekly and monthly mass media. More than 3000 periodicals are published, covering everything from business, law, computing and family to sports, health and how to win the pools. A few publishing firms handle most of the mass circulation and specialist journals, but new ones are often run by an entrepreneurial publisher/manager/journalist. At a minimum of N1.50 per copy, these are not available to everyone, but many people read more than one newspaper every day. Journalists' skills have been upgraded considerably in recent years, but most are still underpaid and notoriety is frequently obtained by being sent to jail. Major papers such as the *Daily Times* (founded in 1926) are nationally distributed, though their main focus is Lagos. Suits for libel are frequent; fortunately most cases are settled by agreement rather than paying the huge damages decreed by the courts (Smythe and Smythe 1960: 149–50; Duyile 1987).

Yoruba distinguish between *mekunnu* (ordinary people), *bale ile ero* or *oga* (entrepreneur/landlord/master) and *enia pataki* (big men). The incomes of *bale ile ero* may be ten times those of *mekunnu*. *Enia pataki* in Agege may be able to dispose of twice as much, while those in more affluent parts of the city have incalculable riches by *mekunnu* standards. An aspect of class relations which sets Lagos apart from most major cities is that all three categories live in the same areas, sometimes in the same houses, since patron–client relations sometimes extend to accommodation. This does not mean that the *mekunnu* are not exploited in wages and rents, but the wealthy are seen as responsible for traditional forms of leadership – prestige depends on having followers (both in the city and at home), who expect generosity. Misers are effectively ostracized or ignored; deference must be earned (Peace 1979b).

Part of this generosity is in providing jobs, licences, loans and advice to the less fortunate. It is visibly expended on ceremonies, such as weddings, baptisms and especially funerals (usually at home rather than in the city), but also at community parties to celebrate events – students returning from overseas, elections, opening new buildings – and contributions to mosques or churches. Information on income is often restricted in order to limit such costs, since increasing capital is essential for business success. A major aspect of social interaction in spite of income differentiation is that successful men and women have often risen through their own efforts; it is most common when they are not well educated and their style of life carries over from their origins. This consolidates the legitimacy of their leadership.

On the other hand, professionals and members of the middle and upper bureaucracy living on low density estates (see Chapter 7), often come from a more advantaged background than businessmen or politicians; they have more education and a more European lifestyle than people in high density neighbourhoods. It is easier for ordinary people to see them in terms of we/they and to resent their corruption and exploitation. However, this segregation is mediated because many *mukunnu* have relatives among the bureaucracy from whom they receive various forms of support. Everyone recognizes inequality, but hierarchies of income are accepted by those who take hierarchies of age and gender for granted. Most people would be more distressed by lack of opportunity than they are by income differences; an unequal society is acknowledged, but not widely resented because social mobility is possible. Rapid rises and falls are visible to all – and are sometimes seen in moral terms (Lloyd 1974: 174–83).

Anarchy and Control

Crime is widely experienced in Lagos by all sectors of society, partly because the have-nots envy the haves and partly because consensus on what is acceptable behaviour is weak. Social control in society draws on norms learned in the family, religious and educational systems, but in Lagos, too many people are far away from the standard-setters of their youth. Local norms are unclear at best, since the daily newspapers are full of stories about people who seek whatever they want in whatever way is most convenient. In addition, the police are widely seen as unreliable at best. Johnson's poem, 'Nightmare: a poem about Lagos' (1982: 42) expresses the widespread fear that crime and violence are everywhere, impossible to escape:

> Fear, funny feelings inside
> when gentle dogs bark at night
> Armed bandits under the bridge
> Robbers loitering in the dark.

People have traditional methods of handling deviants, which continue parallel to the state system and are probably more efficient in minimizing disturbances. Landlords, ward leaders and traditional courts seek to resolve conflict so that people can continue to live together in peace. Cases are heard with an attentive audience which can contradict false evidence. Penalties are imposed on guilty parties with the aim of returning to social equilibrium rather than abstract justice. Religion plays a vital part in that the gods are assumed to punish deviants. However, this system is most useful for extended families and in well-established, relatively homogeneous neighbourhoods. There are many opportunities for escaping it in the mobile and heterogeneous Lagos.

Criminals

Lagos has the highest density of both policemen and criminals of any state in Nigeria. Crime statistics are available in detail only for Lagos State as a whole, but a large majority of crime in the State is committed within the metropolis. Although only four states are officially recorded as having a smaller population than Lagos, it accounts for far more prison admissions than any other state, 13 per cent of the national total. This is only the tip of the iceberg, since few criminals are caught; both civil and criminal offences are usually dealt with informally unless they are committed by strangers and are unduly violent. Crime is often blamed on the unemployed, but incidence is not related to the unemployment rate and many people who are employed also commit crimes – theft, corruption and embezzlement at work as well as in 'spare time' activities (Adeyemi 1989).

Anyone living in Lagos or visiting it faces the real possibility of being attacked and robbed on the street or in their home; houses have iron bars on all the windows, fences, guard dogs, alarms, etc. Watchmen are hired by many householders in elite suburbs, but they have no weapons and can do nothing except try to escape from well-armed thieves. Ten thousand licences for guns were issued in six months in 1987, mainly to businessmen and executives (West Africa 1987: 2048).

Community action is often at least as efficacious as the police in dealing with crime. Some neighbourhoods erect security fences, locked at night, or form vigilante groups (of up to 30 men) to patrol the streets. 'Sleeping policemen' slow getaway cars. Calling for help can bring a crowd; if the offender is caught immediately, the crowd may well deal with him – beating is quicker and more efficient than calling the police. Some robbers get more than a beating; lynching and burning may occur when there is no one in authority to protect the man. Governor Raji Rasaki, who personally caught armed robbers on two occasions, encouraged residents to take the law into their own hands, arguing that lynching those who threaten their homes and families is justified. This approach was rejected by the Nigerian Bar Association and the Civil Liberties Organisation, but some of the beleaguered populace obviously agree (*West Africa* 1990: 436).

The level of crime in an area is affected by the level of need, opportunity and policing. The highest areas of crime (cases in relation to area) are Ajegunle, Surulere, Marina (Island), Ikeja and the Apapa port. The lowest incidence is in Ikoyi, Yaba and Isolo. Ajegunle's title of 'Tiger Town' appears justified. It has the expected characteristics of crime-ridden areas – low income and education, overcrowding, unemployment – but other low-income areas such as Isolo have much less crime. A resident of Ajegunle reported that things were much more peaceful since police night patrols were instigated. The Marina and the docks are obvious areas of opportunity, but also have policemen relatively handy for reporting crime. While much attention is given to crime in high income areas, the problem appears to be greater in Ikeja (which also has low income neighbourhoods) than in Ikoyi or Victoria Island (Adeyemi 1989).

Table 6.1 shows the admissions to prison in 1984, the latest year for which there are detailed data. Many of these people were held and not charged or were found not guilty; discharges and releases in 1984 accounted for 24 774 people, 90 per cent of the number admitted (FOS 1987: 90–1).

Stealing, robbery and armed robbery accounted for one in seven prison admissions; unlawful possession brings this up to a fifth. Nigeria introduced public execution of armed robbers in the 1970s, but it has had little effect. The chance of getting caught is small unless there are resolute bystanders. The police lack the resources to arrest minor criminals and possibly the will to track down the organizers of gangs. People are robbed casually on the streets, drivers are forced out of their cars and sometimes killed, and groups of robbers with guns attack houses and shops. A water supply project was repeatedly attacked, robbing the company of vehicles and equipment and workers of their personal property; this made it almost impossible to get on with the work. Over 950 cars were stolen in the first three months of 1989, compared to 989 in the whole of 1988 (*Lagos Horizon* 29 August 1989).

Only 8 per cent of prison admissions in 1984 were for drugs offences, but the problem has increased considerably since then. Nigeria has acquired an international reputation for providing couriers, mainly through Lagos Airport. This does not just involve poor people carrying drugs to pay school fees or feed their children. In 1989, the daughter of a judge was accused of organizing traffic in drugs. On the same day, N2 bn worth of heroin was

Table 6.1 Prison admissions, Lagos State, 1984, by offence, origin and term

Offence	N	%
Stealing	2432	8.8
Indian hemp	2070	7.5
Assault, affray	1951	7.1
Forgery	1588	5.8
Possession	1523	5.5
Robbery	1480	5.4
Traffic offences	1363	5.0
Native law/custom	1360	4.9
Contempt of court	1347	4.9
Escaped custody	975	3.5
Currency offences	968	3.5
Murder	966	3.5
Immigration	852	3.1
Sex offences	736	2.7
Abduction	301	1.1
Smuggling	301	1.1
Other	7263	26.4
Total	27 476	100.0

State of origin	N	%
Lagos	1453	5.3
Oyo	1625	5.9
Bendel	1592	5.8
Rivers	1554	5.6
Ogun	1442	5.2
Cross River	1437	5.2
Imo	1343	4.9
Anambra	1302	4.7
Kaduna	1281	4.7
Plateau	1176	4.3
Kano	1145	4.5
Benue	1083	3.9
Ondo	1041	3.8
Sokoto	1041	3.8
Kwara	907	3.3
Other north	2805	10.2
Foreign	4147	15.1
Total	27 476	100.0

Term	M N	M %	F N	F %
None	13 105	49.9	679	48.1
Short	10 041	38.5	701	49.7
Long	2920	11.2	28	2.0
Life	na	na	1	a
Death	na	na	1	a
Total	26 066	100.0	1410	100.0

Source: Federal Ministry of Internal Affairs, FOS 1987: 81–8.
[a] Less than 0.1%.

found on an EgyptAir plane from France. The local manager was accused of complicity, but was murdered soon after while attempting to escape the country. There is the usual problem of official probity. A socialite arrested with 18 kg of cocaine and the customs officer who found it both disappeared before charges could be brought.

Local use of drugs has also increased, and moved from Indian hemp (marijuana) to harder drugs. Three men were executed for drugs offences in 1985, but there were 400 arrests of couriers in 1988–9. Some Nigerians acquire the habit while studying abroad; it is also common among pop singers and is spreading among students. Attempts are being made to arrest the 'drug barons', but, as elsewhere, those who are caught are mostly small pushers and carriers. In early 1990, 164 kg of hard drugs, mostly heroin and cocaine, was publicly destroyed at Murtala Muhammed International Airport by National Drug Enforcement Agency (DEA). This had been accumulated through seizures from convicted drug pushers over the previous three years (*West Africa* 1990: 289, 343).

Assault is almost as common as drugs offences; the frequency of murder demonstrates the insecurity of Lagos as a place to live. There were 184 cases of murder, attempted murder and manslaughter reported in the metropolis in 1984, though the numbers in Table 6.1 suggest that several people were arrested for each case or that murderers were sent to Lagos from other states for maximum security. While 184 is one murder every two days, well below major US cities, it is high enough to inspire fear. By 1986, police reported at least two murders accompanying robbery every day and established a special operation to handle it. However, the robbers notified the Commissioner that they knew the complete plan, so it would be useless. Occasionally the victim is well-known. The wife of former President Obasanjo and the Deputy Director of Ciba-Geigy were killed and a sports hero shot while being robbed of their cars (*West Africa* 1986: 1899; 1987: 89, 389, 1835; Adeyemi 1989).

Violence frequently erupts on the streets among people struggling for a livelihood and often distrusting strangers. Guns are easy to buy or steal; there are several licensed gun shops on main streets. Some guns are locally made, but army and police guns also find their way into criminal hands. Abduction may involve violence, though with poor records and communications many people just vanish. Families advertise in the newspapers for missing children, but no more is heard of the case. Rituals may be involved, or the abductors may be seeking child labour.

Large-scale attempts at forgery of banknotes hit the newspapers fairly frequently. This is only one of many attempts to get rich quickly; money-doubling and other confidence tricks are common. Currency offences are more likely to involve wealthy people than robbery and assault, since this includes taking money into or out of the country illegally. Informal money changing flourishes wherever there are travellers who want more than the official rate of exchange and businessmen and women who need cash for trips abroad. Smuggling is closely related, in that the market for cheap goods encourages entrepreneurial activities across borders. Customs officials sometimes collaborate for a price.

The chaotic traffic situation discussed in Chapter 8 is partly a result of Lagosians' anarchic approach to regulations which conflict with their own goals; 1090 people were injured and 463 people killed on Lagos State roads in 1986. That only 2551 accidents were reported (LSG 1987: 95–7) suggests that the police only hear about the worst ones. In most cases, the guilty party escapes or claims are settled by agreement between the parties concerned, since both sides recognize that going to the police could be expensive and unrewarding.

Imprisonment for illegal immigration was common in 1983–4, when a large number of aliens were expelled. Many of these were living in Lagos (see Chapter 3). Some were very brutally treated, but conditions were so much better in Lagos than at home that many returned for another try.

In a city of migrants, it is not surprising that so few of the criminals are of local origin. The figures by state in Table 6.1 are interesting because they suggest considerable differentials in criminality – either because of opportunity, need or inclination – of people from various areas. The majority of migrants to Lagos come from Ogun, Oyo, Ondo and Bendel States, but Ondo produced few prisoners. There are also large numbers of migrants from Imo and Anambra; Rivers and Cross Rivers people are more likely to go to Port Harcourt or Calabar and Kano State people can do as well remaining in Kano. Other northerners also tend to head for Kano or Kaduna, though many Yoruba in Kwara are attracted to Lagos or Ibadan; those who reach Lagos apparently are seldom caught engaging in criminal activity. The large number of 'foreigners' was partly due to increased sensitivity to the offences of aliens in 1983–4; it was probably harder for them than for Nigerians to 'bribe their way through' and thus avoid arrest.

Prisoners and judges

Customary and Magistrates Courts are responsible to High Courts (at both State and Federal Levels), the Federal Court of Appeal and the Supreme Court of Nigeria. Customary Courts deal with 'native law and custom', whereas Magistrates Courts try 90 per cent of criminal cases. The Magistrates' Courts and higher bodies use the English adversarial system, which is not well understood by many people who come before them, since traditional justice seeks conciliation. Generally, compensation or restitution is more efficacious than imprisonment, since the former are understood in traditional terms and prison offers no means of rehabilitation (Adeyemi 1989).

Prisons are run by the Nigerian Prisons Service, under the Federal Ministry of Internal Affairs, rather than by the States. Prisoners may be sent away from their home state, so the local prison population need not correspond to local offenders, but this usually happens only with prestigious prisoners. The main prisons in Lagos are in Ikoyi and Kirikiri; the latter is often used for political prisoners or ex-politicians serving time for offences in office. Another prison about which little is heard is Ita-Oko, an otherwise uninhabited island which was set up in the 1970s by General Obasanjo 'to rid Lagos of ablebodied people unwilling to work'; it appears to have become a detention centre for 'security risks' (*Newswatch*, 19 February 1990, p. 26).

Half of those admitted to prison were not sentenced at all and almost all of the rest served only a short term. This includes women (only 5 per cent of those admitted), journalists who published something the government disapproved of, students and others involved in demonstrations, petty thieves and offenders against minor regulations. Those with long-term sentences included politicians and a few businessmen caught in corruption or other large-scale illegal activities, as well as major criminals not sentenced to death. However, some people disappear into prison and are not heard of for months – no one seems to have a record.

Conditions in the prisons are bad. Overcrowding is the worst problem; Ikoyi prison was built for 800 but holds 2325, while Kirikiri Prison was built for 926 and held 4398 prisoners in 1987, 1663 of them awaiting trial. Food is inadequate in both quantity and quality, and medical and sanitary facilities cannot cope with the needs of prisoners. Several political prisoners held at Kirikiri have been transferred to prisons in the north when they became ill. Seventy-eight prisoners in Ikoyi Prison died in the first nine months of 1989 (*West Africa* 1985: 1246; 1987: 2317; 1989: 1821).

Police cells are at least as bad as prisons, though most people stay only 1–3 days – until they pay the fine (or bribe). Sanitation is very poor and policemen often treat newcomers badly. The legal system operates very slowly, and contact with relatives may be forbidden or granted only after bribes (Ifionu 1987).

Some provision is made for child offenders. There are two remand homes for boys, one for girls and four approved schools – for junior, intermediate and senior boys and for girls. While the approved schools maintain a fairly stable population of about 150 inmates, the remand home population has grown considerably, from 497 children catered for in 1983 to 827 in 1987. Most of these are released or discharged in a few months, but this appears to be as much a problem of space as of resolution of the childrens' problems. Like the prison, conditions are crowded and little can be done in the way of rehabilitation; surplus children are sent to prison with adults (LSG 1987: 127; SMI 1988: 202–3).

Police

The Nigerian Police Force is a national institution; each state has a Commissioner of Police and a system of courts and prisons under the national bodies. Lagos State has 9 sections with 31 stations. Recruitment is a problem, since the force has low prestige and poor pay and conditions. Both policemen and prison warders generally come from the same social stratum as a majority of criminals in education, rural background and occupational alternatives. Applicants must have at least a Primary School Leaving Certificate; an attempt to raise the requirement to four 'O' levels failed for lack of candidates. All sectors of Lagos society see the level of crime as alarming and the police as ineffective. When they experience crime, about two-fifths do not bother to report it to the police because no action is taken or cases take too long to settle. Bribes are demanded, complainants may be locked up or criminals may be notified by policemen who protect them. In 1987, 105 policemen were arrested for crimes including armed robbery, murder and rape; one DPO was caught sharing the loot with robbers. On the other hand, eight policemen were killed in 1988 in encounters with armed robbers (Adeyemi 1989; *West Africa* 1987: 2334; *Lagos Horizon* 29 August 1989).

Several riots in recent years have arisen from mass rejection of police tactics. Policemen are often relatively untrained, with little knowledge of confrontation and as afraid of the public as the public is of them. Inability to speak the appropriate language blocks information on what the problem is. But policemen have guns, and all too often use them with disastrous results. A major riot occurred when a traffic warden stopped a Mr Dawodu and demanded a larger than usual bribe. When a young constable who came along to help the warden shot the driver of the car and his brother, a crowd quickly gathered. The ensuing riot lasted two days, with three killed and thousands of naira of property damage (partly from looting). Even old people joined the demonstration. A Deputy Superintendent of Police was kidnapped by the mob and his uniform shredded. The policeman who caused the riot was arrested and anti-riot policemen were dismissed. The Catholic Archbishop called for more humane action by men in uniform (*West Africa* 1987: 2334, 2464).

Several major riots occurred in 1989, as unrest over traffic and economic problems meant that people were increasingly willing to support protestors. In March, an old man was killed by a lorry evading a traffic warden. The warden escaped to a nearby police station, which was soon besieged. In response to missiles, the police shot three people. Some young men used the occasion to loot houses and shops; it took three days to calm the city. Two months later, five men died when police fired on demonstrators attacking a police barracks. In June, 50 died in riots allegedly started by students against the Structural Adjustment Programme. Tear gas appears to have been lethal in some cases (*West Africa* 1989: 453, 956).

Police unpopularity derives from a well-established reputation for corruption, which they excuse as the product of a corrupt society. There are many cases of collaboration with criminals, molesting of innocent citizens, unlawful arrest and acceptance of bribes. One focus of bribery is the highly unpopular road blocks. These are widely seen as merely an occasion for the collection of 'donations'. In one instance, a road block supervisor was heard to complain to the policeman in charge that he had brought in too little money; someone else who was better at the job would be sent.

Laws about wandering are a holdover from the colonial era. Initially the problem was mainly one of vagrant boys sleeping rough in markets, mosques and open ground. They are readily recruited by criminals and spread the use of drugs to peers who are still in school. Some have been abandoned or thrown out of their homes for delinquency; others want to escape from authoritarian family discipline. 'Vagrants' appear to be less common in the 1990s than in the 1940s, except for newly-arrived school leavers. Children live with their families, but lack supervision from busy parents; the need to trade means that many young people get into trouble with the police (Iliffe 1987: 187–9).

However, the police now use 'wandering' laws for their own ends. Adults may be arrested in front of their own homes at 7 am and given no chance to show that they are going about their proper business. They can be detained for several days unless they can 'rub hands' with the policeman. A woman caught 'wandering' who cannot pay a large fine may be jailed or sexually abused. Landlords can bribe the police to arrest their tenants, so that the room can be let to someone else. A journalist who was falsely arrested had his papers taken from him and was beaten up when he refused to pay 'lika'. He got no help from higher officials because he could not give the badge number of the officers who beat him (Adisa 1987).

Summary

As in any major city, the gap between rich and poor is a large one in Lagos, but the links between them are more evident than in many more industrialized countries. Patron–client relationships, based on kinship, common place of origin or religion, are important in the process of getting ahead, or even surviving through emergencies. It is interesting to find that many people faced with trouble with the police know someone in or near the police to whom they can appeal. The status that so many seek is partly based on having followers; these must be supported through gifts of time, money or goods. Such a system fosters corruption, but also a particularistic concern for the less fortunate which many fear is disappearing. So far, the evidence is patchy. The rich do not give enough, but very few cut themselves off entirely.

This communal concern is not only for self-aggrandisement or survival. Both Islam and Christianity teach the blessedness of helping the less fortunate. Belief in this principle supports many beggars, elderly people and others in need. The formation of numerous small groups which is an important part of religious affiliation in Lagos ensures that many people get support when they need it, though often rather less than they want. Isolates are rare – most often women who have not had the time or resources to form associational links.

Rich and poor

Elite clubs are highly selective and commercial entertainment can be expensive, but these involve relatively few people compared to other, cheaper forms of recreation. Walking around Lagos on a weekend provides many opportunities to observe social life of the streets, with talk, food and drink, drumming and dancing. In spite of the hassle of daily working life, there is still energy for fun. Talk is free and goes on, at high volume, at all hours. Separatist churches also hold noisy all night services. Both day and night markets serve social as well as commercial needs.

The elites are avidly identified by the popular press and their conspicuous consumption provides a model of what success can mean. However, there is considerable pressure to maintain contacts with ordinary people, at least on occasion, because life at the top is insecure and followers may also be supporters in hard times. In addition, those who have risen from humble backgrounds still enjoy many of the activities which constitute ordinary social life and see little advantage in class segregation.

Fear of crime is the greatest threat to social interaction. Life is cheap and robbers aggressive. The police have a long way to go to convince the people that they are in control and supporting the law.

7
Urbanites and suburbanites: land and housing

Ihim Ifejika (1940–) is an Igbo clerical worker employed by a newspaper. His wife Veronica is a seamstress, working from the house. Ihim moved to Lagos from an eastern village about 25 years ago and owns a house in Olaleye Village, a low income neighbourhood in Ebute Metta. He holds the leasehold for this plot (of 18 by 12 metres) from the Olaleye family. The couple and their six children, aged 6–18, share a room and parlour – about 16 sq meters; the 11 tenant households have one room each. There is only one kitchen, toilet and bathroom for all 12 households (some 35 people). Most of the cooking is done on kerosene stoves in the passageway. Water is drawn from a well and public taps and stored in plastic buckets until needed. Unlike most of the tenants, the Ifejika family have cross-ventilation, but their rooms are crowded with furniture, consumer goods and Veronica's work. There is nowhere for the children (in primary and secondary schools) to study. The oldest daughter is learning sewing from her mother. The village, between the railway tracks and Western Avenue, has many 'unauthorized' houses on short-term rental, which are subject to demolition. Environmental sanitation is very poor. Stagnant water breeds mosquitoes and malaria is endemic; dysentery and diarrhoea are also widespread because of inadequate water supplies (adapted from Aina 1990a).

This chapter looks at Lagos as a place of residence, especially in terms of access to land and housing. It starts with a brief discussion of the city's architecture, then goes on to examine how land rights have changed over the last century and the processes involved in acquiring land and building a house. What factors enable some people to become owners while others remain tenants throughout a long stay in the city? What are the political and economic implications of land ownership, and how have these changed in recent years? How is the distribution of housing (in type, quality and size) changing as the city grows? What is the extent of the housing problem in Lagos, in terms of crowding and services. Finally, what contribution does the government make to housing? This chapter sets the scene for the next, which deals with urban planning.

Architects and builders

Akinsemoyin and Vaughan-Richards (1977) produced an excellent discussion of the various styles of architecture found on Lagos Island for FESTAC. They distinguish indigenous, Portuguese, mission, colonial and post-independence influences, providing a history of the city through its notable buildings and showing how architects and builders have responded to the climate and local demand. The earliest houses were of mud and palm leaves; though most building is now with cement blocks, there are still a few houses with bamboo or mud walls and thatched roofs in peripheral neighbourhoods. The traditional Yoruba house has rooms around a central courtyard; these large compounds have been filled over time, producing a warren of small separate houses. Even the *Iga Idunganran*, the *Oba's* Palace, now has separate buildings and a modern frontage.

Wealthy Brazilians put up two- and three-storey houses with gables and ornate plasterwork on the facades. Many of these were destroyed by urban renewal in the 1950s or demolished after long neglect, but Plate 1.2 shows one which is still in good condition. The Shitta Mosque was also built in this style. Christians, both expatriate and local, tended to prefer Gothic architecture, as can be seen at the Anglican, Catholic and Bethel Cathedrals, St Paul's Breadfruit Street and many parish churches.

Colonial house types (carefully graded to the status of the occupier) were copied from one territory to another. Custom decreed that living quarters should be on the first floor, with open space or offices below (see Plate 1.1). This was breezier and safer from thieves. Interior rooms were surrounded by a verandah, often with blinds or shutters to keep out the sun and rain; this left rooms very dark. The iron roofs made conversation impossible when it rained, but were more efficient and less likely than thatch to catch fire. Their widespread use makes West African cities look like vast expanses of rust. Corrugated aluminum is now used, but the rusty image remains. Banks, government offices, commercial headquarters and hotels provided notable landmarks along the Marina (note the rear building in Plate 4.1). Large houses in Victorian style were being built by successful Nigerians by the turn of the century.

Large-scale building was limited during and immediately after the First World War by the lack of materials. Unless specially treated against termites, wood is not considered safe for building in West Africa, and cement had to be imported. The Modernist Movement arrived with designs for the new University, Olowogbowo School, the Bristol Hotel and several banks; most buildings combined new trends with old styles. An imposing set of buildings went up around Tafawa Balewa Square (Racecourse) to provide for the independent government (see Plate 3.1). Building regulations became much stricter from 1952, but were difficult to enforce. While earlier housing had tended to have only a single storey (see Plate 7.1) new buildings were often blocks of flats, using space to better advantage (Plate 7.2). In 1968, Lagos got a modern City Hall with three floors of offices. The major

Plate 7.1 Old Yaba bungalows, water supply and petty trading

Plate 7.2 Tower blocks for federal employees, Victoria Island

contribution of the 1970s and 1980s has been skyscrapers, mainly along Marina and Broad Streets. There is nothing distinctively Nigerian in their design (Plate 4.1).

Off the Island, housing is utilitarian (Plates 4.3, 6.3, 7.5). It is usually the product of builders with the occasional help of surveyors or draughtsmen, not of architects and major construction companies. Periodic collapses indicate that some builders are operating beyond their competence or cutting costs to make more money. Low income housing largely consists of three- or four-storey tenements. Since the maximum allowed is 12 rooms per floor, 6 rooms are aligned on each side of a central corridor, 36 rooms in a three-storey block. There may be another single line of rooms, one or two storeys high, next to the main building; as much of the plot is used as the law allows. Services are at the rear, for common use. Elaborate concrete balconies distinguish expensive houses. Many buildings are painted cream, but the climate and overcrowding soon make them look neglected.

Landowners

Land rights in Lagos have long been a source of wealth and conflict. Real estate has been a much sought-after resource, a route to upward social and economic mobility and to political power; thus it is hardly surprising that disputes over land have kept the courts busy. Among the Yoruba, land is customarily held by corporate descent groups, which means that over the generations large numbers of people share ownership of a plot. The splitting of a descent group was often signalled by the division of family land, but a new descent group can also be established by a migrant to Lagos acquiring land there on which to base a new lineage.

Land could also be transferred through gifts or temporary agreements, which might in time become permanent. The *Idejo* chiefs were the customary 'owners of the land' in Lagos, with the right to make grants to those requesting plots. In the 1850s, the *Oba* of Lagos granted vacant plots to merchants and other settlers. By Yoruba custom, these would have been considered leasehold, for use of the grantee's family only, inheritable but not alienable from the original lineages. Land acquired a religious value through the burial of the ancestors in the compound (see Plate 1.3), but was also seen as belonging to generations not yet born. This fosters egalitarianism in a society where the gap between rich and poor is growing (Okpala 1979: 26–7).

Colonial officials imposed their own ideas of land tenure on the traditional system, especially in large towns. Rising land values for business premises and the possibility of using real estate as security for loans meant that land was increasingly seen in terms of investment and inheritance. Support of the colonial authorities, based on British law, meant that in many cases grantees became de facto owners. The alternative, family ownership, caused many problems. Shared ownership of residential property by extended families over the generations has made legitimate sale very difficult, though families holding *Idejo* chieftaincies continued to sell land on the periphery of the city into the 1970s. Huge rises in land values after independence resulted in a change from freehold to leasehold arrangements (Cole 1975b: p. 22; Hopkins 1980). Much of what follows in this section is based on Barnes (1986: Ch. 3).

The process of acquiring land puts much more emphasis on social networks than on estate agents. Prospective buyers must locate a family which might be willing to sell a plot, usually on the periphery of the city. It might take months or years to get an agreement with the elders as to how much land will be sold and at what price. Sales of family-owned plots have frequently been challenged; members of the descent group who did not share the money could take the new owner to court, demanding that he pay again. Some landlords had to buy their land three times over, even though they had acted in good faith. In addition, boundaries might not be clearly specified, so neighbours could also claim that some of the land was theirs. Few sales were registered before the 1950s; transfers of ownership were often based on verbal agreements in front of witnesses and any written records may be inadequate or lost.

The blend of British and customary law with which disputes were handled has proved inadequate to the task. This is probably the most lucrative field for lawyers in Nigeria, and the cause of periodic violence between communities. Written documents for conveyancing became more popular in the 1960s; courts began to rule in favour of owners who could produce documents showing that they had paid for their land and built on it. Nevertheless, there was still much land whose ownership was ambiguous.

The most important recent change in land ownership stemmed from the Land Use Decree, issued by General Obasanjo for the Federal Military Government in 1978. This vested all land in each state in the hands of its Governor and required that all land boundaries and owners be registered, thus eliminating disputes. Governors are responsible for allocating urban land, while local governments are responsible for allocating rural land. Individually owned urban land can no longer become family owned, as it was in the past. This is a considerable improvement on earlier land tenure agreements, though it can be an expensive hurdle for poor, ill-educated potential landowners.

Certification is also intended to remove sharp practices in land transfers. Descent groups sometimes sold the same plot to several buyers. Speculators who acquired a large plot sometimes subdivided and resold it without actually having established secure rights to the land. Some people just sold land, or tried to build on land, over which they had no rights at all (squatters). The time after purchase, or part-purchase, when the land was not yet built on, was particularly dangerous to the new owner. The land could be lost through inability to defend it – to pay legal fees, court costs or additional payments to claimants. Death of the original owner could also lead to trouble, as rival claims might be made in the hope that the heirs did not have the documents or were unaware of provisions of the agreement.

The elimination of family ownership of land and housing is resisted because considerable money and security are at stake. Forty years ago, a small gift might be enough to acquire a plot in an undeveloped area from one of the major land-owning families. In 1989, a plot in Ikoyi (1000m^2) cost N2–2.5 m; on Lagos Island, it could cost N4–5 m for half that size. Industrial plots in Ikeja cost N200 000 and residential plots N100–150 000. High density plots in Mushin go for N80–120 000; in built-up areas of Agege they cost N50 000, on the periphery N10–15 000 and speculators or the poor pay N5000 for a really 'bush' plot.

The Lagos State Lands and Housing Department is responsible for issuance and revocation of Certificates of Occupancy. The application costs N250 for residential plots and N500 for other uses, plus layout fees of from N250 for places of worship or schools to N5000 for light industry or central commercial plots. The charge for residential plots is inversely related to the number of people to be accommodated – N500 for high density up to N1000 for low density areas.

Each week, the Land Use and Allocation Office advertises in the newspapers the names and addresses of applicants for Certificates of Occupancy, together with a description of the location and status of the property (whether it is developed). Objectors have 21 days to present documentary evidence that they are the true owners of the land. The aim is to provide certificates within three months of application, but it can take longer, especially if the case is challenged. Upon obtaining a certificate, owners must prove that they have paid their taxes and must pay the first year's ground rent plus registration, administration and stamp charges. Corporate owners must certify that the company and two of its directors have paid their taxes and the development levy.

Initially there was considerable building without certificates, but as costs have risen and bank loans are not available without them, they have become necessary. Once the certificate is obtained, no further claims on the land will be entertained. There are about 5–600 applications per month, including some on old houses which had not yet come under the law. Undeveloped plots are supposed to be built on within two years, though this is not well enforced.

One way of defending land awaiting development is to sublease it, collecting rents from the tenants while ensuring that they live on the property and thus prevent interlopers. In Olayele Village, for example, a few large landowners have subdivided their property and let out 60 ft by 40 ft or smaller plots on short leases (monthly, annual or for five years), so that the maximum commercial income can be obtained while waiting for appreciation in value. Shanties built of wood or zinc sheets, providing only minimal shelter, are the only answer to such impermanence of tenure. These houseowners are in no sense landlords (Aina 1990a: Ch. 4; 1990b).

Confusion over tenure is exemplified by the case of Ayobo Village, Agege. Resident farmers signed a 99 year lease on the property in 1923, but the land was sold by the *Baale* of Ayobo in 1965. In 1976, the new owners resold 404 acres to Radio Communications of Nigeria for N560,000. Its owner, Chief Abiola, began large-scale farming in the 1980s. Problems came to a head in 1981, when villagers (the third generation of the original signers of the 1923 lease) went to court because their farmland was being fenced. Apparently they had not been told of the sale; they claimed to have paid the *Baale* N2 annual plot rent until 1976, when he asked them to stop. Some tenants' houses have been destroyed 'as a warning' by Abiola Farms, which says tenants must renegotiate their leases or face ejection. RCN has demanded that they stop building houses and selling plots they don't own, though under Yoruba customary law three generations might be enough to claim ownership. Abiola Farms wants them off most of the land (*Lagos Horizon* 15 and 29 August 1989).

Private Landlord/Landladies

There are at least 100 privately owned houses in Lagos for every house owned by the government (Okpala 1979: 26). Most of the housing provided by the state or federal government is for senior officials or the military, so ordinary people must find accommodation in the private market. The main supply of residential housing comes from individuals who were born in or have decided to remain in Lagos and have managed to save enough to invest in accommodation for themselves and others. Housing is widely seen as a secure and lucrative investment, which enhances the owners' status in the community. Speculative housing and multi-house ownership have increased considerably in recent years, but large numbers of houses are still lived in by owners who rent out surplus flats or rooms to tenants.

Private housing can be divided into buildings which are considered authorized and legitimate by the authorities, those which are on land subject to customary tenure which has not yet been certificated and spontaneous or informal housing – 'temporary' buildings put up wherever the squatter (by government definition) can find room and which may be subject to demolition orders. Houses in the 'legitimate' system are expected to reach a certain standard, though the enforcement of the regulations may be very uneven. Houses on land with customary tenure are usually built to a lower standard, if only because urban facilities have not yet reached the area. They are considered legitimate by owners and tenants, and are often improved as funds become available.

Informal housing is at a very low standard because there is no point investing large sums in a house which may be lost at any time. It is more often on unused government land than on land subject to customary or legal tenure, because customary owners and purchasers usually keep close watch on their property. In addition, some customary houses are now defined as illegitimate by the government. This is justified in terms of raising standards, but a more obvious effect is to clear land for more elitist uses, as at Maroko. Planning regulations will be discussed in the next chapter.

Investors

There has been much less squatting in Lagos than in eastern Africa or Latin America because the low level of government control over construction meant that legitimate houses could be easily and profitably built; housing the poor was good business. On the whole, residential housing has been the safest investment available, producing a quick return on capital. In the 1970s, rents for one to three years could be collected from potential tenants before building had even begun (Peil 1976a).

However, as speculators have moved into the market, land and building materials have become more expensive, regulations have increased and profits declined, there is much less interest in providing housing for the poor. Incomes set a limit on how much rent can be charged. A block of four flats which costs at least N200,000 to build and rents for N250 each per month brings in only N12,000 per year; low-income housing may be only half as expensive, but it brings in less rent. As a result, the housing shortage is growing and squatting has become more common.

Money for building is obtainable from the Federal Mortgage Bank of Nigeria (FMBN), the Nigeria Building Society, the Lagos State Building Investment Corporation (LSBIC) and the United Bank for Africa, but these institutions supply only a small proportion of the money needed. Mortgages are most common for people buying property from the government; most of those who build houses must rely on their own savings, though some get loans or gifts from their families. The FMBN, founded in 1977, is supposed to supply mortgage funds for the whole country, which it is manifestly unable to do. Like so many government institutions, it has suffered from corruption and bureaucratic inefficiency as well as a shortage of resources. Its total assets were N753.9 m in 1988, but only N19 m was given out. Estate agents do not advise clients to apply for loans, because the delays are long and so few are granted. The LSBIC paid out N10 m in 1987 and earned N11 m in 1988 (LSMI 1988: 184–7).

FMBN regulations require that at least a quarter of the cost of the house must be saved before an application can be made and the applicants must wait at least two years to receive a loan; the maximum loan is N80 000, not enough for a house of any size in Lagos. Both land and building costs are rising rapidly, so delay in acquiring a loan can mean that the project is no longer possible. Between 1988 and 1989, the cost of iron rods rose from N800 to N7000, roofing sheets went from N15 to N68, bags of cement from N12 to N45 and unskilled labour from N20 to N25 per day (West Africa 1989: 1307).

Who is most likely to become a landlord? Barnes (1982; 1986) points out that investment in housing is a social and political as well as an economic act. Landlords often become neighbourhood patrons and brokers between tenants and governmental or political authorities. They attract followers, adjudicate disputes and establish new descent lineages for their families. What leads some men and women to decide to undertake these roles, whereas others are content to rent housing in town and build, if at all, at home? Except occasionally as a speculative investment, they are not usually members of the elites. High-ranking government and corporate officials, university staff and other well-educated and well-paid employees usually live in housing which comes with the job, a hold-over from colonial times. They may decide to build a house for themselves as a prelude to retirement, but are unlikely to take in tenants.

Most houseowners are relatively secure but otherwise average men; many live on relative low incomes. Nearly a third of the employees in the ECA study (1980: 116) who owned houses earned less than N918 per year. But owners are often self employed – after if not before they acquire houses. Commerce is a more common background than manual work (skilled or unskilled), because it is easier to build up the stake needed for house building through business. Lower-level manual or nonmanual workers, such as Mr Ifejika at the head of this chapter, may acquire housing gradually, investing in a room at a time as their finances permit. The important factor is motivation. They have usually decided to remain in the city rather than return home eventually, and wish to become more involved in urban affairs as well as to secure their future there.

Men are far more likely to be houseowners than women, just as they are more likely to be household heads. It is difficult for women to acquire sufficient resources to buy land and build a house. Though successful women traders may invest in housing, this is often rented out to high income tenants rather than serving as a family residence. A few women inherit a house from their husbands, but this seldom happens in Lagos because housing is so valuable that the inheritance would be challenged.

Data on the occupation and incomes of houseowners are very limited. Mabogunje (cited by Barnes 1982: 13–14) reported that in the late 1950s most of the housing in Surulere and Yaba was owned by clerks and traders. Barnes' 1971 study found higher levels of ownership by traders and artisans and fewer clerks in Mushin and Shomolu. In my study of 120 Ajegunle houses at about the same time, two-fifths of the 41 resident owners were male manual workers, often seamen or skilled artisans. A quarter were nonmanual workers, including a nurse, a traditional healer and a soldier; a fifth were traders, including four of the five women, and the rest were retired. The occupations of resident owners are probably roughly related to the recency of development of the area. It is easier for manual workers to acquire land in new areas, whereas ownership in more developed areas is biased towards those with higher incomes.

The ECA study found that 2 per cent of government employees and 4.4 per cent of non-government employees lived in their own houses; 5 per cent and 3.4 per cent respectively lived in employer-provided housing, an additional 5 per cent of each lived in family accommodation and the rest were private renters. Wage income made relatively little difference to the proportion of owners up to N2500, then it gradually rose for private employees, with those earning more than N4200 twice as likely as those on lower salaries to own their own houses. Over half of government employees at this income level were living in government housing (ECA 1980: 116).

While overall about 11 per cent of houses are owner-occupied, the proportion is considerably higher in some low income areas, where those who want to become owners have been able to afford land. A third of Mushin and Ajegunle houses had resident owners in 1971; of the Ajegunle sample, 14 per cent lived elsewhere in Ajegunle, 35 per cent in Lagos and 12 per cent further away – often in the east. This suggests that peripheral suburbs have been open to opportunity, but are increasingly subject to speculative, absentee ownership. This is important because the owner of a single house builds for himself and his family, providing for tenants as an extra, whereas the speculator is interested only in profit and does not build if more profits can be made elsewhere. Higher costs keep out both types of builders, for different reasons. While most resident owners intend to remain permanently, some return home without selling their property; rents serve as a pension. Non-residents often place a kinsman in the house as a caretaker, but caretaking may also be done by someone who lives in the neighbourhood; rents may also be collected by an agency. The size of the houses in Ajegunle was not related to whether the owner was resident or to resident owners' occupation. The largest houses were owned by a trader and a seaman; women and retired men tended to have smaller houses than the rest (Barnes 1979; LSG 1981: 7; Peil 1981: 134).

Another interesting aspect of resident houseowners in Ajegunle was their relative youth. Ownership of housing generally increases with age, both because of inheritance and because it takes considerable time to save the money and build the house. But the median age of owners in both Mushin and Ajegunle of the early 1970s appears to have been the early to mid 40s. Where land and housing are reasonably priced, relatively young men and women are able to marshal the necessary resources to become owners. As prices rise in more developed areas and because of inflation, larger multi-storeyed buildings are expected; it takes longer to save money and greater success is necessary to break into the housing market. Only about 5 per cent of household heads are owners, and they are probably older than in the past. However, insofar as the average tenement building accommodates 8–10 households, the proportion of resident owners may not have declined (FOS 1986: 56).

Once one becomes a property owner, he or she has a position to maintain and is on the way to building up the resources to support that position. Landlords/ladies tend to have larger households than tenants; they are more likely to have two or three rooms, but may be almost as crowded as tenants because of polygyny, numerous children and relatives who come to stay with them. Owners are more likely than tenants to be active in the community and in hometown or family associations. This active social life is partly fostered by their long stay in Lagos (many were born in the city), but even relative newcomers are more committed than tenants to a permanent stay and social relations are quickly built up if one has appropriate resources. A high proportion of owners are Yoruba; since they are more at home in Lagos than 'strangers', it is easier for them to commit themselves to permanent residence.

Tenants

New migrants find a room wherever they can, moving on if they find another which is more convenient to their work or where conditions are better. Morgan and Kannisto (1973: 13) reported that about 45 per cent of Lagos residents they studied had moved within twelve months, either within the metropolis or to or from the city. Unfortunately, they do not separate change of residence from migration, but suggests that movement within the city is considerable. Rents tend to be fairly standardized within a neighbourhood, so moving cannot do much to lower costs, but inability to pay back rent may also require a move.

Landlords may shift tenants if they need space for a relative or clear the house for 'redecorating' as an excuse to raise the rent. Another reason for moving is social, to avoid people one does not get on with. House-mates who are noisy or dirty, whose children are ill-behaved or who try to seduce one's wife can be avoided by finding another room. Young men may also choose to disappear so that a girlfriend cannot find them. In a society where information is mainly communicated verbally and where there is no need to leave a postal forwarding address, it is difficult to trace people who have moved.

Tenants have much less commitment to a neighbourhood than owners, especially if they work some distance away. Tenants are generally seen as temporary, low-status dependants in the neighbourhood, regardless of age, whereas owners settle disputes and demonstrate success in local terms. Political activities are largely organized and patronized by owners, who are more likely to be active in local voluntary associations. Owners set the standards of behaviour in their houses and exercise authority to maintain peace. Tenants who work in the area (mainly the self employed) need a good reputation to attract and keep customers, but many tenants spend little time in or near their rooms (Barnes 1986).

However, a distinction needs to be made between poor tenants who have no alternative and those in public housing, who are comfortably accommodated because of their jobs. Some of the latter own houses which they rent out or have built a house at home for retirement. They remain tenants from choice, because it maximizes their resources. They are often politically active, within the constraints of government service, but have no particular commitment to the neighbourhood in which they find themselves. Public housing will be discussed further below.

Rent controls were established in Lagos in 1973. The maximum rent allowed varied by location and type of accommodation. Tenants in single rooms were to pay N11 on Lagos Island, N10 in Mainland and N8 in Ikeja;

flats cost N16, N15 and N10 per room respectively. Tenants are entitled to a deduction if the amenities are not up to standard and can appeal to a rent tribunal. No more than three months rent can legally be demanded in advance, and it is also an offence to demolish or alter a building without permission or to eject or harass tenants to get more money out of them. Unfortunately for tenants, controls are relatively easy to avoid because the market for housing is so strong and the resources for enforcement are so weak. There are few empty rooms and many potential tenants. An owner may ask for large sums as 'key money', or may find other charges which are not classed as rent. For example, owners can charge for water from a household tap or tank (*West Africa* 1973: 485).

Many people spend at least 25 per cent of their income on rent. The alternative is the insecurity of a squatter shack or sleeping in markets, bus terminals, etc. Rents have risen rapidly since the early 1970s, though perhaps less than the stereotype because it is harder to increase the rent of stable tenants than to charge newcomers more. Over 70 per cent of low income families paid more than N10 rent in 1972, and rooms which cost N10 in the mid 1970s cost N40–70 fifteen years later (see Table 6.1). Landlords charge what the market will bear, though more at the upper end than at the bottom (HRRU 1974: 25; Nigeria 1975: 308; *Lagos Horizon* 29 August 1989).

Many property owners prefer to have tenants who are not of their own ethnic group because they are more likely to pay the rent regularly rather than trying to avoid it through claims of kinship, however distant. This increases ethnic mixing because owners are likely to be Yoruba, whereas tenants can come from all parts of the country. The Ajegunle study found that 98 per cent of houses with more than one household were ethnically heterogeneous and 63 per cent of household heads had no co-tenant of the same ethnic group. The proportion of Yoruba in the Mushin population is much higher than in Ajegunle, but only 19 per cent of houses had exclusively Yoruba residents (Peil 1981: 117; Barnes 1986: 71). Ethnic mixing within houses can cause conflict, especially when tenants do not speak the same language, but it also fosters greater understanding of other peoples, which is essential for Nigerian development.

Housing Conditions

As might be expected, most housing in Lagos is badly overcrowded and grossly underserviced. Widespread poverty means that most households have only a single room, for which services are often minimal and shared with other tenants. While improvements in services have been made in the 1980s, densities have increased.

Density

Crowding is high in most areas of Lagos, both in terms of the number of people per hectare and number per room. Although the metropolitan area has expanded very considerably, the density has risen from 19 per hectare in 1931 to 95 in 1963, 137 in 1974 and 189 in 1988 (Table 1.1). Only 1.5 per cent of households have a building to themselves; 5 per cent live in flats and 95 per cent in single rooms. Koenigsberger *et al.* (1964: 1) estimated that 48 000 more houses would be needed by 1972, at 20 occupants per house, but the population grew more quickly and the housing stock more slowly than was planned. By 1976, the city had only 84 500 houses and there was a need for 1.58 million new units, including 317 000 for middle income households and 79 000 for high income residents, to cope with population growth, replacement of substandard buildings and losses to commerce or roads. The need has probably grown rather than declined since that time (Ebong 1979; *Master Plan* 1980: 593; Ayeni 1981: 134; FOS 1986: 54).

Three-quarters of Lagos housing in 1976 was for low income people, at high density; 20 per cent was of middle density; and 5 per cent was for high income people, at low density (*Master Plan* 1980: 593). While the income level of residents is not as closely correlated to density as this suggests, it can safely be assumed that at least 75 per cent of residential space has a very high population density. Areal crowding represents high densities per room because most houses have only one or two storeys. New blocks of rooms or flats often have three or four storeys, but are separated at the minimum permissible distance from other blocks. This intensifies problems of room ventilation.

For historical reasons, both high and low density housing are found in relatively central areas and on the outskirts (see Maps 6 and 7), so there is no clear density gradient (Sada 1969: 122). Nevertheless, residential densities vary considerably in different parts of the city. In 1977, there were under 100 people per hectare in Ikoyi, 607 in Agege, 1200 in Mushin and 2150 on the north side of Lagos Island. Residence per room varied from 1.6 in Amuwo Odofin and Festac Town to 5.4 on the island. There were between 3.5 and 5.0 people per room in Agege, Ajegunle, Iganmu, Ebute Metta/Yaba, Ijeshatedo/Itire, Ikeja, Lagos Island north, Maroko, Mushin, Obalende, Shogunle and north Surulere. Many rooms are less than 8 sq metres and few are larger than 13.5 sq metres. Rooms are full of household goods, since this is the only place for secure storage. There is often only one bed; some of the household members sleep on mats on the floor or in the hallway or verandah. These areas are also used for cooking (*Master Plan* 1978; 1980, vol. 1, p. 115).

Ajegunle/Aiyetoro provides an example of the problem: over the last 20 years the population has increased about eight times, with relatively little areal growth. Open spaces have been filled in and roads have been improved, but there are far too few new houses for the additional residents. New buildings usually have three storeys, with more rooms than the old

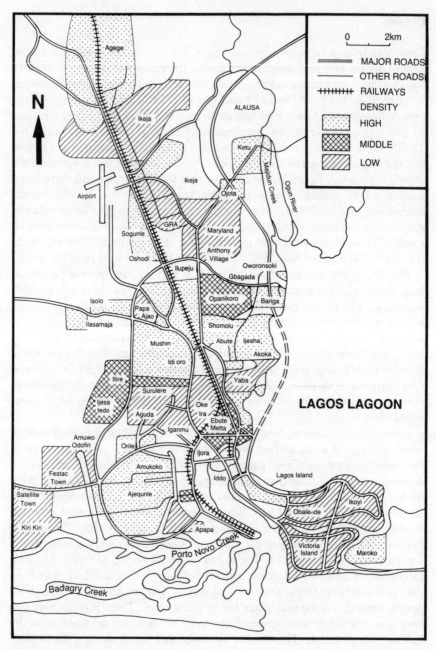

Map 6 Housing densities

Source: Adapted from *Master Plan* 1980: 101

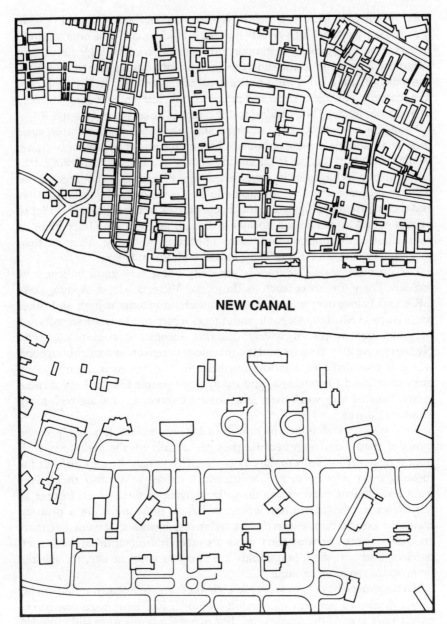

NEW CANAL

Map 7 Across a canal: Ajegunle and Apapa
Source: Adapted from Federal Surveys, Nigeria, 1964

ones, but the great increase in density is something local people must live with. It could be argued that high density housing is efficient in low income countries when transport is expensive in time and money. However, high densities in Lagos are a response to the shortage and cost of housing, not to locational convenience; they contribute nothing to easing transportation problems. The majority of wage earners and many school children have long journeys to and from home. The resulting traffic chaos is discussed in Chapter 8.

Crowding is related to income, ownership, age and migration status, since these factors shape the size of households and the ability to pay for housing. While there is an inverse relationship between income and crowding, it is not as strong in Lagos as in many major cities because of the large size of many middle and upper income households, the shortage of flats and houses and their consequent high cost, and a general lack of concern for the level of privacy which is considered normal in Britain or America. Other items of conspicuous consumption are more important to many Africans than spacious housing, and it is difficult to restrict household size.

For various reasons, address is generally not a very good indicator of income. There are areas (such as Ikoyi and Victoria Island, Apapa, Ikeja GRA and Palmgrove) where average household income is high and other areas (such as Mushin, Ajegunle and Agege) where residents are stereotyped as poor. But people of widely differing incomes live in most areas. Numerous wealthy families find it convenient to remain in a neighbourhood which is crowded and deteriorating because it serves to maintain family links or is good for business, and many poor people live on high income estates because they work there (e.g. domestic servants) or share with more affluent relatives.

New middle and upper income housing estates are less likely to be crowded than older ones because they are usually on the periphery, with poor transportation links to the city centre. This makes the area difficult for those who do not own cars. Families which choose to distance themselves from less affluent relatives can do so by moving to these areas; insofar as self-conscious classes are developing in Lagos, these areas are a primary focus for segregation. Nevertheless, relatives, hawkers, servants, tenants and other visitors or temporary residents make it difficult to establish such barriers, and with time households are likely to grow in size, though the living space remains the same.

Houseowners have a resource which they are frequently called on to share. Whilst 90 per cent of Mushin landlords had more than one room, only 10 per cent of the tenants did. But many landlords were still crowded by international standards; their households were 45 per cent larger than tenant households. Relatives and people from home may ask for a room, or may offer to help out as servants, and clients (apprentices, assistant drivers, junior sales personnel) may be housed if there is room. There may be a steady flow of visitors. In addition, the success which makes house ownership possible often leads to increased family size through additional wives and children (Barnes 1982: 19).

Children are the most frequent cause of crowding. Owners are, on average, older than tenants, and so have had more time to produce children. These are more likely to remain at home when they enter the labour force if they are living in a family house; many owners house an extended family, including a married son and his wife and children, or elderly parents who need support. Siblings or other relatives ask for their children to be fostered or housed while they are sent to school.

Age is important because of its relationship to the life cycle rather than income. Young people on their own are relatively uncrowded. Marriage and children increase density considerably, since the family cannot usually afford to pay for additional rooms. Crowding may decline as the children move out, depending on whether relatives or grandchildren must be accommodated. Young people who are well educated may be earning considerably more than middle-aged people with less education, and the additional income may be invested in better, less-crowded housing if it can be found. However, it may be spent on school fees for younger siblings or on other consumer alternatives.

Regardless of a migrant's economic success, residential density usually increases with the length of time spent in the city, partly because this is related to age and stage in the family lifecycle. Family houses, especially in the inner city, become more crowded over time because access to a room is part of one's inheritance. Sons may build another room on the family house for themselves and their families (see Schwerdtfeger 1982: Ch. 10). There is considerable pressure to rent out any available rooms to tenants. Long-distance migrants are more likely to leave their wives and children at home and are under less pressure from visitors, but some share rooms with friends to maximize their savings.

Amenities

In 1969, the LEDB reported that 40 per cent of Lagos housing was in poor condition, 17 per cent was fair and 42 per cent was good (cited by Abiodun 1974: 345; see also HRRU 1974). Some services improved during the 1970s, but many older buildings continued to suffer the effects of over-crowding and lack of repair. Even new buildings often lack such amenities as flush toilets, running water and waste disposal which urban residents in industrialized countries take for granted. Environmental sanitation is poor and ventilation inadequate. A majority of the housing on Lagos Island is well over half a century old and urgently needs upgrading.

Almost all the city's houses have concrete floors and cement block walls, though the latter need paint. Two-thirds have corrugated iron roofs; most of the rest are of asbestos or cement. Electricity is the most widely provided utility, 93 per cent of houses in urban areas of Lagos State had it in 1984. However, houses in new areas may have a long wait for connection and the supply is not dependable, making air conditioning unreliable for the few

Table 7.1 Household amenities, by area, 1972, and Lagos urban 1984 (percentages)

Location	Water Piped, House	Piped, Other	Well	No	Bathroom Alone	Shared	No	Toilet Water House	Other	None	Kitchen Alone	Shared	No
Ikoyi	100	0	0	0	100	0	0	100	0	0	100	0	0
Ikeja	100	0	0	0	100	0	0	100	0	0	100	0	0
Palmgrove	94	6	0	0	88	12	0	94	6	0	88	12	0
Victoria Is.	100	0	0	0	65	35	0	100	0	0	62	35	0
Surulere	86	1	10	3	58	36	6	82	14	4	60	33	7
Apapa	60	6	32	2	57	43	0	61	39	0	57	42	1
Yaba	78	1	10	1	28	72	b	49	50	1	28	71	1
Ebute-Metta	70	27	2	1	11	88	1	48	50	2	12	84	4
Obalende	64	36	0	0	27	73	0	36	64	0	21	76	3
Island	65	35	b	b	19	80	1	12	87	1	18	80	2
Oshodi	54	0	46	0	24	76	0	17	83	0	29	71	0
Igbobi/Bariga	53	12	28	7	17	83	0	47	53	0	16	82	2
Mushin	59	12	7	22	8	91	1	33	65	2	8	85	7
Agege	6	3	82	9	13	83	4	3	93	4	13	83	4
Ajegunle	0	16	71	13	7	92	1	2	98	0	6	93	1
Lagos urban[a]	47		49	4	88	12	0	19	81	b	13	83	1

Source: Fapohunda, *et al.* 1977: 143, 146, 151; FOS; 1986: 58, 60, 74.

a   1984 figures refer to all urban areas in Lagos State.
b   Less than 0.5 per cent.

who can afford it. Except in elite households, which tend to prefer gas to electricity, kerosene is the main fuel used for cooking. When it is in short supply, firewood may be substituted, but many families do not have the facilities for using wood and it is hard to get. A shortage of kerosene in late 1989 led to queues up to ten hours long (FOS 1986: 62–78; *West Africa* 1989: 2123).

Much of the data in Table 7.1 came from a 1972 survey; in many areas conditions have improved, though rising densities have increased the problems of sharing bathrooms, toilets and kitchens. The data from 1984 refer to all of the urban areas of Lagos State, but a large majority of households live in the metropolitan area. Piped water is less available and wells are more common in smaller towns than in the city. Sharing bathrooms is less common and sharing of toilets and kitchens is more common in peripheral urban areas. The claim that all urban households in Lagos State had access to a bathroom and toilet in 1984 may be questioned. The major problem is the number of people who must share; one toilet for 25 people means that many residents act as if they had none. A single kitchen for a large house is also ignored; people cook either in their rooms or in the hallways.

Water remains a major problem in most parts of Lagos, though the University has a large 'lollipop' tower to supply the campus. In the early 1970s, the water taps in Agege were turned off at the end of the wet season in November and not turned on again until the rains returned in April. The selling of water (brought in by tanker) is good business in Ajegunle. New houses, even in low income areas, usually have a water tank on or near the roof, but in areas with low pressure residents must pay for water to be brought in by tanker and pumped into the tank.

Table 7.1 shows that amenities are much more likely to be available in some areas than in others. High income areas such as Ikoyi, Ikeja, Palmgrove and Victoria Island are well provided for and services are usually kept in good condition. Surulere has adequate amenities because the estates there were built recently and were seen as showpieces of what an independent government could provide. The Apapa estate is considerably older, and in the early 1970s many of the houses still depended on wells. Yaba and Ebute-Metta are conveniently located for water supplies, but the old houses have inadequate and overcrowded bathrooms, toilets or kitchens. Houses in Obalende and on Lagos Island tend to be old and very crowded; while piped water is available in the compound if not in the house, other amenities are grossly inadequate. Oshodi and Igbobi/Bariga have been developed much more recently. Many houses still rely on wells and other amenities are usually shared.

Problems in Mushin are due partly to it having been an outpost of the Western Region until shortly before independence and its extremely rapid growth since then. Being peripheral to the city and inhabited by strangers, Agege and Ajegunle have always been neglected. They demonstrate in extreme form the lack of amenities in high density, low income areas; those that are available are likely to be shared with several other households, especially among tenants. Although the main pipeline from the Iju water-works taking water to Badagry passes under Ajegunle, few houses there are supplied from the mains. Conditions may improve now that Ojo has become a local government area, with most of its population in Ajegunle.

Government as Landlord

Government Residential Areas (GRAs) are a feature of most large cities in areas colonized by the British. One of the first Lagos estates, at Ikoyi, was begun in 1918. The colonial government first became concerned with the provision of housing beyond the needs of its own officials in the 1920s, though in the early years the major interest was in sanitation and ensuring minimum standards from private developers. Neither the colonial authorities nor the government of independent Nigeria has provided much public housing; what was built has been mainly for senior officials or the uniformed services, though Lagos has had its share of 'low income' projects.

The federal and state governments continue to accommodate employees. For example, there are three 20-storey buildings and a large estate of 10 storey buildings (known as the 1001 flats) for federal employees on Victoria Island (see Plate 7.2). The Lagos State government houses the governor and other top officials in Ikeja; it is building more housing for civil servants in

Alausa. There are Army barracks in Ajegunle, Apapa, Obalende and Yaba and Police barracks in Ikeja, Ikoyi and Surulere. Government hospitals provide accommodation for many of their professional staff, especially doctors. Lagos University houses senior staff on campus and in Ikoyi.

Government rents are highly subsidized, at 10 per cent of salary. Large private employers tend to follow the government's lead, since it would be hard to retain senior staff without this perk. The net result is that the high cost of housing in Lagos is particularly burdensome to middle income people – not high enough in the hierarchy to qualify for cheap, employment-related housing, but wanting more than the minimum space which most families must cope with.

The government has also taken up the role of provider of housing to the general population, though on a much smaller scale than in Kenya or Zimbabwe. The main agencies are the Lagos Executive Development Board (LEDB) now the Lagos State Development Property Corporation (LSDPC), and the New Town Development Authority (NTDA). These agencies focus mainly on the provision of serviced land rather than housing, and their contribution to the development of the metropolis has always been hampered by a shortage of resources, inefficient personnel and special interests. They will be discussed in more detail in Chapter 8; the issue here is the housing which has been built.

The approach of independence in the 1950s provided an opportunity to assess government housing in the light of local needs. The emphasis remained on accommodation for senior personnel, but it was clear that there would soon be more of them and that Nigerian officials would demand the same standards as had been provided for expatriates. In addition, the general public wanted relief from the high densities they faced. The Apapa and Ikoyi Estates were extended by providing more building plots in the early 1950s, and low density housing was also developed on Victoria Island. Considerable expensive land reclamation was necessary for this; the land was made available for private development as well as providing housing for Members of Parliament, top federal civil servants and the diplomatic corps. While such provision was seen as necessary at the time because of the demands of independence, it severely limited the resources available for low income housing.

The housing estate at Surelere was the largest undertaken by the LEDB and aroused the most controversy. This highly complex scheme was first proposed in 1951, to supply residential accommodation for people of all income levels. One sector provided 712 freehold plots at 5 to 8 houses per acre, consisting of single-family bungalows, two-storeyed homes and multi-family flats. A second scheme (390 freehold houses) passed from the intended low income population to those who could better afford the amenities provided (see Chapter 8).

Recent government projects have been mainly for sale, either immediately or through long-term payments while living as tenants. A lottery is used to handle the demand, but the requirement of a large downpayment and

Plate 7.3 Dolphin Scheme LSDPC housing, Lagos Island

other bureaucratic procedures limit the access of the poor to LSDPC housing. 'Low income' estates have been built at Ilupeju and Isolo to house industrial workers, though they are far too limited in size for the demand. Since 1979, housing units have also been built at Abule-Nila, Amuwo Odofin, Coker Village, Ipaja and Iganmu.

The Dolphin Scheme involved redevelopment of 167 hectares on the north side of Lagos Island and 74 hectares in Obalende (western Ikoyi). The area has a potential population of 112 000, most of whom want to live in this neighbourhood. The land used was formerly a market for fish, planks and firewood, some of which has been displaced to a nearby swampy area. The three- and four-storey blocks of flats are not impressive in appearance and the standard of building leaves much to be desired (see Plate 7.3), but there is no problem finding tenants/purchasers. Illegal structures have appeared in the spaces between buildings, since the location is convenient for anyone working in the area.

A flat in the initial phase of the Dolphin Scheme cost N1000 down and N30 per month over 15 years to buy; flats in the four-storey buildings of phase II cost N2000 to apply and N50 per month. Residents generally find them better than their former houses, but they have improved the very basic flats provided by plastering and painting internal walls, tiling the living room floors and kitchen walls and improving security by putting iron bars across entrance doorways. Some buildings suffer from rotting wood and leaking roofs. There is considerable turnover; over half the résidents questioned in 1984 had lived there less than a year. Nevertheless, social

159

relations have developed; most people had friends among their neighbours (Fatai 1984).

Estates need more that just houses, and infrastructural provision is often slow to appear. Government bureaucracy and inefficiency makes it less acceptable as a landlord than a private owner, partly because more is expected and partly because housing and environment are seen as a unit. In an address in 1988 Major J.K. Ekunleye (ret.), President of the Isolo Low Cost Housing Estate Landlords Association, complained that the Mushin Local Council 'behaves like . . . imperial Royalty'. Action was asked for on high rates, refuse, drainage, roads and traffic control. The estate needs more primary schools, water and electricity; a clinic, functional market, post office and telephone should be provided. Crime on the estate is a major concern.

Tenement rates in Isolo are twice those elsewhere in Mushin. This may be because the estate was built more recently and hence the houses were more expensive, but residents see the assessment as unfair, especially in the light of the lack of services on the estate. They argue that refuse sites should be designated and cleared regularly. The primary school is overfull, and the only furniture has been provided by the community itself rather than the Local Council. Transportation to other parts of Lagos is time-consuming and seems likely to get worse. Abandoned roads make movement difficult, and armed robbers operate freely when they cannot be chased. There are no functioning street lights and part of the estate still has no electricity; this increases the risk of robbery.

A local post office and telephone would greatly enhance the residents' links to the wider community, including calling the police when they are needed. There has been no water for over a year and one-third of the estate has no pipes laid; it is estimated that residents spend N1.6 m per year buying water from tankers. Government regulations on market hours are inefficient from the community's point of view. The Isolo community does not expect the government to provide everything, but it would like support from the Local Council. Residents are ready to help with building a health centre and community centre, which they feel would be of great benefit. While similar lists of needs could be produced by many low income neighbourhoods, having government as a landlord increases expectations and strengthens their case.

Festac Town was initially built on the main road to Badagry, to the west of the city, for visitors to the International Festival of African Arts and Culture in 1977. After the festival, it was decided to sell the flats even though the infrastructure had not yet been developed. The first phase covered 460 hectares, divided into three communities. The complete town, with ten communities on 2230 hectares, should provide 24 000 dwelling units in all. Plot size and the width of roads vary with the expected income level of occupants. Most of the housing is four-storey blocks of flats (see Plates 7.4 and 7.5), though there are some detached houses.

Plate 7.4 Festac Town flats

Plate 7.5 Omuwo Odofin flats

161

Plate 7.6 Third Mainland Bridge housing scheme
Source: Lagos State Ministry of Information and Culture

A ballot for houses was held in 1977–8. While quite a few middle income people got low income units, some low income people are living in units intended for high or middle income families. Residents moved there from more central locations because more space was available and they could buy their flats; most came from middle rather than low income housing, though quite a few came from deteriorating neighbourhoods. A majority of residents are relatively well educated, migrants and Christians, employed as civil servants or clerical workers in central Lagos. Given the inadequate bus service and long journey to work (15 km in heavy traffic), there is considerable advantage in owning a car. Those who changed workplace on moving to Festac Town were mainly self employed or teachers. There was considerable dissatisfaction at the small number of posts available in local schools (Oyeleye 1981; Oynemenam 1983).

It appears that a high proportion of government housing money is going to people who could afford to build their own houses or rent from private land-lords. A new 'middle income' scheme is opening along the Third Mainland Bridge link to Ebute Metta (Plate 7.6). These flats cost N140 000 to buy, at a time when university lecturers earn less than N20 000 per year, so they are effectively out of reach of many 'middle income' people. In an effort to 'cater for all segments of people in the society', the government is spending over N37 m on flats at Ijaiye, 76 duplexes at Amuwo-Odofin (Satellite Town) and

82 houses at Ojota-Ogundu GRA. A block of six maisonette flats on Victoria Island cost N1.4 m; expensive duplex houses in the Ikoyi sector of the Dolphin Scheme are being completed and residential blocks of six flats are being built at 'luxury' level for medical doctors (*Lagos Horizon* 29 August 1989). A larger contribution to the Federal Mortgage Bank of Nigeria might encourage cheaper and more efficient private building. Aspects of the planning of these projects will be discussed in Chapter 8.

Summary

Housing is a perennial problem in Lagos, as in all major cities. Architects and builders have produced a few notable buildings (especially in Brazilian style), but on the whole comfort and design have been of less concern than supplying basic needs. The population is growing much more rapidly than the housing supply. This shortage and widespread poverty inevitably produce high densities and some squatting, but there is less 'informal' housing than in many Third World cities because successive governments have operated a laissez faire policy rather than enforcing strict regulation.

The Yoruba customary system of land tenure was complicated during the colonial period by British ideas of property, and major changes have occurred in access to and registration of land since the 1978 Land Use Decree. Security of tenure has improved, though rising costs have made it difficult for poor people to move into the housing market. Though there are now clearly regulated ways of acquiring land, traditional customs may have a strong effect on what actually happens. Families of Idejo chiefs still control and lease property on the periphery of the city, and plots of land which have been acquired through customary arrangements are still seen as legitimately owned, though subject to challenge to a greater extent than Certificated land. Access to land is essential because there is very little resale of houses in Lagos; houses have belonged to families rather than to individuals and those who want to acquire a house must build one, unless they can acquire one of the few built by the government.

A much higher proportion of housing in Lagos is privately owned than in countries such as Kenya and Zimbabwe, where colonial governments tried to control housing for Africans. On the whole, various Nigerian governments have not been concerned with providing housing except for their own employees, and most of what has been built for the public is for sale. Thus, private landlords/ladies make the market, and the security and profitability of investment in housing has been the main reason why the city was relatively well provided for. The opportunity to get a higher return for commercial investment in the 1970s oil boom and the rapid inflation of building costs in the late 1980s have deterred private builders, increasing the shortage. Personal savings are less likely to be sufficient for entry into the housing market than in the 1960s. With the economy in the grip of a recession and returns on house building falling, there is no chance that enough accommodation will be available for the huge numbers of migrants pouring into Lagos. What is built is largely flats for the affluent, not tenement rooms for the poor. Even the rich have to wait for the expensive accommodation now being built.

Ownership of land and housing is prestigious and opens up political and social roles which are seldom available to tenants. Owners have tended to come from middle and lower income levels and to share their houses with tenants; it was a way of securing one's position in the city. Family housing provides rooms for members of widely differing income levels and encourages successful members to remain in the neighbourhood rather than moving out to exclusive estates. These factors have served to minimize class barriers and encourage ethnic heterogeneity in residential areas. The situation may be changing, in that wealthy speculators in the housing market have the rent collected by an agency and have no personal contacts with their tenants; severe overcrowding in older areas encourages those who can afford it to move out. More research is needed to establish how much contact residents of Ikoyi, Victoria Island and Festac Town have with relatives elsewhere in Lagos.

The buildings in many areas of Lagos look weary of trying to combat climate, overcrowding, underservicing and lack of upkeep. Newcomers often start by sharing a room with relatives or friends; few households have more than one room and most are living at densities greater than three per room. This crowding speeds building deterioration, as does the widespread sharing of facilities such as toilets and kitchens. Nevertheless, housing conditions are better in the capital than in rural areas, in that most buildings are of cement and have access to piped water and electricity, even if water is in short supply and electricity irregular.

Several government estates have been built for the wider population in recent years, but low income families get little of what is provided, since the government seeks to at least recover its investment. The infrastructure on government estates may not be much better than is available elsewhere in the city, though as in other areas it is gradually improving over time. Government planning and provision of infrastructure are the major concerns of Chapter 8.

8
Planners

The Oneru chieftaincy family claims that Maroko land was originally theirs. Early settlers are said to have fled there from the Gold Coast and Dahomey; others settled there for fishing under the leadership of the Oniru (chief). The population grew rapdily when the Lagos Executive Development Board (LEDB) moved people there in 1958 so that Victoria Island and Ikoyi could be developed for Europeans and wealthy Africans. By 1962, there were 22 villages, each with its own *Baalę*. Since then, migrants have come from all over the country, since this largely unserviced settlement is convenient for wage employment as well as for fishing and trading and provides some of the cheapest housing in Lagos. The first primary school opened in 1979 and a government secondary school a few years later. A small nursery school and a maternity clinic were built by USAID and run by volunteers. A government clinic was provided in 1980, though it was often short of drugs. The community was built on swamps, and the sandy roads were in very poor condition (see Plate 8.1); some houses were surrounded by water even in the dry season. The rusty-roofed, 4–6 room houses had no safe water supply, no drainage and irregular electricity.

It is convenient to call the residents squatters, but in practice most were allotted or purchased their land, with procedures which were legal at the time. The government demolished houses at Moba, near Maroko, in 1984 with the promise of resettlement; by late 1989 nothing had been done. Bulldozing of Ilado (part of the Maroko settlement) was also started to foster development of the Lekki Peninsula, but was stopped by the Akhigbe administration. Nevertheless, as the price of Lekki Peninsula plots rose rapidly, the threat of being pushed off their land hung over the area. Maroko was bulldozed in July 1990, making about 300 000 people homeless (Wemambu 1988; *Lagos Horizon* 15 August 1989; *West Africa* 1990: 2166).

This chapter looks at planning problems. Governments today usually assume that urban growth (housing, transportation, water, electricity, and so on) should be planned. But the extremely rapid growth of Lagos and resource constraints impede the fulfilment of plans. Introducing Lagos State's regional plan for 1980–2000, Governor Jakande lamented the

Plate 8.1. Boys playing football at Maroko, slum housing

helplessness of government in the face of 'de facto townships', including greater Ajegunle, most of Somolu local government area, Maroko, Coker Village and several new developments. The *Master Plan* was accepted to strengthen government resolve and control, with the goal of improving the quality of life of residents (LSG 1981).

Cynics may argue that national plans have more to do with political aspirations than with realistic development programmes. Expensive consultants are brought in, but their glossy projections remain largely on paper. Most residential development takes place informally rather than as a result of planning, and planners are left to make sense of an already established situation. Urban policy is more crucial for the development of services than of housing because the latter can be provided privately, but local practice tends to be more responsive to vociferous demand than advance planning. The provision of basic services in Lagos is examined here from the points of view of planners, decision-makers and the ordinary people who feel the effects of their action or lack of action. The focus is on important developments over the last 35 years in government housing estates, transportation and other services, financial commitments and the winners and losers in the planning process.

Planning and development are big business, honeypots for politicians, contractors and international lending agencies. In the process of building up its own planning capacity, Lagos has had at least three plans by imported consultants: Koenigsberger *et al.* (1964), Doxiades (1973), whose plan was partially rejected, and the *Master Plan* (1980) drawn up by Wilbur Smith and Associates with United Nations aid. The *Master Plan* provides much more information on which to base planning than had previously been available and suggests short range (to 1985) and long range (to 2000) development programmes. The 1980 Regional Plan recommends peripheral development to take pressure off the central city, upgrading and filling of industrial areas, land reclamation, improving environmental and employment conditions for low income people and improving transport links within the city and with the countryside (LSG 1981: 8–9).

Although there is a long way to go, much was done in the 1980s with the resources available. For example, in 1987 Lagos State spent N18.3 m on infrastructural development, chiefly in the Central Business District, Ikeja, Amuwo Odofin, Gbagada, Magodo, Omole, Lekki Peninsula and Victoria Island. This included the building of 60 km of roads. An additional N35 million was spent on housing. Smaller projects were also carried out by local governments. Finance for major projects often comes from federal and international rather than state or local sources; such funding may be more difficult to acquire when the capital moves to Abuja.

LEDB and its successors

The Lagos Executive Development Board (LEDB) was established in 1929 in response to the 1924 outbreak of bubonic plague, which had necessitated demolishing slum houses. Its first job was to clear swamps and drain lagoons to produce more land for expansion of the city. In 1930, it organized Yaba for people displaced from Lagos Island, rejuvenated Ebute Metta and laid out Apapa as a separate residential area for Europeans. The Town and Country Planning Acts of 1932 and 1946 set out rules for zoning, land occupancy and other forms of control and development. New residential estates were built at Ikeja and Ilupeju.

From 1948, in the run-up to independence, it was charged with urban redevelopment, to rid the capital of slums and produce a city worthy of the new nation. It developed the GRA (Government Residential Area) at Ikoyi, a safe distance from the crowded, unsanitary conditions of Lagos Island, and housing estates for senior staff in Apapa, East Marina and Victoria Island. These estates were far too small to cater for the demand and little provision was made for the poor – even those moved from the East Marina site. Between 1957 and 1966, the LEDB built 6714 units on 259.2 hectares; 36 per cent of the units (2400, mostly one or two rooms) were for rehousing but did not replace all the accommodation demolished in central Lagos. Of the rest, 30 per cent were freehold houses for medium and high income families at 1.3 per hectare; these absorbed 77 per cent of the money spent. The 'moderate' and low cost units, built at 10.3 per hectare, were blocks of small flats at minimum standards. It was also responsible for industrial developments in Apapa, Ikeja, Ilupeju, Mushin and Oshodi, including the Apapa Port (Okpala 1979: 36; LSMI 1988: 185–6).

Lagos Slum Clearance Scheme

This project deserves special comment as a major example of urban planning and the political problems which it involves. It was planned to redevelop 70 acres of land on Lagos Island, which housed about 30 000 people. The Scheme was proposed in 1951, but discussions continued until 1954. This provided plenty of time for opponents to build a following and the AG to become their champion. Owners were promised that their land would be returned to them after redevelopment, though this was obviously impossible. Fewer plots would be available and owners could not afford the price charged for added services. It was originally planned to use some land to enhance central commercial and public facilities, but the government was forced to promise that none of the acquired land would be resold to outsiders and plots were only 9 by 30 metres, preventing modern redevelopment (Abiodun 1974: 346; Akinsemoyin and Vaughan-Richards 1977: 55).

The LEDB was in charge of slum clearance, but the boundary between it and the Lagos City Council (LCC), which was responsible for public utilities and bye-laws, was vague. The LCC was subject to election and controlled by the Action Group from 1953. Its considerable delaying powers were fully used, and it stopped this extremely unpopular scheme in 1962, after only part of the area had been cleared. Politial interference continued, with the Minister of Lagos Affairs illegally taking over the distribution of compensation and requiring the LEDB to build 'temporary' shops in the vacated area. The Minister allocated these shops as he wished – to party supporters rather than LEDB clients. Professional planners lost creditability, and further urban renewal has been impossible (Aribiah 1974; 1976).

Roads, drains and other necessary infrastructure were the responsibility of the LCC, the Public Works Department and the Electicity Undertaking. When the first tenants moved in, much of the infrastructure was not yet in place. Traders found themselves a long way from their former customers and from a market in which to start over. The compensation of N400 (later only N70) for loss of business bred great discontent. Early problems of the new estate included isolation from family and friends and increased costs of daily living. Former owners had to pay rent and those who continued to work in central Lagos had to pay for transportation. Some indigenous Lagosians saw Surulere as 'bush', and were afraid of being attacked by thieves. A Residents' Association, founded in 1956 at the suggestion of the LEDB, helped to develop community spirit and support demands for better services (Marris 1961; Aribiah 1976).

The LEDB never managed to serve low income residents as promised. Land prices rose 100–320 per cent over the compensation paid to owners, making repurchase impossible. Surulere was planned to be a temporary home for people who would move back after redevelopment; since very few moved back, no Surulere houses were freed for another stage of urban renewal. Many people who did not want to leave Lagos Island moved in with relatives or displaced tenants rather than going to Surulere, which meant that the north Island area became even more crowded. Others rented out their Surulere house and found cheaper accommodation in Mushin or Shomolu (Mabogunje 1968: 302).

Since many *de jure* owners on Lagos Island were not *de facto* residents, economic factors were more important than traditional ties in people's attitude towards the Slum Clearance Scheme. The Lagos Island houses were 'owned' by far more people than actually lived in them. But the LEDB agreement made it responsible for housing non-resident and resident owners. While the former really lost in the rehousing scheme, since they became tenants and had less space available for their families, non-resident owners were net gainers. In addition to sharing the compensation paid by the LEDB for all the houses it acquired, they were allotted a house which they could either live in or rent out. Any rent which they might have obtained from the Lagos Island house, or any money which might have come to them on its sale, was repaid by these new property rights (Aribiah 1976: 51–2).

Planned redevelopment in communally owned areas of African cities needs to take this factor into account – either in selectively reimbursing residents or only rehousing those who have actually been displaced. In practice, urban populations quickly learned the lesson of urban renewal. The Ghana government found it impossible to organize a similar scheme in central Accra in the 1960s.

The Surulere estate is easily differentiated from neighbouring areas by the 'government quarters' style of buildings – smaller and far more regular in design than is normal in Lagos housing. Only 913 'low cost' houses were built. These were terraced to save land; they had one to four rooms, water and electricity. They were thus more suitable for middle income people with young families (former tenants) than for the large families of central Lagos houseowners. While 4000 people were housed in Surulere, some of these were migrants to Lagos who illegally got their names on the housing list. Only 8 per cent of the houses went to low income tenants; the rest provided 'better-class housing' to those who could pay, including senior civil servants and politicians. In 1971, only 15 per cent of estate residents were Lagos indigenes, though 82 per cent were Yoruba (Sada and Adefolalu 1975: 88–91; Aribiah 1976: 44–53).

Units were rented for 25 shillings a month per room. This represented a considerable subsidy given the cost of construction, but was more than many former residents of central Lagos family housing could afford. Keeping the rent at this level over a long period ensured the permanence of tenants; only 11 per cent of the 1971 residents had arrived in the last ten years. Subsidized rents were only 55 per cent of commercial rents in 1964 and by 1971 a two-room house with water taps, bathroom, toilet and kitchen similar to those in Surulere would have cost at least four times as much elsewhere in Lagos. However, this stability was bought at considerable price to the LEDB. Rents were too low to recover the costs of administration and new building, especially given the declining value of the naira. While residents would have strongly objected to paying the market value of their accommodation, some increase in rent was justified (Ohadike 1968: 86).

While most residents settled down in Surulere, acknowledging that the housing was better than what they had left, former landlords were less satisfied and more willing to return to central Lagos than tenants (Aribiah 1976: 45). The permission given in 1979–80 to buy Surulere houses provided a welcome return to ownership and security of tenure. This has also applied to the nearby Shitta Bay Resettlement Area and more recent housing schemes.

Promises that public ownership of land would control urban development for the good of all citizens, increase efficiency of land use and social justice, promote security of tenure and keep down land speculation proved false in the Lagos case. People went on building wherever they could get access to land, because this was cheaper than LEDB property, and tenants can lose LEDB houses through inability to pay rent. This problem was partly handled by the agreement that defaulting tenants could only be evicted with a court order, which gave them a long time to pay their back rent. The Land Use Decree of 1978 controlled some of the anarchy in the housing market by requiring land registration and building permission, but has not eliminated it; there are many ways to get around the regulations. Land speculation has greatly increased, both in reselling government plots and developing areas outside government planning areas (Aribiah 1976; Okpala 1979; Aina 1990b: 93).

Another lesson which the LEDP and its successors have only partly taken to heart is their clients' potential for economic 'progress'. Side streets in Surulere are narrow, since it was assumed that residents would be using public transportation. However, partly because houses went to middle income families and partly through economic growth in the 1970s many residents now own cars, for which no parking space was planned. Residential developments beyond the estate bring considerable additional traffic to Surulere roads, which were not planned to accommodate them. The streets are wider in Festac Town, which was designed for middle income residents, but new low income projects must also be planned for upwardly mobile people – the most likely customers.

Reorganization

As the city developed, the LEDB faced the problem that the area under its control was far too small. Ikeja had its own planning authority, which led to considerable confusion and inefficiency. The creation of Lagos State and reorganization of local governments made it possible to integrate the LEDB, the Ikeja Area Planning Authority and the Epe Town Planning Authority into the Lagos State Development and Property Corporation (LSDPC) in 1972. Planning is in the hands of Lagos State ministries (or departments under military governments) dealing with land, housing, physical planning, development and waste disposal.

The LSPDC is charged with acquiring land and developing housing and industrial estates for sale to the public. Roads, paths, bridges, sewers and drains on these estates are its responsibility until the local government takes them over. The Corporation must gain state approval for its plans and does not have the power to allocate plots. Clients must make a downpayment years in advance; some 1980 depositors had not yet been allocated a flat in 1986. The Dolphin Scheme was briefly discussed in Chapter 7; part of this was the politically popular provision of low income flats at the north end of Lagos Island. 'Jakande houses' at Abule-Nia, Iponri and Ijeh were so poorly built that 500 had to be demolished in 1987 'to avert disaster' (*West Africa* 1986: 645; 1987: 1605).

Controlling land became necessary. The government demolished 4383 illegal structures in 1984–6 because they were on government land, on land reserved for industrial use, built without approved plans, too close to the road or under high-tension electric cables. These were not all houses, but illegal buildings are evidence of the increasing shortage of low income accommodation (*West Africa* 1986: 747).

LSPDC and other government building remains at a low level; only 1500 LSPDC units were completed between 1972 and 1979. The Third National Development Plan (1975–80) allocated N11 m to the Federal Housing Authority for 46 000 housing units in Lagos State, but only 8616 were built. The new civilian administration in 1979 proposed 50 000 housing units over the next four years. Duplexes, bungalows, houses and high rent commercial units were provided in Ikoyi and Victoria Island, but relatively few houses were built for the poor. In 1987–90, the LSPDC expected to provide 412 duplexes, 504 'medium cost' flats and 2000 'low cost' units, at a cost of N131.9 m (LSMI 1988: 184–7; Okoye 1990: 81). The duplexes and flats have four bedrooms, tiled toilets and bathrooms, terrazzo floors, ground water tanks and parking spaces, while over 90 per cent of the city's population lives in single rooms.

In an attempt to make the Corporation more commercial, the Military Government promoted the development of shopping centres at Falomo (Ikoyi, see Plate 4.6), Lagos Central, Surulere (Adeniran Ogunsanya) and Iponri. The Ikeja Plaza and Suru Ultra Modern Market are under construction. The LSPDC has also built community recreation centres, a cinema, and commercial/office blocks on Lagos Island. In 1988, rental income totalled N15 m. Capital receipts were N42 m from sales of low cost housing and N96 m from middle and upper income schemes. Capital expenditure on housing in 1988 was only N9.2 m, though an additional N22.4 m was spent on town and country planning. Capital receipts and rental income were higher in 1989 than in 1988, but expenditure was down. Allottees are continuing to buy houses, but the Corporation has less money to build, at a time when each building costs more (LSMI 1988: 180–3; LSG 1989b: 43–5, 69–70).

Some of the original functions of the LSDB have been taken over by the New Towns Development Authority (NTDA), which was established in 1981 to handle site selection, provision of infrastructure, commercial or industrial development and housing in new suburbs beyond the urban perimeter. One of its largest projects is the Amuwo-Odofin Town Scheme (see Plate 7.5). Satellite Town, included in this project, will cover 2400 acres, part of it used for federal government housing. Another major project is the Lekki Peninsula Scheme, which is expected to provide middle and high income housing and recreational facilities along the Atlantic coast. A new federal port may be built at Iberekodo. Though recommended by the *Master Plan*. Lekki development is moving slowly. However, it was announced in 1989 that 2000 of an eventual 3579 residential and commercial plots were ready; people were warned to move in and develop their plots quickly. This area is ripe for speculators (LSMI 1988: 182–3; *Lagos Horizon* 29 August 1989).

Transporters

Residents and visitors complain at length about Lagos' transportation problems, especially traffic jams, known locally as 'go slows'. About a third of Nigeria's cars are registered in Lagos; vehicle registration increased at nearly 7 per cent per year between 1963 and 1975 and traffic flows on main roads increased about 200 per cent between 1966 and 1975. Considerable improvements have been made since the mid 1970s, widening roads, constructing flyovers and improving drainage and surfaces. Mass transportation has also expanded, supplementing the public system and handling huge numbers of people. However, urban growth has been so rapid that the roads have never caught up with the volume of traffic. The Central Licensing Authority in Lagos registered over 60 000 public transport vehicles between 1980 and 1985, though the numbers dropped sharply after 1982. In 1987, 1311 commercial vehicles were registered and 38 078 re-registered, compared to 4108 new and 129 483 re-registered private vehicles. Firms now own nearly as many vehicles as commercial providers of transportation (Olanrewaju 1981: 64; LSG 1987: 8–9).

Planners argue that Lagos transportation needs unified control, planned development and the enforcement of discipline; transportation is handled by too many government bodies and too many drivers ignore the rules. The Federal Ministry of Works and Housing is responsible for major roads linking Lagos to the rest of the country and a few routes within the city; the Federal Ministry of Transport and Aviation controls some ferries; the Federal Ministry of Finance must approve major plans which attract federal support, such as the Third Mainland Bridge; and the Nigerian Airports Authority, the Nigerian Ports Authority and Nigerian Railway Corporation handle their respective sectors (Onakomaiya 1981).

At State level, the Department of Works and Transport constructs and maintains major roads; the physical Planning and Development Department supervises building plans, including the provision of roads in new estates by the LSPDC and NTDA; and the Lagos State Transport Corporation (LSTC) runs bus and ferry services. Local councils are responsible for minor roads in their areas. Decisions are often taken by one of these bodies without consulting the others. The judicial system is occasionally involved when land is repossessed for new roads and the police (both regular and traffic division) attempt to maintain discipline on the roads.

Onakomaiya (1981) makes the case for a Lagos Metropolitan Traffic Authority (LMTC), which would coordinate research, planning, road construction, maintenance and mass transportation services. Road plans, including walkways, would be required before any new area could be developed. Improving road discipline needs close ties between the LMTC and the Police. Traffic policemen need more training and better wages and conditions to cut out bribery. Speed and parking limits should be set and enforced, varying with the type of road. A Highway Patrol Section could be formed to arrest offenders. Traffic lights at major junctions and better signposting would at least notify drivers of who has the right of way. More rigorous testing of new drivers to ensure that they know the Highway Code and have no visual defects would also be helpful, as would measures to certify that all vehicles on the roads are mechanically sound and insured. Unfortunately, drivers' attitudes are hard to change. While improvements in the 1980s were considerable, there is still a long way to go. No LMTC exists or is planned.

Traffic wardens, a decentralized branch of the police, do their best to keep Lagos' chaotic roads under control. The service was inaugurated when the country changed from driving on the left to driving on the right in 1972. Their orange and blue uniforms are now a familiar sight, and their patience in handling traffic jams is admirable. While they cannot make up for the overcrowded roads, they do help to make major junctions, which seldom have traffic lights, function much better than would be possible without them. The Lagos drivers' habitual disregard of regulations is at least restricted where it matters most. However, the job of warden also offers opportunities for bribery, which makes the public justifiably suspicious. Two occasions when their activities resulted in riots were discussed in Chapter 6.

Roads

The Lagos–Badagry, Lagos–Ibadan and Abeokuta Expressways make it relatively easy for Nigerians to reach the urban network, but it is much more difficult to get into the city once one is forced to leave the expressways and cope with narrow, overcrowded streets. Map 8 shows the major thoroughfares of Lagos. East–west traffic is severely limited by the few roads crossing the south–northeast railway and canals through the swamps in Ajegunle and their extensions into Surulere. While it is much easier now than in the early 1970s to cover long distances, the time saved may be lost getting on and off expressways and bridges.

Location on an island added to the congestion of Lagos traffic from an early period; the need for bridges to maintain contact with the mainland has

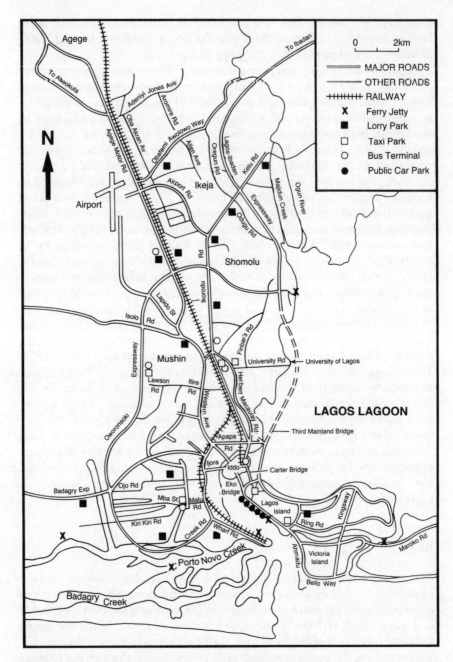

Map 8 Major roads, bus terminals and parking areas

Source: Adapted from Shell 1985; Adefolalu 1986

continued to be a source of blockage. Canoes and small boats are still used for crossing the lagoon and creeks. The city is expanding its ferry services, but most commuters travel in vehicles crossing the three bridges. The Carter Bridge was opened in 1901; it has been replaced twice, in 1933 and in 1979. It now has eight lanes and runs for 1.2 km, connecting north Island with Iddo and Ebute Metta. Eko Bridge was built in 1970 for N17.5 m as the first link in the expressway system and rehabilitated in 1989. It runs from Western Avenue to the western end of the Marina and the Inner Ring Road. The Third Mainland Bridge runs from Ikoyi and the eastern end of the Island to Herbert Macaulay Street, Ebute Metta; eventually it will extend 15 km to the end of the Apapa–Oworonshoki Expressway in Shomolu. This was part of the Dolphin Scheme, designed to link the Inner Ring Road and Ikoyi to the mainland but also, by filling swamps and redevelopment, to provide additional housing in a very crowded area (see Chapter 7). Bridge construction was halted by the military government, but work began again in 1987. The second phase is estimated to cost N555 m, of which the Federal Government will pay N495 m (Sada and Adefolalu 1975: 97–104; LSMI 1988: 117). Three short motorway–standard bridges link Apapa to Tin Can Island and Victoria Island to the Inner Ring Road and to Ikoyi.

Most of the expressways listed in Table 8.1 were built, or at least started, under Governor Jakande, though most had extensive support from federal funds. The Federal Government spent about N1 billion on Lagos roads between 1975 and 1980. This included making Western Avenue–Agege Motor Road, Ilupeju Road and Herbert Macaulay Road into dual carriageways, with central barriers and limited access, greatly increasing the number of cars they can handle. Other expressways were completely new. The Inner

Table 8.1 Expressways

Route	Length (km)	Lanes
Lekki Peninsula: Victoria Island–Lekki	65	4
Apapa Port–Isolo–Oworonshoki: links Tin Can Island to Agege Motor Rd, Airport and Ibadan Expressway	28	8
Apapa Wharf–Ikeja: linked to Ikorodu Rd at Jibowu	14	8
Ikorodu Rd.: Yaba–Ojota, linked to Ibadan Expressway	13	10
Inner Ring Rd: Island, links to 3 bridges, Ikoyi and Victoria Island	11.5	8
Herbert Macaulay Rd: Ebute Metta–Yaba, linked to Ikorodu Rd	6	8
Maryland–Ikeja–Airport	5	8
Iddo–Ijora–Iganmu: crosses Apapa Wharf Rd, linked to Badagry Expressway at Ijora	4.5	8
Obafemi Awolowo Way: Ikeja–Secretariat (Alausa)		8

Source: Adefolalu 1986.

Ring Road, around Lagos Island, required filling the MacGregor Canal in 1976. It is used mainly by people who want to bypass the Island on their way to and from other areas. The old streets on the Island are still choked with traffic.

Lekki Peninsula roads are planned to reach Epe, but so far have little traffic. The Apapa–Oworonshoki Expressway is the western and northern section of the outer ring road. It starts as the Tin Can Island Expressway, linking the two ports. Obafemi Awolowo Way is the main route to the Lagos State Secretariat; it can be reached from Airport Road, Ikorodu Road – or the Lagos–Ibadan Expressway through the Oworonshoki link. The Third Mainland Bridge will complete the outer circle of motorways, drawing through traffic off mainland streets (Ayeni 1981: 151).

The major problems of these roads are inadequate links to the rest of the network and no planning for pedestrians. Traffic frequently backs up waiting to enter non-express roads or negotiate flyovers. Expressways have few footbridges, often only one every 2 km, even when they run through crowded residential areas. It is much easier to run across the road, even if this requires leaping over a three foot barrier, rather than climbing up and down a footbridge. A six day count at two footbridges found that 2015 people used the footbridge and 9938 crossed the road at Adekunle Bus Stop in Ebute Metta (near a police station); at Sabo market in Yaba the figures were 2324 and 15 745 (Adefolalu 1986).

The number and size of motor parks and bus terminals run by local governments is increasing to cope with demand. The major ones are shown on Map 8. One of the oldest and largest is at Iddo (37 000 sq. metres). Shomolu has six to handle buses and lorries leaving for the north; the largest, at Ojota, can handle 2000 vehicles. These cater for public and private buses and taxis as well as lorries, and are a source of revenue to the council. Some motor parks are merely large, unserviced open spaces, very muddy during wet weather. Local councils are gradually providing facilities – tarring, adding fences, drains, water, toilets and market stalls – to improve conditions of those waiting for transportation. The plan to redevelop Yaba Bus Stop (a large open space with a modern Presbyterian church as its major landmark) was shelved when there was no nearby area which could replace this major transfer point for commuters. It is crowded throughout the day (Adefolalu 1981; 1986). The construction of official bus stops (a place to pull off the road and a small shelter) along major routes in recent years has been welcomed by passengers and drivers, since stopped buses obstruct traffic.

Although building regulations have long required that houses be well back from the road, major road developments through crowded areas often require demolishing buildings. For example, squatters, mechanics, fishermen and traders were ejected from the lagoon shore by the Dolphin Scheme and construction of the ferry jetty at Oworonshoki. Houses were pulled down without compensation to widen the Agege Motor Road; 10 000 people were displaced, though their houses had been built with government approval (Fapohunda and Lubdell 1978: 77, 87).

Indigenes are likely to get a more sympathetic hearing than 'strangers'. Alhaji Abubakar Abdullahi, a transport owner and cattle dealer in Agege, sued the government for damages when first his fence and later his house were demolished in 1986. He bought the land in 1975 and had building approval, but the land was wanted for a channelization project so his right of occupancy was revoked. He not only lost the case, but was told by the judge that his fence was a public nuisance and he should return to Kano: 'leave Lagos for Lagos people' (*West Africa* 1986: 1497).

Other carriers

Road transportation is supplemented by planes, trains and ferries. Murtala Muhammed Airport, operated by the Nigerian Airports Authority, is by far the country's busiest, for both international and domestic flights. In 1986, 1.1 million international passengers used this airport (85 per cent of the national total), as did 2.7 million domestic passengers (72 per cent of those using the three international airports). In a country the size of Nigeria, domestic flights are becoming increasingly important; several private airlines compete with Nigeria Airways for local traffic. A new N31 m domestic terminal was scheduled for completion in 1990 (*West Africa* 1987: 1936; 1988: 571).

Trains are also a federal responsibility. The main terminus for long distance trains continues to be at Iddo, where railway service began in 1896; the Apapa Wharf station is used mainly for freight traffic to and from the port. Though a tram line ran (at a financial loss) from 1902–13, commuter trains are a relatively new innovation. They run 14 and 22 km from Apapa and Iddo to Oshodi and Agege, from 4:30 am until 7:30 pm, with shorter hours and fewer trains at weekends. The early trains are popular with market women and school children, since the service is cheap and faster than buses. Although the *Master Plan* advised against it, a metroline was started under President Shagari. It was stopped by the Military Government in 1985 as far too expensive; N78 of the estimated N700 m cost had already been spent (Sada and Adefolalu 1975: 97–8; *West Africa* 1985: 235).

The Nigerian Port Authority, which handles international shipping, was discussed in Chapter 4. Ferries are run by the Inland Waterways division of the Federal Ministry of Transport and by the Lagos State Transport Corporation (LSTC). The first government ferry service, Marina–Apapa, began in 1956. In the early 1980s, two 800-passenger ferries made 16 trips each way daily, but the charge was so small that even with 10 000 passengers daily there was very little profit. Nevertheless, new ferry services have been inaugurated or planned. Three LSTC ferries operate from Mile 2 on the Lagos–Badagry Expressway (near Festac Town) to the Marina, taking an hour and carrying about 105 000 passengers per month in 1988; the charge is only 30 k. The operators complain of too much pushing/ shoving at the jetty to get on the ferry (Adefolalu 1981: 1986).

Planners

Six 75-seater ferries are on order, and jetties are being developed at Ebute Ero and Tarkwa Bay to help fishermen, at Oworonshoki for commuters and at the Federal Secretariat to provide a ferry link with Ebute Metta. Private ferries carry about 10 000 people daily across Five Cowrie Creek to and from the Falomo shopping centre, Ikoyi, Victoria Island, Maroko and the Creek Hospital (LSMI 1988: 115–7).

Users

The mainly unplanned growth of Lagos and the housing shortage make commuting across the city essential for a large proportion of residents. Often the husband goes in one direction, the wife in another and the children to schools in other areas. While the majority of workplaces are on the Island or in Apapa, Ebute Metta, Ilupeju or Ikeja, the low income population is concentrated in places such as Agege, Ajegunle, Mushin and Shomolu. Only in Apapa, Lagos Island and Victoria Island are the majority of residents working locally, and thousands of commuters also pour into these areas. Residents of Agege in particular face long journeys to reach jobs in Alausa, Mushin or further afield. Direct transportation is often unavailable unless one can afford a taxi; a transfer at Ikeja, Mushin, Yaba or Ebute Metta adds to the time needed for the trip. The average resident spends 2.4–3.2 hours daily travelling (Fapohunda and Lubdell 1978: 69; Ayeni 1981: 142; Banjo and Brown 1981).

Plate 8.2 Tinubu Square traffic jam, LSDC and *molue* buses
Source: Lagos State Ministry of Information and Culture

178

Plate 8.3 Dual carriageway and pedestrians
Source: Lagos State Ministry of Information and Culture

Roads in Lagos also suffer from mixed use. Cars, motorcycles and buses in motion compete with handcarts and cattle, moving much more slowly; parked and sometimes double-parked cars; and pedestrians, traders and beggars. The four major types of mass transportation – buses, *molue* (small buses), *danfo* (minibuses) and taxis – compete along major roads. People walk in the streets because walkways are full of traders and parked vehicles or are non-existent, because they cannot afford the fare or cannot find a taxi, and because walking is often faster than riding.

Plate 8.2 shows traffic congestion around Tinubu Square, with a *molue* followed by LSTC buses (bottom left), cars and buses coming out of Bamgose Street (left of the church) and heading into Broad Street (right) and Tinubu Street (centre). Parking is provided by Development House (top right). One corner has a Brazilian house in poor condition (far left). Plate 8.3 shows a jammed dual carriageway, with taxis and *molue* collecting passengers (left) and pedestrians walking through stalled traffic (right). The barriers are high enough to stop people crossing the street, but there is no footbridge. Note the wide variety of housing along this mainland street.

A field survey of three major streets on the Island (Marina, Broad Street and Nnamdi Azikiwe Street) found an average of 6–7500 vehicles and 10–15 000 pedestrians per hour; in each case Broad Street carried the most and Nnamdi Azikiwe Street (leading to Carter Bridge) the least. Parking along these streets (especially in front of the Central Mosque) may bring this traffic down to one or two lanes. Off the Island, the major crossroads at Oju

Planners

Elegba (Surulere) catered for 6000 vehicles and 10 000 pedestrians per hour. In more peripheral areas, truck pushers and cattle can slow traffic to a walking pace, but unmade roads can make it unsafe to go much faster.

In 1977, the government introduced a system whereby before 6 pm cars with licence plates starting with odd numbers can only use city streets on Monday, Wednesday and Friday and those with even numbers on Tuesday and Thursday. Government and diplomatic vehicles and taxis are exempt. Many elite families bought more cars to beat the system and taxis have gained business, but on the whole it has been enforced (violators are fined on the spot) and effective in cutting down traffic. Some Asian cities have considered emulating Lagos.

Cars make up at least 80 per cent of the traffic on the Island and up to 70 per cent on the mainland (*danfos* are prohibited on Lagos Island and *molue* are restricted). Only a few firms and ministries provide parking for staff. The oldest carpark in Lagos, at Martins Street, often holds nearly twice its official capacity. Six surface carparks on reclaimed land along the Marina hold 5000 cars; some spaces are saved for government officials. The charge of 50k is not enough to deter drivers, so it is difficult to find an empty space. A park and ride scheme was introduced in 1978, accommodating 600 cars at the National Theatre, but deterioration of the air-conditioned buses led to the service becoming known as 'park and roast'. Illegal parking is much more convenient, and unlikely to be penalized (Adefolalu 1986).

Buses and taxis

Mass transportation is a complex mix of public and private provision – dirty, crowded and dangerous, but seldom dull. In recent years, commuters have faced a large-scale decline in services. The estimated 50 000 commercial vehicles in Lagos in 1982 were down to 20 000 by 1989; losses were mainly due to high operating costs and the unavailability of spare parts. Nevertheless, the contribution of buses and taxis to traffic congestion is still considerable (*West Africa* 1989: 917).

There were several short-lived bus services in the early part of the century. The largest and most successful was run from 1928 to 1958 by a Lebanese firm, J. and A. Zarpas. The Lagos City Council bought it in order to establish a municipal monopoly, but this was impossible because lack of resources and inefficiency made it easy for other services to compete. However, the Lagos City Transport Service did make a profit until it was taken over by the State (LSTC) in 1974; it has largely operated at a loss since then. This is partly due to overmanning of a public company; the LSTC averages over 12 employees per bus.

The LSTC covers the whole state, though most of its buses operate on eight routes in the city. They run from 6 am until 11 pm; low volume and the danger of armed robbery makes it uneconomic to operate later. The 100-passenger buses are slow and usually overcrowded; at least a third of

Table 8.2 Mass Transportation, 1985

Vehicle	Estimate
LSTC buses	73
Other (large bus)	1850
Molue/bolekaja (small bus)	5345
Danfo (minibus)	19 498
Taxi	30 671
Car hire	6498

Source: Central Licensing Authority.

their time is spent at bus stops. Because so many are off the road (down from 245 in 1980 to 73 in 1984), the service averaged only 146 000 passengers per day. In 1989 the state provided N23 m to buy new buses and refurbish old ones, but maintenance continues to be a problem. Plans to buy 100–150 buses every year and ban private buses from many routes seem likely to falter on financing (Sada and Adefolalu 1975: 99–100; *West Africa* 1989: 917).

Most mass transportation is provided by private owners. Transporting is a profitable, competitive and hazardous business. Many private buses and taxis are in as poor mechanical condition as LSTC buses and have the same problems with spare parts, but operators do anything necessary to keep their vehicles on the road, since they have no government subsidy to rely on. The major skill required of an owner is in choosing and controlling the drivers who rent his expensive vehicles; a large bus which costs 100 times its weekly income can be destroyed in a minute of inattention, with loss of life as an additional hazard. Drivers pay the daily rent in advance; any surplus after rent and petrol belongs to the driver. This encourages speeding between stops so that so that he can pick up as many customers as possible, changing of routes to ensure maximum capacity, overcharging passengers at peak periods and less than optimal care of the vehicle in heavy Lagos traffic. Clutches, gear boxes and engines are especially at risk. The LSTC tried contracting their buses, but were unable to maintain the necessary control (Peace 1988).

The owner's or manager's check on the vehicle at the end of the day exercises some restraint on drivers, but more important is the ability to choose among applicants. Most drivers work only a few days each week, and a careless driver will not find anyone willing to give him a chance. Experienced drivers with good records, on the other hand, become clients who are helped with loans and accommodation, perhaps even to marry and buy a vehicle.

The LSTC had only 73 buses on the road in 1985; other numbers in Table 8.2 are estimates based on vehicle registration between 1980 and 1985. Quite a few of these did not last more than a year or two, but such is the ingenuity of local mechanics that a majority were probably still on the road in 1985. Full-size buses are operated by four major private operators: Benson Transport Service, Oshinowo Transport Service, Union of Nigerian Transporters and Elias Transport Service. All of these have been in business for many years and some provide long-distance bus transportation as well. Other large buses are operated by major firms for their staff. Most of the next category were *molue*. These and *danfos* may be individually owned or part of fleets. *Molue* are supposed to carry a maximum of 40 passengers, but often have as many as 60. *Bolekeja* are long-distance lorries which also carry passengers. They are not supposed to operate in the city, but some cannot resist the lucrative demand.

Danfos are 14–20 seater Volkswagen minibuses which stop more often than their larger competitors and run more varied routes, though they also cover major roads. They seldom turn away a passenger if there is breathing space. These are the cheapest to buy and most likely to be owned by their drivers. They fill quickly and thus can do more trips per day than buses. A *danfo* driver paid his owner N30–50 per day in 1986; the rest of his earnings were his own, to be saved for basic needs and buying his own vehicle. Unlicensed commercial vehicles (*kabukabu*) are illegal, but operate wherever there is an unfilled demand – especially at night and off regular routes. In the late 1970s, there were more unlicensed than licensed providers of mass transportation, but regular checking of papers has cut this down somewhat. However, civil servants, soldiers and even policemen may drive *kabukabu* for extra income. Long distance travellers also pay for rides in private vehicles (Adefolalu 1981: 114; *West Africa* 1989: 139; *Lagos Horizon* 22 August 1989).

Private carriers are painted yellow, as are taxis; they tend to follow the same routes and stop at LSTC bus stops. The same fares are charged on LSTC and private buses, *molue* and *danfos* – 50k except for very short runs, which cost 30k. Change is a major problem, with the collector moving up and down trying to find someone with coins or 50k notes that can be repaid to other customers. Though government approval is supposedly required, fares may rise with inflation, congestion or industrial action.

Taxis are ubiquitous unless you want one, and the private hire business is growing rapidly. Taxi drivers (licensed and unlicensed) prefer major roads, taking as many passengers as they can from one busy location to another. People stand along the street shouting out where they want to go; taxis only stop if the journey is along their usual route or seems profitable. Although official rates are glued to the window, meters are not used and rates for longer distances are subject to negotiation. There are standard rates for short trips (e.g., N1 if the taxi is full). Requests for a journey off the main road, (e.g., to a local council office), to a traffic blackspot (the Island or Agege) or a long journey (the Alausa Secretariat) meet with stiff resistance or a charge of N20. It is cheaper to rent the taxi for the day, at N20–25 per hour, to be sure that the driver is waiting and will go wherever you want. (These are 1989 figures, subject to inflation.)

Many taxi drivers are self employed; their livelihood depends on keeping one vehicle on the road and carrying as many passengers as possible. Rapid inflation and a severe shortage of spare parts has made it very difficult to stay in business. In 1989, the government imported 200 Skoda taxis, 1000 tyres and spare parts for the Lagos State Taxi Drivers Association, but this will cater for only a small part of the demand. Drivers must deposit N5000 for a new taxi (*Lagos Horizon*, 29 August 1989).

Case Studies

1. Alhaji Gbadamosi is a composite of the transporters studied by Peace (1979b; 1988) in Agege in 1971–2. Although conditions have changed somewhat, not least because of closer government regulation, transporting still provides an opportunity for migrants without much formal education or financial support to achieve economic success. Alhaji Gbadamosi arrived in Lagos from Ijebu about 1935, after a few years of primary education. He served as a conductor (collecting fares, calling the destination, washing the vehicle, running errands) until he passed his driving test. (The licence charge of N1 was supplemented by a N50 bribe, paid with a loan from an owner.) After working up from casual to regular driver, he saved enough money, with a gift from his sister, to share the purchase of a second-hand produce lorry with a close kinsman. They transported food and passengers between the city and the hinterland; smuggling was a lucrative sideline.

He was lucky; the vehicle was not lost in an accident or otherwise put off the road, leaving him again in the position of client driver. It took seven years to save enough for a bus, but with careful management his fleet eventually expanded to several vehicles, which required additional drivers. Each bus could earn about 20 times a craftsman's weekly income, minus overheads, if it could be kept on the road. Many of his fellow drivers from the early days failed to become owners; these tended to move into trading, factory employment or vehicle repair. Some of the mechanics worked for Alhaji Gbadamosi.

Success is often measured in political activities. Alhaji Gbadamosi was active in the Nigerian Motor Transport Owners' Union, through which he maintained contacts with other owners and discussed problems such as official limits on fares, bribes demanded by the police and where to obtain spare parts. He built a large house in his village, inviting the state governor and important ex-politicians and civil servants as well as business colleagues and fellow villagers to the formal opening. This elaborate and expensive event served to demonstrate his success, but also reinforced his position as a kinsman and patron to the less fortunate. The latter may dislike his ruthlessness, but he is admired for his attainment, expertise and what he contributes to the advancement of others. Eventually, he found the anxieties of the transporting business onerous, and built a three-storey house in Agege whose rents would ensure a comfortable old age. Most of his vehicles were sold off to drivers aspiring to follow his example.

2. 'Baba' (old man) has been driving since 1956, when the Queen visited Nigeria. His taxi licence number is painted on the door. The inside and outside of his taxi demonstrate its age and its owners's lack of 'progress'. The vehicle is started by manipulating two wires; the knob must be shaken to start the windscreen wipers, but they are adequate for heavy rain. The seats are comfortable and reasonably well covered, but there is no lining along the frame or doors. The driver's door is held by a latch; other door and window handles are gone and doors must be opened from the outside. The hood needs periodic slamming, on both sides. The engine died in heavy traffic at the bottom of Herbert Macaulay Road, where the traffic from the Third Mainland Bridge joins vehicles coming up from the Carter Bridge. A pedestrian helped to push briefly; then (lacking other volunteers), the traffic police pushed us through the junction. Since the car still wouldn't start, Baba pushed it across several lanes of traffic in both directions into the corner petrol station. Another push there was equally unsuccessful, so Baba got a stick from the boot to hold up the bonnet and began work.

He is a patient and generally conservative driver, able to go 50 kph on expressways and wait in dense traffic for the right moment to move. Petrol is bought in relatively small quantities, as money is available; he may need to borrow from the customer. Stations offering cheaper petrol for commercial vehicles are preferred, but he sometimes uses stations for private drivers because they are more convenient. He carries a wad of papers to be produced at periodic police checks.

Baba had little education; he can cope with directions in English, but cannot read maps. He has five children. Three sons who completed School Certificate could not find wage jobs and are now a mechanic, a panel beater and an auto electrician – all useful to their father, though his taxi is almost beyond their help. The last two are in secondary and primary school.

3. Clarence has only been driving a taxi for two years. His father borrowed money to send him to the UK after his O levels. After ten years in the UK, he returned to Nigeria in 1979 with one A level and a certificate in business from part-time study at North London College. After nine months of unemployment following redundancy in 1987, he reluctantly agreed with his wife, family and friends that he should use one of the two cars he had brought back as a taxi. (The other was stolen on the Lagos–Ibadan Expressway; he is grateful to the robbers for his life.) He felt ashamed to descend to taxi driving, but had to support his family. He painted the car yellow and paid N600 for a taxi licence. Since he grew up in Akoka, near the University, he concentrates on the University–Yaba Bus Stop link. He works 7 am–5 pm Monday to Friday, with an hour for lunch, and 7–12 on Saturdays.

Since he lacks the contacts and qualifications necessary to get a managerial post, he is likely to be stuck with taxi driving. A man who sees himself with less status than he deserves, Clarence keeps to himself. Any improvement in his position will be very difficult. Though he takes good care of it, his vehicle is disintegrating through the rigours of Lagos traffic. Spare parts are very expensive. He had not heard about the government's importation of spare parts for the Taxi Drivers' Association and he will probably have no access to them. When an army vehicle bumped his taxi, he was very upset and refused to move on though he was tying up traffic at a Broad Street crossing. The traffic policeman finally convinced the soldier to get out and look at the damage, but it was clear that no payment would be made.

Service providers

Electricity, telephones, water and sanitary services are all essential for urban life today, but get less attention than transportation from Lagos planners. They were all dealt with in the *Master Plan*, but economic constraints have made the fulfilment of plans very difficult. The inadequacy of these services is assumed in the expression 'That's Lagos!'; it makes life difficult for industry, commerce and private individuals.

NEPA and NITEL

The National Electric Power Authority is universally known as NEPA, which has become a term of derogation. The inadequate supply of power and frequent blackouts are widely blamed on inefficient management. The lights can go off several times in 24 hours, or be off for days. Lagos first got electricity in 1898 and uses about a third of the national supply, down from two-fifths in 1977. New estates wait months or years for a supply and firms which require electricity to operate must buy their own generators. Poor repair of NEPA generators, unmotivated staff and inefficient debt collection add to its problems; workers responsible for a major blackout in 1988 were jailed (*Master Plan* 1980: 540; *West Africa* 1989: 767).

Table 8.3 Electricity consumption in Lagos State, by consumer, 1970–87

	1970	1978	1987
Consumers			
Residential	69 212	175 858	318 808
Commercial	12 969	26 772	44 846
Industrial	347	541	1805
Total	82 537	203 171	365 459
mKWH consumed			
Residential	281.1	680.9	3247.9
Commercial	124.3	385.5	240.3
Industrial	192.2	532.4	725.8
Total	597.7	1598.7	4213.9

Source: LSG 1987: 75.

However, NEPA also faces resource problems not of its own making. The demand is growing faster than new generators can be brought on stream. Sales rose 16 per cent per year from the 1950s to the 1970s. Table 8.3 shows that consumption in 1987 was seven times that of 1970, with 4.4 times as many consumers; the number of industrial customers went up more than five times. There was also more use by residential consumers – eleven times as much electricity in 1987 as in 1970 – though commercial and industrial consumers used less on average because many rely partly on their own generators. An attempt to require users to pay NEPA for all the electricity generated privately was impossible to enforce.

Generation from the Kainji Dam, the cheapest source of electricity in the country, was hit by inadequate rainfall in the 1980s. The use of oil for generation for the Lagos market has been far more expensive. The conversion of six thermal generators at Egbin, near Lagos, to gas (brought by pipeline from Bendel State) will reduce the cost considerably. However, though this improvement was supposed to be completed in 1985, it was only finished in 1989. At full capacity, the Egbin plant will supply 40 per cent of Nigeria's peak demand for electricity. But delivery continues to be a problem after leaving the plant. Thieves periodically steal cables, street lights and other equipment. A fire at Badiya in 1989, started by a candle, did N5 m damage to NEPA poles and transformers and left several parts of the city in darkness (*West Africa* 1986: 2301; 1989: 121, 244, 767).

Service is gradually getting better, but more through catching up than planning. To improve services, it is essential that charges reflect costs. Commercial electricity charges went up sixfold in 1989, from N7000 to N42 000 for a five-storey building. This is shared equally by all firms in the building, regardless of use. The provision of meters would be a far more equitable way to charge and would cut down use, but NEPA would have to find honest meter readers.

There is a saying that an African country's telephone system is inversely related to its level of development. The more developed countries have had telephones for a longer time and cables tend to be worn; newer services are likely to be in better condition. Nigerian Telephone's service began in 1897 and NITEL fulfils the stereotype in providing poor service. Thieves regularly steal telephone cables for the copper, but corporation inefficiency and a shortage of skilled labour causes far more problems. A large proportion of the country's telephones are still in Lagos, but it can be faster to visit a contact than try to get through on the phone. The country is now divided into several sectors, and contact between sectors is even more difficult than local calls; paradoxically, international calls are relatively simple – unless they must be passed on by the Lagos exchange.

It takes a long wait to get a telephone installed or mended, and continuous service is not to be expected. Many telephones only provide half service: the office of a top state civil servant could only receive calls, whereas the University Guest House could handle outgoing but not incoming calls. Completing a call during business hours is difficult even if both phones are working because demand is more than the lines can handle. Phones can be arbitrarily cut off for nonpayment of bills which have actually been paid and repairmen, when they finally arrive, often refuse to fix the instrument without a bribe. A few pay telephones have been installed on the streets and more are wanted, but it is difficult to keep them in order. Realistic resourcing for explosive growth is badly needed.

Water

The Iju Waterworks were commissioned in 1915, with a maximum of 650 000 gallons. They were extended in the 1940s and additional water was brought from the Ogun River in 1954, raising the capacity to 24 mg/d (million gallons per day). The system was expanded further in the 1970s and 1980s, but is still grossly inadequate. Consumption was 49 215 ml in 1984 and 94 495.82 ml in 1988, 135 ml/d (million litres per day) and 259 ml/d respectively. Two-thirds of this is produced by the Iju Water Works. The *Master Plan* estimated that demand for water would be 939 ml/d by 1985 and 1547 by 2000, including some increase in per capita use. It seems unlikely that this demand can be met. Though the designed capacity is 354 ml/d average daily production (204.5 of which is at Iju), it was as low as 232 ml/d in February 1989 and only topped 277 ml/d in March (Fapohunda and Lubdell 1978: 79; *Master Plan* 1980: 536; LSG 1987: 83–4; LSG 1989c: 53–5).

Many people lack access to a piped water supply (see Table 7.1), and must get water from streams, wells or the lagoon – all frequently polluted. Only 3 per cent of metropolitan Lagos had water-borne sewerage in 1970; 7 per cent had septic tanks and the rest had bucket latrines or nothing. Where nightsoil was collected, it was often dumped directly into the lagoon. There were an estimated 5000 wells in 1972. By 1986, 47 per cent of the population had access to piped water but only 19 per cent had water-borne sanitation (Ola Daniel 1975: 161; Fapohunda and Lubdell 1978: 80; FOS 1986).

Even piped water may not be safe. Typhoid and cholera viruses and dangerous levels of mercury were found in the LUTH water supply in 1979, but no action was taken. There were over 80 deaths from typhoid in Lagos in mid 1989; over 1000 people were treated in hospital. The outbreak was blamed on cracked and corroded water pipes too near to sewage. Wells and boreholes are also sited too close to soak-away and refuse pits (*West Africa* 1989: 1574).

People who lack access to piped water or wells must buy it. Hawkers and owners of water tanks in low income communities such as Ajegunle and Agege do a good business selling water by the tin or bucket (25k in 1980). This water may already be contaminated, or becomes unsafe while in storage. Widespread diarrhoea and gastroenteritis are the inevitable result of impure water supplies.

Paradoxically, sometimes there is too much water. The sand ridges on which Lagos is built often provide poor drainage, and swampy areas encourage malaria. Drainage ditches have been dug off and on since 1930, but buildings often block drains, which increases flooding in the area. Constructing too many buildings on reclaimed land encourages subsidence; buildings crack and wastes pollute the water table. Given the shortage of land, some houses are built in swamps – as at Ajegunle and Maroko. Houses with cement block foundations have a better chance of survival than those built on wooden poles, but in either case the environment is unhealthy. There is no safe way of installing sanitary facilities for the inhabitants.

Environmental sanitation

Lagos won a place in the 1983 *Guinness Book of Records* as the dirtiest city in the world. While conditions have improved somewhat since then (people killed in traffic accidents are usually picked up within 24 hours and refuse is collected more regularly), Lagos continues to suffer from water, air and noise pollution. Water pollution comes from the dumping of faeces, industrial refuse and oil into the lagoons and canals and from digging latrines too close to wells. Port facilities do not cater for the clearing of tanks on shore, so ships discharge into the harbour or coastal waters; fish stocks along the coast are declining as a result. The shortage of facilities for rubbish collection also depreciates the environment. Rubbish is thrown into the streets or lagoons, especially in crowded, low income areas with no collection service, making walking difficult and aiding in the spread of disease (Inyang 1978).

Air pollution comes from industrial wastes discharged directly from factory chimneys, domestic and industrial fires and traffic fumes. The sea helps to diffuse these, but the prevalence of light winds and frequent calms increases the concentration of pollutants over the city. Paved surfaces re-radiate heat, raising temperatures.

Noise pollution is also high. While horns are used less continuously than twenty years ago, traffic still contributes considerable noise. Radios and record players blast away, both from homes and shops. Muezzins call the Muslim faithful to prayer with strong electronic assistance. Even casual greetings on the street can seem unnecessarily loud to strangers used to a quieter environment.

One response has been Environmental Sanitation Day. On the last Saturday of every month, residents must stay home between 7 and 10 am and clear up their environment. No one is allowed on the streets except on cleaning duty. Piles of refuse are left at the side of the road to be collected by the Waste Disposal Board. This programme grew out of the War Against Indiscipline launched by the Military Government in 1984. In 1985, civil servants were required to spend Saturdays cleaning the streets and mobile courts were set up in a War against Filth. The emphasis was on getting rid of street traders as producers of rubbish; this was discussed in Chapter 4. Regular publicity on the problem does help, and Lagos now appears cleaner than it used to, though some people merely rest or clean their own room at the appointed time.

Sunday mornings may also be used to clear accumulated rubbish from the gutter in front of one's house, though there is still a problem of what to do with the result. In the absence of rubbish bins, litter is dropped freely by a public that does not take environmental cleanliness very seriously. Sanitary inspectors, a feature of the colonial era, were brought back in 1984 to check houses for mosquito control, water supply and sewage disposal and to inspect markets, motor parks and public toilets for conformity to hygiene regulations and illegal structures. They are supposed to educate as well as fine those they meet in the course of duty, but have a reputation as bribe-takers which is hard to overcome. They are in a position of power, enforcing regulations which many do not consider necessary or reasonable.

The Waste Disposal Board (WDB) started collecting in 1978, with 170 000 metric tonnes. The amount produced has increased rapidly; it collected 2.4 m metric tonnes of waste in 1988, which was estimated to be only 40 per cent of the volume generated. The Ministry of Environment and Physical Planning estimates that only 3 per cent of Lagos industrial firms have made arrangements for handling their own wastes. Many just dump them wherever it is convenient. Waste was collected by local governments for a period, then recentralized. A state-wide service at least takes some of the pressure off local councils, whose efficiency in dealing with rubbish varied considerably. However, the large fee they must pay to the WDB is more than they would pay for doing the work themselves.

Several 'refuse houses' were constructed, but they have not been successful; they are not convenient for dumping and are not emptied often enough. Collection of domestic rubbish from numerous tips by lorry has generally been more efficient. More vehicles have been purchased, but the problem is keeping collecting lorries on the road. A 1986 investigation found unmaintained tip sites, abandoned vehicles and other problems with equipment and personnel (*Business Times* 21 August 1989).

The results of dumping rubbish to create new land at Akoka, Ajegunle and Ijora have been mixed. The Akoka project has been successful, creating a playing field at St Finbar's School on what was formerly a sandy swamp. Filling the Achakpo Street swamp at Ajegunle (see Plate 8.4) has gone on for at least fifteen years, at considerable cost to the nostrils of neighbouring residents, without releasing land for settlement. The dumping at Ijora is far more problematic, since the lagoon is coastal; the refuse does not settle and becomes a danger to the poor living along the coast.

Plate 8.4 Dumping rubbish to fill swamps, Ajegunle

Summary

On the whole, planning in Lagos is done by politicians, not planners. Planning for infrastructure, industry and housing are often done by separate bodies. That the result makes the city an inefficient and uncomfortable place to live should hardly be surprising. While part of the problem lies with inadequate management by insufficiently trained specialists and part is due to inadequate finance to carry out plans, this is not the whole answer. Some blame must be put on politicians who are busy feathering their own nests and civil servants who are unable to see the whole picture. Is the city necessarily relegated to short-term crisis management, or are there possibilities of long-term plans being fulfilled?

One's perspective tends to depend on what has happened recently to encourage optimism or pessimism. There can be no doubt that the size and complexity of the problems make solutions difficult, especially in times of continued financial stringency. The removal of national government from the city may well help, in that an increasingly efficient local and state government apparatus can operate with less interference from national politicians or the military. However, there is so much money to be made in Lagos that interest groups will continue to compete to control it, and money spent to house some people and speed them to their work cannot be spent on others.

As the city grows northward, some coordinated planning with Ogun State is necessary. The *Master Plan* (1980) recommended a Greater Metropolitan

Lagos Planning Authority. Transportation and industrial development are especially important here, but water and electricity supplies would also profit from greater coordination. However, decentralized services by local governments responsible to their constituents may be more efficient than centralized bureaucracies.

Local responsibility could also help to focus both civil servants and residents' minds on honest and adequate revenue collection and expenditure, which is essential if the city's problems are to be solved. Plans for Lagos, as for other cities in Nigeria, have tended to be out of date before they were produced, and commitment to fulfilling the directions of outsiders has always been weak. Response to demand may be a better solution, even if it results in piecemeal action rather than overall strategy. However, the costs will continue to be well beyond what local councils can afford, and those paying the bills will expect to make the major decisions.

9
Conclusion: whose city?

IT IS A HOT PULSATING SPOT
where life is faster than a race
Workers beat the starting guns –
clock alarms, imam's Allahu akbar
before they're jolted out of bed.

Early morning goodluck requests –
Corps and wardens praying for culprits
Workers seeking promotions due
motorists wishing free traffic
Poor peddlers looking for go-slow.

. . .

When the daily race is over
workers and labour let out steam.
Zealous fans of action films
jam Indian movie houses in town
chanting with the fiery choice actors.

Young Amuluduns in see-through
sugar mommies, sugar daddies
pockets stuffed with banknotes
steal the show, shaking and spraying
under the spell of powerful afrobeats.
                    M.A. Johnson (1982: 40–1)

This is a convenient time for summing up what Lagos has become, what the future is likely to hold and what it means to the people who live there. Growth has slowed somewhat and its problems seem to be slightly more under control. Its image is of a poor city, with the energy to become a great city in its own rather than in EuroAmerican terms – a city which takes what it needs from other countries but remains culturally African. The characters of Ekwensi's *People of the city* (1963) are still living there; though now there are also many people in new roles, the same aspirations for success and limitations of their environment shape their lives.

Looking back

In the 400-plus years since its foundation, the 130 years since the beginning of the colonial period and the 30 years since independence, Lagos has become something none of the founders of these eras foresaw. The village or small town is now a primate city, a metropolis which provides a hard life for many but opportunities which continue to draw ambitious men and women from all over Nigeria and beyond. Yet it retains its Yoruba roots: chieftaincy, masquerades, extended families and petty trading. Other groups have brought other ways of doing things, some of which have become part of the Lagos way of life. The heterogeneity of the metropolis draws on the rural roots of much of the population, but the colonial input into urban structure, law and government and multinational imperatives in employment have also been syncretized by local people into something which suits their needs and goals. Large numbers of people, in all walks of life, continue to use local languages and wear local dress, though they switch to European language and clothing when the occasion warrants it.

Housing the national government has been beneficial to Lagos, though more to the educated, affluent and politically active residents than to the mass of the population. Colonial centralization brought it advantages over the rest of the country, and local response to the limitations of colonialism played a considerable role in the drive for independence. Local government structures have changed many times over the years, eventually returning to indigenous control. Local people encourage the perception that migrants should look to their home areas and leave urban affairs to their hosts. However, as more local councils are set up, sometimes in areas which have few indigenes, owners of land and houses who have decided to stay in the city exercise increasing influence. Market women and tenants seek patronage and occasionally mobilize to support their interests, but on the whole they concentrate on survival and leave politics to relatively affluent men.

Baker (1974: Ch. 10) summarized Lagos politics in the late 1960s as indigenized and communalized. The same can be said for the city in the 1990s, though in a wider sense. There are many interest groups in Lagos, but leadership cannot be summarized in terms of pluralism on the American pattern or class stratification; leaders tend to be brokers, patrons and family elders all in one. Who they are leading and in which direction depends on the situation. Communal and economic interests at various levels continue to be an important ingredient in decision making, though the city's increasing size and heterogeneity make it more difficult to maintain the expected personal ties.

The indigenes still have an important role, especially in state politics, but the city is now too large for them to control. The Yoruba also have an important communal role, but structures are too complex for them to have total control either, and competition between Yoruba subgroups is an important factor in some decisions. One must concentrate not just on the leaders involved in particular situations, but also who the followers are. Allies today may be on opposite sides tomorrow. Communal identities continue to be reflected in language use and in social relationships, even though much of the population can now communicate in English. Many newcomers make no attempt to learn Yoruba.

The flexible and infinitely divisible communalism makes it difficult to predict what will happen next, except that face-to-face groups will always concentrate more on their own than on the public good. This is important for most aspects of urban life, since it can never be assumed that residents will cooperate with plans or obey laws, even when, in principle, they approve of them. They therefore continue to trade and park at their convenience, bribe policemen, avoid taxes, publish libels, build houses without permission and generally get on with business as if the wider community does not matter, while expecting government to provide efficient services at minimum cost. At the same time, they prefer to use the system rather than trying to overthrow it. Recent riots may indicate changing attitudes, at least on the part of the unemployed young, but the belief in individual success continues to emphasize joining rather than subverting those in control.

Lagos is a commercial rather than an industrial city, in spite of its large share of Nigeria's industrial production. Its role as a port was vital to its growth, and it is commerce which gives Lagos its dynamism. Entrepreneurship, large or small, is seen as the prime opportunity for getting ahead – the main reason for coming to Lagos in the first place. Even the rare communists are often businessmen, and politics and trade unions tend to be run like a business, for private profit. Large numbers of people not officially in business have something going on the side, and other supposedly settled wage employees are looking for a gap in the market which they can exploit. This shapes their attitudes toward their jobs and the city (Waterman 1976). One reason for federal civil servants not wanting to move to Abuja is that they and their wives would lose their business sidelines. Government as a shareholder is acceptable, but wholesale nationalization would be strongly resisted. Opportunity is far more important than equality in this highly hierarchical society.

Universal primary education is a reality, and secondary education is well developed, producing one of the best-educated populations in Africa. Large numbers of newspapers and periodicals keep people informed of their political and economic rights and responsibilities. Publications and performances help to keep local languages alive. Radio and television are used primarily for entertainment, but they also inform people who are usually fully occupied with their own affairs about the rest of the country and the wider world.

The gap between rich and poor may be widening in economic and spatial terms, but there are increasing numbers of middle income families whose aspirations must be taken into account. Social relations readily cross income boundaries because power is based on personal relationships, but, as the city grows, a tendency to segregate rich from poor could make it more difficult to maintain these links. This has always been overwhelmingly a city of the poor, but a poor whose standard of living has improved over time. The rising cost of living hurts people at all levels, helping to unite them against government attempts at structural readjustment. Private education and health care, available to those who can pay, are recognized as a source of relative advantage or deprivation, but they are widely used and approved of because they provide jobs and choices, opportunities for reaching goals.

Religion is firmly based in local culture, as important to the successful as to the marginal. Adherence to Christianity or Islam, in their mainstream or separatist manifestations, provides a measure of security and also a source of support in times of trouble. Traditional religion is less visible because it is based on homes rather than special buildings, but it remains important in the lives of residents. Religion affects attitudes towards medical care and education; it structures social relationships, use of leisure time and even business ties. Small sects provide face-to-face relations in a situation of equality, which deflects attention from the problems of everyday life and the leaders who may be responsible for them. So far, politically active religious fundamentalism has not been notable in Lagos, where Christians and Muslims tend to cooperate for their mutual benefit. Shared primary and secondary education probably contributes to this.

Commercial recreation in Lagos is similar to what is found in most large cities – sports, cinemas, clubs, bars, restaurants – but most people spend their spare time in casual conversation with family and friends. This is partly due to poverty and the energy needed for travel and work in a hot, humid climate, but it is also the legacy of an oral culture, where people prefer personal over impersonal contacts and value extended family ties. Isolated nuclear families are rare; most migrants maintain contacts with the family at home, whether or not they have relatives in Lagos.

Crime is the desperate underside of Lagos society, a threat to all, every day. It is interwoven with problems of corruption, anarchy and opportunism. Societal values applaud the wealthy, regardless of how the wealth was obtained, insofar as some of it is redistributed to needy relatives and clients. There is a strong feeling that the 'cake' should be shared, by helping oneself to the detriment of a stranger if necessary. Violence readily erupts when people feel strongly or are under too much pressure trying to survive in what many feel is a hostile place. One sometimes gets the impression of living in an armed camp, though gun ownership is limited compared to American cities.

There are still a few houses of bamboo or mud in areas which were once villages, but most houses are built of concrete blocks. With few exceptions, housing is utilitarian, designed to fit in as many tenants or family members as possible, at the least possible cost and using as much of the plot as the law allows. Gardens are a colonial import which only a few of the elite take seriously. While some estates were laid out all at once on a common pattern (mostly by the government), most residential areas were built up piecemeal over a long period, by private owners of widely varying resources. Therefore, most streets have a mixture of buildings, in size, height, age and condition. Since most old houses are owned by families which have no intention of selling, redevelopment is rarely attempted; the Slum Clearance Scheme for Inner Lagos was a salutary warning. Speculation in land and housing has increased as profits have grown, but it is likely to be greatest in areas being developed for the elites.

The provision of services – roads, water, electricity, telephones, sanitary services – has clearly improved in recent years, making Lagos a more pleasant place to live except in the newest suburbs. New roads, in particular, make it possible to move around the metropolis at a speed unhoped for twenty years ago. However, the environment is still a major problem. It is manifestly dangerous to the elderly who can no longer race across busy streets and the young who drink polluted water or have no protection from malaria. It is a continual problem for people in low income neighbourhoods with shared toilets and unmade roads. It is dangerous in a different way for the rich behind their barred gates or driving their air-conditioned cars down lonely roads. There is still a long way to go to cure the endemic 'go-slows' and provide the level of services to which the public should have a right. Unfortunately, the days when Lagos could claim a lion's share of the country's development money are gone.

Lagos is clearly a primate city, but the classification of parasite sits less well; there is give as well as take. Lagos is dependent on what the rest of the country produces, especially on oil revenue, and the rest of the country is to some extent dependent on decision-making in Lagos, as on any capital. Lagos provides a focus for development which people feel free to join, and the competitive nature of Nigerian society means that other cities make notable contributions to their own hinterlands, develop new ideas which Lagosians may want to copy, and start industries which promote local development. For example, Ijebu Ode has a more 'modern' market than any in Lagos.

Much of the income produced in Lagos goes back through remissions to the migrants' home areas. The standard of living for the poor is better in Lagos than in many other cities, but not that much better considering local costs. At present levels of population growth, many young adults cannot remain down on the farm. It is hardly surprising that large numbers continue to head for Lagos. Nevertheless, the declining rate of migration to Lagos shows that people are aware of relative advantage, but are finding other towns where the social and psychological costs are lower. In 1990, Lagos is clearly a world city, a distinctively African city, a city of poor people who want more than they are getting.

Looking forward

What sort of city is Lagos likely to be in 2000? The 1980s can serve as a model, though a great deal depends on the price of oil and what sort of political stability Nigeria can achieve. By the year 2000, it is estimated that Lagos will have about 12 million people. It will need more houses, roads, jobs, schools and health facilities for this doubling in population (LSMI 1988: 188).

However, it may be comforting that this will represent a declining level of growth from the over 9 per cent per annum, 25 000 per month and 34 per hour which characteized the 1970s. The 1981 forecast for the metropolitan area in 2000 was between 13 and 16 million people, even if growth in the 1990s declined below 5 per cent. As it happened, recession meant that the 1990 population estimate was less than forecast and the 1990s seem likely to continue the trend. The government recognizes that it is impossible to stop the growth of Lagos, since it will retain economic primacy and is a state capital (LSG 1981: 1–8). While other state capitals are being promoted as growth centres, there is not enough money available to give these a real chance of competing with the opportunities in Lagos. Abuja may become another Brasilia – a civil service city where anyone who can manage it spends as little time as possible because the real action is in the economic capital.

The city's location and structure will continue to compound its problems, and a gradually increasing standard of living is important for political stability, whatever its effect on the environment. Modern roads can cut the costs of space and new industrial estates could make it possible for many people to work relatively near their homes. Therefore, a city of 12 million may not seem much larger to its residents than today's city if residential areas include markets and room for self employed craftsmen to carry on their businesses. If the government tries to legislate against small-scale commerce and industry in the name of planning, low incomes and unemployment could increase civil unrest.

It is estimated that the city needs 80 000 new houses per year, costing more than N1 billion, to provide 1.5 million housing units by 2000. Yet this would only provide one unit for each eight people. As the cost of housing rises faster than incomes and entrepreneurial earnings go into more profitable ventures than housing the poor, the high densities of low income areas are likely to increase. The extra six million people will arrive (as many by birth as by migration unless the fertility rate declines sharply), but the housing will not be built. The forecast drop in household size from 6.3 to 5.5 should help to alleviate crowding, but would require even more housing units. Lower fertility, encouraged by birth control programmes, the cost of education and economic insecurity, would contribute to smaller household size and lower housing demand (*Master Plan* 1980: 593; LSMI 1988: 188).

Infilling at high densities has already taken place in many areas, so much new housing will have to be further out; there is no prospect of low density areas being turned into high density areas. New towns will not have much effect; they can only be successful in attracting residents away from Lagos if they provide a wide range of employment and services, and Nigeria's record suggests that this will not happen. Rather, new areas such as Satellite Town and Lekki will house families which can afford cars to get to central jobs and schools. It will be much more difficult for the poor who find rooms in the northern suburbs – beyond the developed areas of Agege and Ikeja, toward Ikorodu and Ogun State as well as villages to the west. These will have to wait for paved roads, buses and urban services; even the provision of schools will depend on the strength of the economy. Lagos State's emphasis on rural development could be helpful insofar as new centres of population can attract attention, but being composed of strangers will be a disadvantage, since the programme is aimed at indigenes. Few villagers will complain about urban encroachment unless they lose control of their land, since tenants are usually more profitable than crops.

Some attempt will probably be made to improve traffic on Lagos Island, but more high-rise office buildings will increase the density of its working population. Further urban renewal will continue to be resisted, but upgrading houses could be acceptable if it avoids massive displacement of residents. The move to Abuja will not have much effect on Lagos, since federal civil servants who are willing to move (about 300 000, including families) can easily be replaced by new migrants (ECA 1980: 212). The older federal buildings, some going back to the early part of the century, will be replaced by larger and more efficient office blocks, by private capital if the government does not need the space. The construction of a ferry jetty at the Federal Secretariat is a useful indicator that it will be needed for government agencies remaining in Lagos.

The city will be more bureaucratically run, though to whose benefit is not clear. Insofar as there are more secure jobs and more efficient government, ordinary people should find life easier. But the personal ties which ease problems today may be harder to mobilize and the self employed may be increasingly harassed. There will be little money for social welfare, though the proportion of elderly people will rise. Crime seems unlikely to decline, since this too is a business and capital punishment has had no deterrent effect; increasing economic hardship and ownership of guns could make things much worse.

An important question is what will become of the recent tendency to riot – the fact that there are now far too many disappointed people, who feel that the system offers far less than they hoped, against whom the Structural Adjustment Plan seems to be biased. It does not take very many people to start the ball rolling, and the disappointed young in particular feel that they have little to lose. A larger city will not necessarily be more or less just, and an increasing number of jobs may still provide none for them. They will not blame it on international dependency (though the World Bank may come in for a few harsh words from the better educated), but on inefficient and corrupt local leadership, or lack of leadership. A central government in

Abuja may well seem less concerned for their welfare and thus more guilty than leaders who are visible on the streets from time to time.

The city is important not just for residents, but also for visitors. Even when it is no longer the national capital, it will have an allure, a reputation, as a place to be experienced. Some services cater for its hinterland as well as for residents. Visitors see only a small part of the city – the airport, Museum and Bar Beach if they are tourists; a bus terminus and Ajegunle, Shomolu or Mushin if they are visiting family members; perhaps Lagos Island in both cases. However small their experience of it, each will think, 'That's Lagos!'

Bibliography

Abiodun, J.O., 1974, Urban growth and problems in metropolitan Lagos, *Urban Studies* 11: 341–47

Adamolekun, L., Rowland, L., 1979, *The new local government system in Nigeria*, Heinemann Educational Books, Ibadan

Adefolalu, A.A., 1981, Intra-urban transport services in Lagos, 95–122, in D.A. Oyeleye (ed) *Spatial expansion and concomitant problems in the Lagos metropolitan area*. Occasional paper 1, Department of Geography, University of Lagos

Adefolalu, A.A., 1986, Transport facilities in Lagos, Department of Geography, University of Lagos

Adefuge, A., Osuntokun, J., Agiri, B. (eds), 1986, *A history of the peoples of Lagos State*, Lantern, Lagos

Aderibigbe, A.B. (ed), 1975, *Lagos: the development of an African city*, Longman, Lagos

Adesina, S., 1975, The development of western education, 124–43, in A.B. Aderibigbe (ed), *Lagos: the development of an African city*, Longman, Lagos

Adeyemi, A.A., 1989, Ordinary crime and its prevention strategies in metropolitan Lagos, in *Urban crime, global trends and policies*, U.N. University, Tokyo

Adisa, I.O., 1987, Bureaucratic corruption in the police force – Lagos State Police Command, undergraduate Sociology project, University of Lagos

Aig-Imoukhuede, F., 1975, Contemporary culture, 197–226, in A.B. Aderibigbe (ed), 1975, *Lagos: the development of an African city*, Longman, Lagos

Aina, T., 1990a, *Health, habitat and underdevelopment in Lagos*, Earthscan, London

Aina, T., 1990b, Petty landlords and poor tenants in a low-income settlement in metropolitan Lagos, Nigeria, 87–101, in P. Amis and P. Lloyd, (eds), *Housing Africa's urban poor*, Manchester University Press, Manchester

Ajisafe, A.K., 1948, *History of Abeokuta*, Kash and Klare Bookshop, Lagos

Akeredolu-Ale, E.O., 1973, A sociohistorical study of the development of entrepreneurship among the Ijebu of western Nigeria, *African Studies Review* 16: 347–64

Akeredolu-Ale, E.O., 1975, *The underdevelopment of indigenous entrepreneurship in Nigeria*, University of Ibadan Press, Ibadan

Akinola, R.A., Alao, N.O., 1975, Some geographical aspects of industries in greater Lagos, 108–23 in A.B. Aderibigbe (ed), *Lagos: the development of an African city*, Longman, Lagos

Akinsemoyin, K., Vaughan-Richards, A., 1977, *Building Lagos*, 2nd edn, Pengrail, Jersey

Aluko, O., 1987, The expulsion of illegal aliens from Nigeria, *African Affairs* 84: 539–60

Anikulapo-Kuti, F., 1989, Animal can't dash me human rights, *Index on censorship* 18 (9): 12–13

Aribiah, O., 1974, The politics of rehousing, *Lagos Notes and Records*, 5: 5–13

Aribiah, O., 1976, Community creation in a rehousing estate, *Urban African Notes*, Series B, (2), 39–54

Aronson, D.R., 1978, *The city is our farm: seven migrant Ijebu Yoruba families*, Schenkman, Cambridge, MA

Asuquo, M., 1987, The magnetic pull that is Broad Street, *The Guardian*, Lagos, 7

Ayeni, B., 1981, Lagos, 127–55, in M. Pacione (ed) *Problems and planning in third world cities*, Croom Helm, London

Baker, P.H., 1974, *Urbanization and political change: the politics of Lagos 1917–1967*, University of California Press, Berkeley

Balogun, F., 1987, *The cinema in Nigeria*, Delta Publications, Enugu

Bamisaiye, A., DiDomenico, C.M., 1983, The social situation of the elderly in Lagos, Nigeria, report to Help the Aged, London

Banjo, A.G., Brown, P.J.B., 1981, Time budget expenditure and travel time variation in Nigeria, 192–211, in S. Carpenter and P. Jones, (eds), *Recent advances in travel demand analysis*, Gower, Aldershot

Barber, K., 1987, Popular arts in Africa, *African Studies Review*, 30: 105–32

Barbour, K.M., *et al.* 1982, *Nigeria in Maps*, Hodder and Stoughton, London

Barnes, S.T., 1979, Migration and land acquisition: the new landowners of Lagos, *African Urban Studies*, no. 4: 59–70

Barnes, S.T., 1982, Public and private housing in urban West Africa, 5–32, in M.K.C. Morrison and P.C.W. Gutkind, (eds), *Housing the Urban Poor in Africa*, African Series No. 37, Maxwell School of Citizenship and Public Affairs, University of Syracuse, Syracuse, NY

Barnes, S.T., 1986, *Patrons and power: creating a political community in metropolitan Lagos*, Manchester University Press for the International African Institute, London

Barnes, S.T., 1987, The urban frontier in West Africa: Mushin, Nigeria, 257–81, in I. Kopytoff (ed), *The African frontier: The reproduction of traditional African societies*, Indiana University Press, Bloomington

Barnes, S.T., Peil, M., 1977, Voluntary association membership in five West African cities, *Urban Anthropology*, 6: 83–106

Biobaku, S.O., 1960, Madam Tinubu, 33–41, in K.O. Dike *et al.*, *Eminent Nigerians of the nineteenth century*, Cambridge University Press, London

Bonacich E., 1973, A theory of middleman minorities, *American Sociological Review*, 38: 583–94

Brydon, L., 1985, Ghanaian responses to the Nigerian expulsions of 1983, *African Affairs*, 84: 561–85

Business, 1987–9, monthly, Lagos

Business Times, 1989, weekly, Lagos

Campbell, I., 1990, The Nigerian military: the transition to civilian rule, 28–41, in A. Hughes (ed), *Towards the third Nigerian Republic*, Occasional Papers 1, Centre of West African Studies, Birmingham University, Birmingham

Cohen, A., 1969, *Custom and politics in urban Africa: a study of Hausa migrants in Yoruba towns*, Routledge & Kegan Paul, London

Cole, P., 1975a, Lagos society in the nineteenth century, 27–57, in A.B. Aderibigbe (ed), *Lagos: the development of an African city*, Longman, Lagos

Cole, P., 1975b, *Modern and traditional elites in the politics of Lagos*, Cambridge University Press, London

Bibliography

Cox, E., Anderssen, E., 1984, *Survive Lagos*, Spectrum Books, Ibadan

Crowder, M., 1962, *The story of Nigeria*, Faber, London

Daily Sketch, 1988, Lagos

Danmole, H.O., 1987, The crisis of the Lagos Muslim community 1915–1947, 290–305, in A. Adefuye *et al.* (eds), *History of the peoples of Lagos State*, Lantern Books, Lagos

Davies, P.N., 1976, *Trading in west Africa: 1840–1920*, Croom Helm, London

Doxiades Associates International 1973 *Nigeria: development problems and future needs of major urban centres – Lagos*, Doxiades, Athens

Duyile, D., 1987, *Makers of Nigerian press*, Gong Communications, Lagos

Eades, J.S., 1980, *The Yoruba today*, Cambridge University Press, London

Ebong, B.J., 1979, Urban growth and housing problems in Nigeria: a case study of Lagos, *African Urban Studies*, no. 4: 71–82

Echeruo, M., 1977, *Victorian Lagos: aspects of nineteenth century Lagosian life*, Macmillan, London

Economic Commission for Africa (ECA), 1980, *Report on demographic survey of households, housing and living conditions in Lagos*, United Nations, Addis Ababa

Ehimiagbe, O.J., 1983, Manpower utilization and labour turnover in a large government bureaucracy, undergraduate Sociology project, University of Lagos

Ekwensi, C., 1961, *Jaqua Nana*, Hutchinson, London

Ekwensi, C., 1963, *People of the city*, Heinemann Educational Books, London

Ezeala, E.O., 1983, Senior employee perception of indigenous management development in a private sector enterprise – Mandilas, undergraduate Sociology project, University of Lagos

Fafunwa, A.B., 1974, *History of education in Nigeria*, Allen & Unwin, London

Famisjo Surveys, 1983, *Map of Mushin Local Government area*, Lagos

Fapohunda, O.J. *et al.*, 1977, *Population, employment and living conditions in Lagos*, Human Resources Research Unit, University of Lagos

Fapohunda, O.J., 1978, *The informal sector in Lagos*, Human Resources Research Unit, University of Lagos

Fapohunda, O.J., Lubdell, H., 1978, *Lagos: urban development and employment*, International Labour Office, Geneva

Fapohunda, O.J., Ojo, F., 1985, *The costs of children in Lagos*, Heinemann, Lagos

Faseyiku, O.S., 1988, Aspects of horizontal interaction between expatriate managers and their Nigerian counterparts, *Nigerian Management Review*, 3: 111–16

Fashoyin, T., 1986, *Incomes and inflation in Nigeria*, Longman, Lagos

Fatai, O.S., 1984, New settlement creation: Iganmu and Dolphin low income estates, Sociology project, University of Lagos

Federal Government of Nigeria (FGN), 1966, *Report of the tribunal of inquiry into the affairs of the Lagos City Council*, Ministry of Information, Lagos

Federal Government of Nigeria (FGN), 1974, *Public Service Review Commission, main report*. Ministry of Information, Lagos

Federal Ministry of Information (FMI), 1967, *Annual abstract of statistics 1965*, Lagos

Federal Office of Statistics (FOS), 1963, *Population census of Lagos, 1963*, Lagos

Federal Office of Statistics (FOS), 1970, *Industrial survey 1970*, Lagos

Federal Office of Statistics (FOS), 1972, *Industrial survey 1972*, Lagos

Federal Office of Statistics (FOS), 1985, *Social statistics in Nigeria 1985*, Lagos

Federal Office of Statistics (FOS), 1986, *National integrated survey of households*, Household Surveys Unit, Lagos

Federal Office of Statistics (FOS), 1987, *Annual abstract of statistics*, Lagos

Federal Office of Statistics (FOS), 1988, *Consumer price index April–June 1988*, Lagos

Federal Office of Statistics (FOS), 1989a, *Consumer price index: May 1989*, Lagos

Federal Office of Statistics (FOS), 1989b, *Statistical News*, No. 117, Lagos
Federal Surveys, Nigeria, 1964, *Lagos*, Sheet 330/888/16, Lagos
Folami, T., 1982, *A history of Lagos, Nigeria: the shaping of an African city*, Exposition Press, Smithtown, NY
Fry, R., 1976, *Bankers in West Africa: the story of the Bank of British West Africa Limited*, Hutchinson Benham, London
Gale, T.S., 1979, Lagos: the history of British colonial neglect of traditional African cities, *African Urban Studies*, no. 5: 11–24
Gbadamosi, G.O., 1975, Patterns and developments in Lagos religious history, 173–96 in A.B. Aderibigbe (ed), *Lagos: the development of an African city*, Longman, Lagos
George, A.M., 1989, Incidence of divorce cases in Lagos, undergraduate Sociology project, Lagos University
Gravil, R., 1985, The Nigerian aliens expulsion order of 1983, *African Affairs*, 84: 523–37
Guardian, 1988–89, daily, Lagos
Guardian Financial Weekly, 1989, Lagos
Hopkins, A.G., 1966, The Lagos strike of 1897, *Past and Present*, 35: 133–55
Hopkins, A.G., 1980, Property rights and empire-building: Britain's annexation of Lagos, 1861, *Journal of Economic History*, 40: 777–98
Hughes, A., Cohen, R., 1978, An emerging Nigerian working class: the Lagos experience, 1897–1939, 31–55, in P. Gutkind, *et al.* (eds), *African labour history*, Sage, London
Human Resources Research Unit (HRRU), 1972, Population, employment and living conditions in Lagos, *Research Bulletin* 2/001, University of Lagos
Human Resources Research Unit (HRRU), 1974, Some aspects of population and housing conditions in Lagos, *Research Bulletin* 2/002, University of Lagos
Ifionu, O., 1987, Dreadful state of jails, *African Concord* (Hastings), 27 August, 7–10
Iliffe, J., 1987, *The African poor*, Cambridge University Press, London
Inyang, PEB, 1978, Environmental pollution in some Nigerian towns, 169–77, in P.O. Sada and J.S. Oguntoyinbo (eds), *Urbanization processes and problems in Nigeria*, Ibadan University Press, Ibadan
Iroh, E., 1985, Of aliens and foreigners, *African Business* (Lagos), June, 23
Johnson, M.A., 1982, *Wooden dolls*, Four Wind Press, USA
Kennedy, P., 1988, *African capitalism*, Cambridge University Press, Cambridge
Koenigsberger, P. *et al.* 1964, *Metropolitan Lagos*, United Nations Commission for Technical Assistance, New York
Krapf-Askari, E., 1969, *Yoruba towns and cities*, Clarendon Press, Oxford
Lagos Horizon, 1989, weekly, Lagos
Lagos Life, 1989, weekly, Lagos
Lagos State Government (LSG), 1973, *Statistics of education*, Ministry of Education, Lagos
Lagos State Government (LSG), 1981, *Lagos State regional plan, 1980–2000*, Ministry of Economic Planning and Land Matters, Ikeja
Lagos State Government (LSG), 1987, *Digest of statistics*, Office of Military Governor, Statistics Division, Ikeja
Lagos State Government (LSG), 1989a, *Monthly statistical indicators*, Part I (January), Statistics Division, Ikeja
Lagos State Government (LSG), 1989b, *Monthly statistical indicators*, Part I (July), Statistics Division, Ikeja
Lagos State Government (LSG), 1989c, *Monthly statistical indicators*, Part II (April), Statistics Division, Ikeja
Lagos State Ministry of Commerce and Industry (LSMC), 1989, *Directory of manufacturing companies*, Alausa

Bibliography

Lagos State Ministry of Information and Culture (LSMI), 1988, *Lagos state handbook*, Alausa

Lagos State Survey Division, 1987, *Lagos State*, Military Governor's Office, Ikeja

Lagos Street Finder, 1981, Nigerian Mapping Company Limited, Lagos

Leighton, N.O., 1979, The political economy of a stranger population: the Lebanese of Sierra Leone, 85–103, in W.A. Shack and E.P. Skinner (eds), *Strangers in African societies*, University of California Press, Berkeley, CA

Lesthaeghe, A. *et al.*, 1989, Child-spacing and fertility in Lagos, 3–24, in H.J. Page and R. Lesthaeghe (eds), *Child-spacing in tropical Africa: traditions and change*, Academic Press, New York

LeVine, A.A., 1966, *Dreams and deeds*, University of Chicago Press, Chicago, IL

Lloyd, P.C., 1974, *Power and independence: urban Africans' perception of social inequality*, Routledge & Kegan Paul, London

Lucas, D., 1974, Occupation, marriage and fertility among Nigerian women in Lagos, *Research Bulletin* 3/001, Human Resources Research Unit, University of Lagos

Luckham, R.A., 1971, *The Nigerian military*, Cambridge University Press, London

Mabogunje, A.L., 1962, *Yoruba Towns*, Ibadan University Press, Ibadan

Mabogunje, A.L., 1968, *Urbanization in Nigeria*, University of London Press

McNulty, M.L., Adalemo, I.A., 1988, Lagos, 212–34, in M. Dogan and J.D. Kasarda (eds), *Metropolis era*, vol. 2, *Mega-cities*, Sage, Beverly Hills, CA

Mann, K., 1985, *Marrying well: marriage, status and social change among the educated elite in colonial Lagos*, Cambridge University Press, London

Marris, P., 1961, *Family and social change in an African city: a study of rehousing in Lagos*, Routledge & Kegan Paul, London

Master Plan for Metropolitan Lagos, 1978, Bulletin 3, Residential densities in Metropolitan Lagos, Lagos State Government Ministry of Works and Planning, Ikeja

Master Plan for Metropolitan Lagos, 1980, vol. I and II, Wilbur Smith and Associates for the State Ministry of Physical Planning and Land Matters, Lagos

Mba, N.E., 1982, *Nigerian women mobilized: women's political activity in southern Nigeria, 1900–1965*, Institute of International Studies, University of California, Berkeley, CA

Morgan, R.W., Kannisto, V., 1973, A population dynamics survey in Lagos, Nigeria, *Social Science and Medicine*, 7: 1–30

National Concord, 1988, daily, Lagos

National Population Bureau, 1986, *Nigeria fertility survey, 1981–82: Lagos State*, Federal Ministry of Health, Lagos

Newswatch, 1990, Lagos

Nigeria, 1975, *Third national development plan, 1975–80*, vol. I, Central Planning Office, Lagos

Nwafor, J.C., 1982, The development of manufacturing industries and regional planning in Nigeria, *African Urban Studies*, no. 13: 75–94

Nwapa, F., 1971, *This is Lagos and other stories*, Nwankwo-Ifejika & Co., Enugu

Nwosu, T., 1989, The place for bargains, *Business*, Lagos, 2 (5): 34–5

Obuji, C.C., 1987, Housemaids: understanding their roles, recruitment and self employment characteristics, undergraduate Sociology project, University of Lagos

O'Connor, A., 1983, *The African City*, Hutchinson, London

Ohadike, P.O., 1968, Urbanization: growth, transitions and problems of a premier West African city, Lagos, Nigeria, *Urban Affairs Quarterly*, 3: 69–90

Okoye, T.O., 1990, 'Historical development of Nigerian housing policies with special reference to housing the urban poor', 73–85, in P. Amis and P. Lloyd (eds), *Housing Africa's urban poor*, Manchester University Press, Manchester

Okpala, D.C.I., 1979, Accessibility distribution aspects of public urban land management, *African Urban Studies*, no. 5: 25–44

Okpala, D.C.I., 1983, Finance for urban management: evolution and status of property rate revenue in Nigeria, *African Urban Studies*, no. 15: 1–16

Ola Daniel S., 1975, Health and social welfare, 143–72, in A.B. Aderibigbe (ed), 1975, *Lagos: the development of an African city*, Longman, Lagos

Olanrewaju, S.A., 1981, Modeling the urban traffic problem: some Nigerian results, *African Urban Studies*, no. 9: 57–74

Oloko, A., 1990, Children's street trading in Nigeria: informal education, economic participation or child abuse, in W. Myers (ed) *Protecting working children*, Zed Books, Oxford

Olowu, D., 1990, *Lagos State: governance, society and economy*, Malthouse Press, Lagos

Olurode, L., 1989, *LKJ in the eyes of the people*, John West Publications, Lagos

Onakomaiya, S.O., 1981, Towards an efficient transportation service for metropolitan Lagos, 57–62, in P.O. Sada and J.S. Oguntoyinbo (eds), *Urbanization processes and problems in Nigeria*, Ibadan University Press, Ibadan

Onenekan, T.P., 1987, Social clubs and social stratification in the city of Lagos, undergraduate Sociology project, University of Lagos

Onokerhoraye, A.G., 1984, *Social services in Nigeria*, Routledge & Kegan Paul, London

Orewa, G.O., Adewumi, J.B., 1983, *Local government in Nigeria: the changing scene*, Ethiope Publishing Corporation, Benin City

Osuntokun, J., 1987, Introduction of Christianity and Islam in Lagos State, 128–41 in Adefuye, A. *et al.* (eds), *History of the Peoples of Lagos State*, Lantern Books, Lagos

Oyeleye, D.A. (ed), 1981, *Spatial expansion and concomitant problems in the Lagos metropolitan area*, Occasional paper 1, Department of Geography, University of Lagos

Oynemenam, C.C., 1983, Urban adjustment of rural migrants at Festival Town, undergraduate Sociology project, University of Lagos

Peace, A., 1975, The Lagos proletariat: labour aristocrats or populist militants?, 281–302 in R. Sandbrook and R. Cohen (eds), *The development of an African working class*, Longman, London

Peace, A., 1979a, *Choice, class and conflict: A study of southern Nigerian factory Workers*, Harvester Press, Brighton

Peace, A., 1979b, Prestige, power and legitimacy in a modern Nigerian town, *Canadian Journal of African Studies*, 14: 26–51

Peace, A., 1988, The politics of transporting, *Africa*, 58: 14–28

Peel, J., 1968, *Aladura: a religious movement among the Yoruba*, Oxford University Press, London

Peil, M., 1971, The expulsion of West African aliens, *Journal of Modern African Studies*, 9: 205–29

Peil, M., 1973, The cost of living in Lagos, *Lagos Notes and Records*, 4: 12–16

Peil, M., 1975, Interethnic contacts in Nigerian cities, *Africa*, 45: 107–22

Peil, M., 1976a, African squatter settlements, *Urban Studies*, 13: 155–66

Peil, M., 1976b, *Nigerian politics: the people's view*, Cassell, London

Peil, M., 1979a, Urban women in the labor force, *Sociology of Work and Occupations*, 6: 482–501

Peil, M., 1979b, West African urban craftsmen, *Journal of Developing Areas*, 14: 3–22

Peil, M., 1981, *Cities and suburbs: urban life in West Africa*, Holmes and Meier, New York

Peil, M., Ekpenyong, S.K., Oyeneye, O.Y., 1988, Going home: migration careers of southern Nigerians, *International Migration Review*, 22: 563–85

Peil, M., Bamisaiye, A., Ekpenyong, S., 1989, Health and physical support for the elderly in Nigeria, *Journal of Cross-Cultural Gerontology*, 4: 89–106

Bibliography

Pittin, R., 1983, Houses of women: a focus on alternative life-styles in Katsina City, 291–302, in C. Oppong (ed) *Female and male in West Africa*, George Allen & Unwin, London

Punch, 1988, weekly, Lagos

Sada, P.O., 1969, Differential population distribution and growth in metropolitan Lagos, *Journal of Business and Social Studies*, Lagos, 1: 117–32

Sada, P.O., 1970, The rural–urban fringe of Lagos: population and land-use, *Nigerian Journal of Economic and Social Studies*, 12: 225–241

Sada, P.O., *et al.*, 1978, Periodic markets in a metropolitan environment: the example of Lagos, Nigeria, in R.H.T. Smith (ed), *Market-place trade-periodic markets, hawkers and traders in Africa, Asia and Latin America*, Centre for Transportation Studies, University of British Columbia, Vancouver

Sada, P.O., Adefolalu, A.A., 1975, Urbanisation and problems of urban development, 79–107, in A.B. Aderibigbe (ed), 1975, *Lagos: the development of an African city*, Longman, Lagos

Sada, P.O., McNulty, M.L., 1974, Traditional markets in Lagos: a study of the changing administrative processes and marketing transactions, *Quarterly Journal of Administration*, January, 149–65

Sada, P.O., Oguntoyinbo, J.S. (eds), 1981, *Urbanization processes and problems in Nigeria*, Ibadan University Press, Ibadan

Schwerdtfeger, F.W., 1982, *Traditional housing in African cities*, John Wiley, Chichester

Shell, 1985, *Street Guide of Lagos and Environs*, Shell Petroleum Development Company, Lagos

Smythe, H.H., Smythe, M.M., 1960, *The new Nigerian elite*, Stanford University Press, Stanford, CA

Sonuga, G., 1987, *Lagos State Life and Culture*, Gabumo Publishing Company, Lagos

This Week, 1987–9, Lagos

This Week 100, 1989, Special edition, The top 100 companies, no. 139, Lagos

Thomas, O., 1985, Factors in prostitution: brothels in the Surulere area of Lagos, undergraduate Sociology project, University of Lagos

Uchendu, V.C., 1965, *The Igbo of southeast Nigeria*, Holt, Rinehart & Winston, New York

Udenwa, O., 1988, Fela: 50 years of a bitchy life, *Quality*, Lagos, October 13, 18–22

Waterman, C.A., 1988, *Asíkò, sákárà* and palmwine: popular music and social identity in inter-war Lagos, Nigeria, *Urban Anthropology*, 17: 229–58

Waterman, P., 1976, Conservatism amongst Nigerian workers, 159–84, in G. Williams (ed), *Nigeria: economy and society*, Rex Collings, London

Waterman, P., 1982, *Division and unity amongst Nigerian workers: Lagos port unionism, 1940s–60s*, Research Report 11, Institute of Social Studies, The Hague, Netherlands

Waterman, P., 1983a, *Aristocrats and plebians in African trade unions? Lagos port and dock worker organisation and struggle*, Katholieke Universiteit van Nijmegen, Netherlands

Waterman, P., 1983b, H.P. Adebola: the man, the myth, the movement, *The other side* (New Delhi) August, 35–8

Wemambu, M.E., 1988, The history of new settlements in Lagos metropolis; case study of Maroko, undergraduate History project, University of Lagos

West Africa, 1973–1990, weekly, London

Whitaker, C.S., 1970, *The politics of tradition, continuity and change in northern Nigeria, 1946–66*, Princeton University Press, Princeton, NJ

Whitford, J., 1967, *Trading life in western and central Africa*, F. Cass, London (1st edn 1877)

Who's Who in Nigeria, 2nd edn, 1971, Daily Times, Lagos

Williams, B.A., 1975, The federal capital: changing constitutional status and intergovernmental relations, 59–78, in A.B. Aderibigbe (ed), *Lagos: the development of an African city*, Longman, Lagos

Williams, B.A., Walsh, A.H., 1967, *Urban government for metropolitan Lagos*, Praeger, New York

Yemitan, O., 1987, *Madam Tinubu: merchant and kingmaker*, Ibadan University Press, Ibadan

Yesufu, T.M., 1968, Population, employment and living condition in Lagos, Human Resources Research Unit, University of Lagos

Index

Index

Index